the pole of passage, fixed is to be ornamented with composition.
the curtain tacked to this piece.
two spikes, like this, driven into the wall to support the cornice.

9. feet

The windows of Din'g R. Monticello 5/09. from out to
out of architrave, within. consequently all the proportions ought to be as 09.9:609. or as 5:4

5:4 :: 6:5   x
        20:24 = 2
        30:26½ = 2.2½
        39:31 = 2.7½
        65:40½ = 5.0½
        100:80 = 6.8.
        108:86½ = 7.2½

The curtain cornice pro-
jects, consequently the
difference projects from
the returned end of the
-jection of the architrave
17.2½ I. diminish will be requisite for each window at Monticello

dimity 2f. 1 I. wide
the window from out to out of
the architrave 9½ I. wide

for working fire engine

for breaking plaister

the lowest wheel
may be on the main shaft
or put on it's axis by a
socket

1796. Nov. Bill of scantling.
    Sleepers, sills, plates, joists, principal rafters 10. I. by 3 I.
    rafters 3 I. thick. 6 I. deep at lower end, 4 I. at upper
    Studs 4. I. by 3. I.   except where otherwise ment'd

Cellar floor. 76 studs 9. f. long for partition + 2. 2 I. from cent. to center
Ground floor. Girders. 10 I by 4 I. 1. 14 f. long for front of alcoves of the 2. octagons
                                    1. 28 f. long across the Hall
        Sleepers 10 I. from center to center.
                66. 16 f. long. for 2 octagons, 2 square rooms & North passage
                11. 11 f. for South passage
                36. 16 f. for Hall
        Studs. 2. I. from cent. to cent.
                22. 12 f. long for partition of bedrooms above of Din' R. closets

Upper floor. Girders 10 I. by 4 I. 2. 20 f. long over back of Alcoves
            10 I. by 6 I. 2. f. long for Nursery
                        2. 16 f. long. diagonal for gallery of Hall.
        Sleepers. 6 I. by 4 I. 16 I. from center to center
                46. 21 f. long for 4. bedrooms
                24. 11 f. for N. passage & wide part of S. passage
                11. 6 f. for   narrow part of do
                8. 16 f. long for S. Bow
                16. 12 f. long for Nursery.
                9. 16 f. long for gallery
        Studs. 68. 9. f. long for partitions, alcoves, closets

Roof. Plates. 2. 28 f. long over front of alcoves
            1. 28 f. long over front of N. E. Portico.
            2. 12 f. long for flanks of do
        Girders 2. 25 f. long. 12 I. sq. across hall, under the sills of lopers over
joists support center to center
            46. 19 f. long over bedrooms includ'g one projn for cornice
            24. 16 f. long for N. passage & wide part of S. passage.
            22. 22 f. long. for Din' room & Chamber & 1. projn.
            16. 18 f. long for N. & S. bows & 1 projn.
            20. 28 f. long for Hall & Entry.
            7. 36 f. long for N. E. portico & 2. projns.
            12. 22 f. long for 2. piazzas & double projd.
            8. 23 f. long for do. bevelled part.
            60. 4 f. long for hanging cornice to.
        Studs. 136. 6 f. long to support cornice to
        Purlins. 12. 24 f. long to support purloins
        Hip rafters. 16. 24 f. long to support middle of rafters.
        Rafters. 72. 20 f. long for plain faces of roof, piazzas, & N. E. portico
                61. 20 f. long to be cut each into 2. for angular faces of roof
        Trans. Sills. 10 I. sq. 6. 24 f. long
                    2. 25 f. long across hall.

External

the void of arch 65.3 I.
the impost from floor of Piazza 1 . 3
                to top of impost   6.375
                                        6.45

Scantlin studs

the flank arches will need no ce-
-stian blinds.
those need be treble folds of the stone
than blinds only against one of
the middle piers. double folds

Arch
5 f.e.

A

THOMAS JEFFERSON

THOMAS JEFFERSON

THE MAN . . . HIS WORLD . . . HIS INFLUENCE

EDITED BY LALLY WEYMOUTH

G.P. PUTNAM'S SONS, NEW YORK

SBN: 399–11166–2
Library of Congress Catalog Card Number: 73–78612

Designed by Robert Conrad
Printed and bound in Great Britain.

CONTENTS

FOREWORD

Lally Weymouth

We have an interval, and then our place knows us no more.... Our one chance lies in expanding that interval, in getting as many pulsations as possible into the given time.

Walter Pater, *The Renaissance*

It is hard to think of man who did get more into his interval on earth than Thomas Jefferson. He served as President of the United States, Vice-President, Secretary of State, and Governor of Virginia. He wrote the Declaration of Independence and the Statute of Virginia for Religious Freedom. Whenever he was not occupied with affairs of state, he spent time expanding his own knowledge: studying architecture, building and rebuilding Monticello, reading, playing the fiddle, inventing a plow and various other devices for the use of himself and his friends, keeping records of the temperature, and farming his large estate.

This collection of essays attempts to give the reader some idea of Jefferson's achievements as a public servant, his interests as a private citizen, and his influence on American history and on America today. But Thomas Jefferson had so many interests and accomplishments in his long lifetime that it is impossible in one volume to do more than touch on a few aspects of his life and expose a range of diverse views of a complicated, fascinating man who has become an American myth.

INTRODUCTION
Dumas Malone

Thomas Jefferson was half a dozen persons rolled into one, and his world was one of the most spacious that a mortal man ever lived in. The latter statement is paradoxical, to be sure, for in the physical sense his world was sharply delimited. Born on the fringe of western settlement in British North America, he never crossed the dividing line between his native Virginia and North Carolina that his father had helped survey. In middle life he went as far north as Lake Champlain, but the man who dispatched Lewis and Clark to the Pacific never set foot farther west than the Shenandoah Valley. Though he spent five years on the vaunted scene of Europe, he never got much beyond the Rhine. Of Africa, Asia, and South America he had no firsthand knowledge whatsoever. Within the physical limitations imposed by the difficulties of transportation in his slow-moving age he was a fairly extensive and notably observant traveler; and on his own continent, he was the greatest patron of exploration of his time – perhaps of any time.

His capacious mind recognized no restrictions of space. As a distinguished French visitor to Monticello observed, he set his mind as he did his house on an elevation from which he could contemplate the universe. Though always interested in the heavens he was no mere star-gazer. From these heights he descended into the world of human affairs for a lifetime of public service; and he is notable in history for his humane spirit as well as for his omnivorous mind.

The particular world into which he was born and in which he grew up was an uncrowded rural world in which one could live close to nature. This gentleman-planter, who invented a moldboard of a plow and regarded the introduction of a useful plant as one of the greatest of human services, loved every bud that opened and was interested in every wind that blew. Throughout life he kept records of the temperature, and he never ceased to find joy in the observation of plants and animals. To call him an agrarian would be to employ an inadequate term and rob him of his universality. He was a genuine foe to all sorts of artificiality, however; and, like Antaeus, he maintained his strength by contact with mother earth.

If he himself is to be believed, he entered reluctantly into the world of law and government and by force of circumstances remained in public life far longer than he expected or desired. For some forty years he was almost continuously in public office of some sort and it was in this connection that he gained his fame. It is not surprising, therefore, that students of his life and times have given most scrutiny to this particular world of legislation and administra-

tion, of war and diplomacy and politics. In view of his ability and industry, one may doubt if he would have been obscure in any period, but he chanced to live in one of extraordinary stimulus and challenge. It was a momentous era, not only in the history of his own country but also in that of western civilization – what we used to call *the* age of revolution – and because of his public services he became one of the most memorable figures of this great generation. Important aspects of his political career are dealt with in various chapters of this book, but volumes would be required to deal adequately with this long, distinguished, and often controversial career. Therefore, these admirable chapters should be regarded as suggestive, not as fully descriptive of him as a public man.

Jefferson's own comments on the political world and his distaste for it need not be accepted at face value. Others besides him have expressed a profound sense of relief when retiring from the Presidency of the United States. None the less, his parting comment to his friend Du Pont de Nemours clamors for quotation. "Nature intended me for the tranquil pursuits of science," he said, "by rendering them my supreme delight." It should be noted that he used the word "science" to mean knowledge, all knowledge. He found delight in the pursuit of it in almost any form, and it was in this ever-expanding world of knowledge that his spirit was most at home. He recognized no barriers within it, and in modern terms he was both scientist and humanist. Nor did he recognize any barriers of time. While preferring the dreams of the future to the history of the past, he looked back to Rome for noble architectural models and carried on a dialogue with the writers of classical antiquity to the end of his days. He has been aptly called a Renaissance man and properly described as the American embodiment of the Enlightenment. In the annals of the country he did so much to establish he appears sometimes as a master politician and always as a great patriot. From the pages of world history he stands forth as the nearest American approximation, and one of the closest human approximations, of the universal man.

This is certainly not to claim perfection for him. His reach exceeded his grasp. Being an imperfect human being, he did not always live up to his own principles, and his judgement regarding public policy was not always good. While the clouds of partisan misinterpretation which long obscured him may have largely lifted, opinions of his statesmanship still differ widely. In such judgements as the contributors to this volume pass on him full agreement is not to be expected. Nor should such a multi-faceted personality be expected to look the same to every observer.

There is something in him for practically everybody. Visitors to Monticello who may be quite indifferent to his political principles and practices can be fascinated by the ingenious inventions and devices of this inveterate tinkerer. Persons who may be wholly unfamiliar with the great documents he drafted can respect him as the surveyor of his own land and admire him as an architect and builder. If he is not appealing as a bibliophile who collected books he may be as a naturalist who collected seeds and fossils.

His diverse activities and achievements are endlessly fascinating. To many, however, including some who have studied him most, his personality seems elusive. This is partly because he was a man of great personal restraint, who rarely revealed his deeper feelings even though he wrote incessantly. He guarded his private life with unusual jealousy. There is much testimony to his amiability in personal relations and this is one of the explanations

of his political popularity and success. He was characteristically undramatic, however, and one cannot help asking if he really had charisma.

Quite clearly he did not have it in dramatic form, but he had extraordinary ability to command personal loyalty and he became the symbol of causes of immense appeal. That the symbol and the man did not perfectly coincide at all times may be conceded, and fortuitous factors were unquestionably involved in the growth of his fame. But as the author of the American Declaration of Independence and of the Virginia Statute for Religious Freedom, he almost inevitably became first a national and then an international symbol of human liberty and self-government. As such he may be said to have reached the pinnacle of his fame at the height of the conflict with totalitarianism during and soon after the Second World War. During his Presidency of the United States he was designated as the "man of the people" by his own supporters. There is something paradoxical in describing this aristocrat by birth and taste as a major patron of democracy, and he was a more discriminating democrat than numerous popular leaders who came after him – Andrew Jackson, for one. But he consistently opposed artificial aristocracies of birth and wealth, as he did vested interests generally, and while he never would have agreed that the voice of the people is the voice of God, he thought it the most trustworthy voice available and was unquestionably the people's friend. Among his own countrymen he has also become a symbol of universal public education. His patronage of learning in all its branches and his lifelong emphasis on the freedom of inquiry have been recognized and valued in our century more than at any time since his death.

To sum up such a man in a few words is manifestly impossible. In fact his proportions varied under varying circumstances in different periods of his long life. Far from being a statue on a pedestal he was a living, growing, changing man. But he always believed that light and liberty go together, and rarely was there a time when he did not put human values first.

THOMAS JEFFERSON:
A BRIEF LIFE

Merrill Peterson

One of the penalties that a great man exacts from posterity is to compel it to understand him. In the case of Thomas Jefferson the task has not been easy. The political rage that engulfed his life pursued him far beyond the grave. It was impossible to feel dispassionate about him because among the nation's founders he had most deeply involved himself with the destiny of American democracy. He became a political symbol, and the twin hysterias of exaltation and denunciation evoked by the symbol obliterated the authentic human figure. His teachings remained significant, whether for good or ill, and so he was repeatedly trotted out, like a trick dog in the circus, for the entertainment of those present. Through the generations he was implicated in the successive crises of the democratic experiment. Looking back it almost seems that American history has been one prolonged litigation, negotiations and hearings, suits, trials, and appeals without number, concerning Thomas Jefferson. Taking possession of Jefferson for their own purposes, Americans did not possess the man himself.

Sufficiently elusive and complex, however, was the man himself. He lived eighty-three years, helped to found a nation, reflected deeply, wrote voluminously, and applied himself to countless tasks. He was a prodigy of talents, not only a statesman but a scientist, architect, agriculturist, musician, inventor, geographer, and linguist. Posterity could comprehend him only in fragments. His life exhibited bewildering conflicts and contradictions: philosopher and politician, aristocrat and democrat, cosmopolitan and American. He was an idealist – "visionary" was the favorite epithet of his enemies – yet on the evidence of his works he was also uncommonly hardheaded and practical. Indeed, what his critics then and since could never forgive him was that he stole the wisdom of conservatism, the mastery of reality, for his dreams of the future. He never reduced the vast corpus of his thought to a system. An ill-arranged cluster of meanings, uneven, opaque, protean, it invited men of all descriptions to split it into pieces and offer some fragment as the essence of the whole. Every man has been his own Jeffersonian – especially in politics. "What *principle* in the political ethics of our country might not be *sanctioned* and refuted by the writings of Mr Jefferson?" a newspaperman asked more than a century ago, and many Americans have felt his exasperation. Jeffersonian political craft have sailed under many colors: democracy, state rights, agrarianism, anti-statism, civil libertarianism, isolationism, welfare statism. And none of these flags, with others unnamed, is entirely fraudulent. Jefferson's personality has proved

An aerial view of Monticello.

to be as elusive as his thought and politics. Almost every other American statesman, Henry Adams wrote, could be portrayed with "a few broad strokes of the brush," but Jefferson "only touch by touch with a fine pencil, and the perspective of the likeness depended upon the shifting and uncertain flicker of the semi-transparent shadows."

There is, then, no simple clue to this labyrinthian figure who has been so much a part of America's ongoing search for itself as to eclipse his identity in the past. Yet the duty of historical understanding remains, and it can begin only by seeking the man himself in the actions and passions of his own time.

Thomas Jefferson was born at Shadwell, in Virginia, on 13 April 1743. Some years before his father, Peter Jefferson, had patented a thousand acres in this wilderness country, then cleared a tract for planting and built a good house, to which he brought his wife and infant daughters prior to the birth of his son. Albemarle, as the new county would be named, lay on the western fringes of settlement, though it could hardly be considered frontier when young Jefferson was growing up. His democracy, whatever its sources, was not an offspring of the frontier. Yet the freedom, openness, and simplicity of upcountry life enforced a sense of man's proper relationship to nature that colored all his values; and throughout his life the West tugged at his imagination. His father, a self-taught surveyor and map-maker, had been in the vanguard of Virginia's explorers and pioneers, even penetrating the distant Allegheny Mountains when Jefferson was a child. This was always a source of pride in the son, who in his sixtieth year would send a younger son of Albemarle, Meriwether Lewis, to explore the uncharted vastness from the Missouri to the Pacific shore.

Jefferson was only fourteen when his father died. Of his mother, Jane Randolph, though she lived until 1776, he had almost nothing to say, except that she was the daughter of a princely family who "trace their pedigree far back in England and Scotland, to which let every man ascribe the faith and merit he chooses." The pedigree assured him social position in colonial Virginia, but he obviously valued more the enterprising example of his father. From modest beginnings Peter Jefferson had built a fair estate, risen through the local offices to membership in the House of Burgesses, and died the first citizen of his county. The pathway to power had been blazed for his son. Most of the estate – several thousand acres of land and the slaves to work them – descended to Jefferson. Habits of industry, system, and responsibility are acquired early, and in Jefferson's case they were learned from his father. Looking back he sometimes wondered why, when this force was removed at a tender age, he did not lose his bearings and become quite worthless to society. Instead, the early thrust to maturity hardened the grain of habits already formed.

Peter Jefferson's education had been "quite neglected," but he prized books and learning, for which his son was eternally grateful. Schooling commenced at five; at nine he began to study Latin and Greek; and at seventeen, having become a proficient classical scholar, he left the hills of Albemarle to attend the College of William and Mary in the provincial capital, Williamsburg. A raw country lad, tall and lanky, with a freckled face and reddish hair, he soon acquired the tastes and manners of the capital without, however, succumbing to its vices or rejecting the values of the youthful society whence he came. At the college he became the student and companion of Dr William Small, of Scotland, the one truly en-

The Rev. William Small, Jefferson's professor at the
College of William and Mary and an important
influence in his life.

lightened man on a faculty otherwise composed of clerics of the Church of England. From him, Jefferson later wrote, "I got my first views of the expansion of science, and the system of things in which we are placed," and it was this influence that "probably fixed the destiny of my life." A hardworking student at all times, strenuous in the pursuit of knowledge, Jefferson learned that high seriousness was the condition of any worthy endeavor and that the world was malleable to the hammers of the mind. The Baconian axiom, "knowledge is power," became the core of his faith; and he was never more typically a man of the Enlightenment than in the conviction formed under Dr Small's tutelage that reason and inquiry might lead men away from whatever was false or capricious in human affairs toward the truth inherent in the nature of things.

His own nature, he often said, destined him for the sciences. But no careers opened to science in Virginia, and upon his graduation from college in 1762 he took the path of the law. Here his mentor was George Wythe, a man of exemplary learning and character. A few months' desultory reading and brief apprenticeship in a law office might prepare a man for practice in Virginia's courts, but Jefferson studied law as a branch of humane learning and put five years of his life into it. Admitted to the bar in 1767, he was successful, though he never attained the celebrity of Patrick Henry, who had taken the tradesman's route and whose golden throat and folksy ways won for him an unprecedented popular following. "Mr Jefferson," it was said, "drew copiously from the depths of the law, Mr Henry from the recesses of the human heart." Law led into politics and was finally significant as a preparation for statesmanship in the American Revolution. When events forced him to abandon his practice in 1774, Jefferson did not abandon the law but turned what he had learned to the greater cause of the Revolution.

His political career commenced at the age of twenty-six in 1769, when the freeholders of Albemarle elected him to the House of Burgesses. He served for six years in that body – the oldest representative assembly in the New World – and despite his youth rapidly rose to a position of leadership. At the same time he began to build Monticello, the lovely home perched on a densely wooded summit in Albemarle. Given the cultural impoverishment of his own environment, Jefferson learned architecture, as he learned most things, from books, and the versatility he demonstrated in this endeavor marked a permanent trait, which would explode in all directions. He discovered his master in the Renaissance Italian Andrea Palladio, who had gone to Roman antiquity for his models. Monticello was a modified Palladian villa, and all of Jefferson's later architectural masterpieces – the Virginia Capitol, the University of Virginia – were in the Palladian style, though original creations in their own right. In architecture the scientific modernist went back to the ancients because there, rather than in the vernacular of his own time and place, he found a definition of beauty that was as universal, chaste, and orderly as the Newtonian laws of motion. Jefferson was a dozen years building Monticello; a decade later, dissatisfied with the first version, he rebuilt it; indeed, such was his love of putting up and tearing down, he seems to have been always building Monticello. It was a lifelong obsession. Perhaps nothing else he ever did so well expressed his heart and mind.

In January 1772, before the mansion was habitable, Jefferson brought his bride to Monticello. Martha Wayles Skelton was an attractive and well-to-do young widow from the

A view from Jefferson's window, showing the revolving chair he designed which the Federalist press satirically called "Mr Jefferson's whirl-i-gig."

Thomas Jefferson.
A Philosopher a Patriote and a Friend
Dessiné par son Ami Tadée Kosciuszko.
Et Gravé par M. Sokolnicki.

low country around Williamsburg, "mild and amiable," it was said, and accomplished in the arts cultivated by Virginia ladies of that day. Legend has it that she favored the rawboned and ungainly Jefferson over more gallant suitors because of his love of music; certain it is that Monticello later resounded to their music, she on the harpsichord, he on the violin. But little is known about Martha or what she contributed to his life during ten years other than six children and an abiding love, because Jefferson buried with her all memory of the marriage. Only two of the children survived infancy and only the eldest, Martha, survived him. Despite the pain and the sorrow, perhaps because of them, he came to prize domestic felicity above any other and would have gladly traded worldly fame for a larger portion of it.

Jefferson rose to fame in the councils of the American Revolution. As a young law student in 1765 he had stood in the door of the Burgesses to hear Henry's fiery speech against the Stamp Act. "He appeared to me to speak as Homer wrote," Jefferson later recalled; and from the moment of his own entrance into the assembly, he was associated with the "young hotheads" around Henry in the controversy with the mother country. Unlike Henry, however, whose talents were oratorical, Jefferson excelled in legislative business, especially as a legislative draftsman, and he was careful not to alienate himself, as Henry had, from the "old guard" leadership in the assembly. At each of the turning-points on Virginia's road to independence, Jefferson played an important, if not a conspicuous, part. In 1774, after the royal governor dissolved the unruly assembly, he was elected a delegate to the colony's first revolutionary convention, which, in turn, was to elect delegates to the First Continental Congress. Falling ill on the way to Williamsburg, Jefferson forwarded the "instructions" he had drafted. Although the convention considered them too bold for its approval, Jefferson's friends published his paper as a pamphlet under the title *A Summary View of the Rights of British America*. Drawing his argument from the most venerable tradition of the English constitution, that of a Saxon golden age, Jefferson reached the radical conclusion that the Americans possessed the natural right to govern themselves. This appeal to the past in behalf of modern principles, this blending of the legalism of the English constitution with the rationalism and universalism of the natural rights philosophy, was thoroughly characteristic of Jefferson. The logic of the argument pointed to independence. He was not ready for this leap, however. It was enough for the present that the next step be taken, the wholesale repudiation of Parliament's authority over the colonies, leaving allegiance to a common king as the only bond of empire. In this sense Jefferson's *Summary View* opened a new chapter in the polemics of the Revolution.

The fighting had begun when, in June 1775, Jefferson took one of the Virginia seats in the Second Continental Congress at Philadelphia. His reputation had gone before him. He brought into Congress, as John Adams said, "a reputation for literature, science, and a happy talent for composition." This talent was at once put to work. Jefferson drafted Congress's reply, as he had earlier drafted Virginia's, to Lord North's "conciliatory proposition," and he co-authored with John Dickinson the momentous Declaration of the Causes and Necessity of Taking Up Arms. Jefferson was now ready for the final step, but the moderates of the middle colonies, for whom Dickinson was the spokesman, were not. Having learned in Virginia that prudence, not audacity, was wanted in order "to keep the front and rear together," he was even more impressed with this political wisdom in Philadelphia, lest

A portrait of Jefferson drawn by Kosciuszko and engraved by Sokolnicki.

George Wythe, Jefferson's law professor, whom he
called "one of the greatest men of the age."

division and civil war be the sequel to independence. So he waited patiently for the
moderates, negotiation at last exhausted, to join the thickening host at the Rubicon.

In June 1776 he found himself, surprisingly, appointed at the head of a five-man committee to draft a united Declaration of Independence. Although two of the committee
members, Benjamin Franklin and John Adams, were decidedly senior and better known
than he, the task of drafting the document fell to Jefferson for political reasons and also
because he possessed that "peculiar felicity of expression" wanted in a state paper of this
kind. He showed a preliminary draft to Franklin and Adams, who suggested only minor

changes, revised it to his own satisfaction, gave it to the committee, and from there it went unaltered to Congress. After adopting, on 2 July, the Virginia resolution for independence, Congress debated the proposed declaration line by line for two and one-half days. Jefferson squirmed under this ordeal. The philosophical preamble was speedily approved, but the delegates made many changes, mostly stylistic, some of substance, in the body of the work, the long indictment of George III. Jefferson seemed to think the Declaration lost more than it gained in this process; in fact, it gained in every respect.

Yet the Declaration of Independence bore unmistakably the stamp of Jefferson's genius. Its language was bold but elevated, neither harsh nor recondite but simple and eloquent in its appeal to the reason of mankind. Its argument, though founded in English law, suppressed the particularism, the local patois, of the English constitution to fundamental human values. Jefferson encapsulated a cosmology, a political philosophy, and a national creed in the celebrated second paragraph. The truths there declared to be "self-evident" were not new; indeed, as Jefferson later said, his purpose was "not to find out new principles, or new arguments ..., but to place before mankind the common sense of the subject." For the first time in history, these truths were laid at the foundation of a nation. Human equality, the natural rights of man, the sovereignty of the people, the right of revolution – these principles endowed the American Revolution with high purpose united to a theory of free government. They heralded the democratic future, and not alone in America, though no one at the time, certainly not Jefferson, realized the far-reaching importance of this act of 4 July 1776. Many years passed before his authorship was generally known, but in due time the Declaration of Independence became his first title to fame.

Jefferson soon returned to Virginia, won election to the reconstituted legislature, and plunged into the work of revolutionizing the colonial government. The constitution adopted while he was in Philadelphia fell distressingly short of his ideas. Although it did away with the monarchical executive, it left the old elite entrenched in power, excluded one-half of the citizenry from the political process, and was silent on feudal land tenures, the religious establishment, and other aristocratic abuses. Worst of all the constitution had been adopted without the "consent of the governed" laid down as a first principle in the Declaration. Jefferson had drafted a more democratic instrument and sent it to Williamsburg, but it arrived too late for serious consideration. Now he postponed the objective of a new constitution for the duration of the war and, from his seat in the House of Delegates, sought liberal reforms by ordinary legislation.

These reforms, Jefferson said, composed "a system by which every fiber would be eradicated of the ancient or feudal aristocracy, and a foundation laid for government truly republican." The abolition of entail and primogeniture removed vestiges of feudal practice and established a uniformly individualistic system of land tenure. If the action was not as radical as Jefferson supposed, it nevertheless tended to break the pride and opulence of aristocratic families and contributed to that "revolution of property" from generation to generation which Alexis de Tocqueville would later view as one of the foundations of American democracy. More important was the Virginia Statute for Religious Freedom. Finally enacted in 1786, when Jefferson was in France, it climaxed a decade-long campaign for religious freedom and separation of church and state in Virginia. The statute became a

Locket with miniature of Martha Jefferson, the oldest child of Thomas Jefferson.

"Nobody in this world can make me so happy, or so miserable, as you," Jefferson wrote to his daughter.

powerful directive for the unique relationship of church and state in the American polity, and by its bold assertion that the opinions of men are beyond the reach of civil authority, one of the great charters of the free mind as well.

Unfortunately, Jefferson did not have the same success with the other major reforms of his system. A remarkable bill – as remarkable for its erudition as for its principles and objectives – to revolutionize Virginia's criminal code would have taken a long stride toward humanitarian standards of criminal justice. But the Virginians seemed to prefer their own bloody code, and the bill was defeated. The same fate befell Jefferson's Bill for More General Diffusion of Knowledge. "If a nation expects to be ignorant and free in a state of civilization," he once wrote, "it expects what never was and never will be." His "quixotism" on this subject was, therefore, rooted in his political principles, and education became a paramount responsibility of republican government. He proposed a complete system of public education from elementary schools at the bottom to a state university at the top. In this conception, in its substitution of the citizen-republicanism of the new nation for the religious ideal of New England education and its social aim of replacing the "pseudo aristocracy" of wealth and privilege with the "natural aristocracy" of talent, Jefferson's plan was a landmark in the history of American education even if it did not come to fruition in Virginia. Slavery was still another formidable obstacle to the hopes of republicanism. A plan of gradual emancipation was part of Jefferson's system. It was held back on the plea of expediency, however. Convinced that "the public mind would not yet bear the proposition," and unwilling to martyr himself uselessly, Jefferson looked to the younger generation to turn the fate of this question.

On the whole, then, despite one of the most monumental enterprises in the annals of legislation, the achievement fell far short of the goal. Nearly all these bills, and over a hundred others, were to form a revised code of law for the new commonwealth, but this rational aim also miscarried. Jefferson was most successful with the reforms that tore at the aristocratic fabric of Virginia society, such as feudal landholdings and the religious establishment. His more constructive measures such as public education were rejected, with the result that the new republican fabric was a thing of bits and patches. Most Virginians did not share his vision. They followed him, kicking, only part way, and the defeat of his most earnest reforms tended even to rob his victories of character. Nor would he succeed when the war ended in remaking the Virginia constitution. It remained for the rest of his life a stumbling block on the road to democracy.

On 1 June 1779, after leading the popular party in the assembly for two and one-half years, Jefferson was elected to succeed Patrick Henry as governor of the commonwealth. The republican convictions, benevolent temperament, and philosophical turn of mind that had given him eminence in the legislative forums of the Revolution would be less serviceable to executive leadership in a situation pregnant with disaster. The war had entered an ominous new phase. The British, unable to destroy General Washington's army in the north, had decided to "unravel the thread of rebellion from the southward." If successful, Virginia must become the crucial battleground. At the risk of the state's own meager defenses, Jefferson sped all possible assistance southward. But he struggled against enormous odds. Inflation ran rampant; arms, stores, and ammunition were desperately short; there were

never enough fighting men; and as the war dragged on, morale dipped so low that militia balked in the counties. These problems had deep roots and had probably passed beyond the power of government to solve. The executive office was weak, and Jefferson, with his aversion to anything bordering on arbitrary rule, was not the governor to strengthen it. While showing commendable zeal and industry, he was unwilling to yield his temperate civilian demeanor to one of high-toned military energy, which, in his opinion, the people would never endure. If the Revolution was to be worth anything to the survivors, freedom and self-government must vindicate themselves in the ultimate victory.

Early in January 1781, the traitor-general, Benedict Arnold, invaded the state from the coast, sped through the lowcountry all the way to Richmond, now the capital, and put the government itself to flight. Jefferson met the crisis bravely, and upon his return to the capital acted with more vigor than before, still to no avail. In the spring General Cornwallis marched his southern army into the defenseless state. The government moved to safer quarters, at Charlottesville, in Jefferson's neighborhood. The redcoats followed, and on 4 June, after his term of office had expired but before a successor could be named, he was chased from Monticello. At this crescendo of humiliation and defeat, the House of Delegates voted an inquiry into the conduct of the executive. In December, several months after the British surrender at Yorktown, Jefferson attended the legislature on this business; but no inquiry was held, the assembly instead voting him a resolution of thanks for his services, which if not a vindication erased all idea of censure.

Exhausted by his ordeal, wounded by criticism, and disgusted that his exertions had been of so little account, Jefferson resolved to quit the public stage for ever. Every effort, by Congress, by the General Assembly, even by his Albemarle constituents, to draw him back into service was rebuffed. A series of personal misfortunes, culminating in his wife's death in September 1782, plunged him into the darkest gloom. Yet it was Martha's death that finally led him back into the path of destiny. The idealized life he had sought at Monticello suddenly passed out of reach. "Before that event my scheme of life had been determined," he wrote to a friend in December. "I had folded myself in the arms of retirement, and rested all prospects of future happiness on domestic and literary objects. A single event wiped away all my plans and left me a blank which I had not the spirit to fill up." Fortunately, Congress threw him a lifeline: renewal of the commission previously declined to negotiate peace in Paris. Peace came before he could sail, however, and Jefferson wound up in Congress instead.

Jefferson would have agreed with Poor Richard's definition of leisure: a time for doing something useful. During his retirement he wrote, in large part, his first and only book, the *Notes on the State of Virginia*. Actually it did not begin as a book or with any view to publication but as a direct response to a series of questions about Virginia posed by the Secretary of the French legation in Philadelphia. Becoming fascinated with these matter-of-fact questions, Jefferson converted the task into an intellectual discovery of his own country. The manuscript grew as he worked at it, and he was induced finally to publish it in a private edition, in Paris, in 1785. A melange of information and opinion on many subjects, from cascades and mountains to constitutions and mammoths, the *Notes on Virginia* is uniquely interesting as a guide to Jefferson's mind as well as to his native country. It exhibits his insatiable

curiosity, multifarious interests, and speculative bent. It reveals the man of science, disciplined to empirical fact and eager to possess nature for the mind, but also the man of
almost romantic sensibility enraptured by the size and the wonders of the American environment even in his quest for utilitarian knowledge. The book was a virtual manual of
Jefferson's political opinions, and some of its passages – on slavery, on the virtues of husbandry and the vices of cities, on the errors of the Virginia constitution – would become so
well known that they were said to be "stereotyped in the public voice." Of unusual interest
was Jefferson's vindication of American nature against current European theories of
impotence and decay. According to these theories the New World exhibited fewer species
than the Old, and, of the animals common to both, those of America were smaller, meanly
formed, "very few ferocious, and none formidable." The native race of Indians was also
weak in body and mind – all the result of a cold, damp climate – and even the transplanted
European, some had said, was doomed to waste and decay in the niggardly New World.
Jefferson's refutation of the European savants was ingenious, on the whole valuable as
science, and a significant expression of incipient American nationalism. The book whetted
the appetite of the tiny community of American philosophers and ensured Jefferson a
scientific and literary reputation on both sides of the Atlantic.

Jefferson's service in Congress was brief, from March 1783 to May 1784, but highly
productive. In planning for the new nation he sought to replace the chaos of custom with
the plain dictates of reason. Thus it was that he proposed the decimal system of coinage on
the dollar unit, which was subsequently enacted. After Virginia and several other states
ceded their western lands to Congress, Jefferson authored the first plan of government for
this immense trans-Appalachian domain. The Ordinance of 1784 established the principle
of creating new, free and equal self-governing states as Americans took possession of the
wilderness. To Jefferson's great regret, his provision to bar slavery from the West was
defeated, though Congress later rectified the error, in part, in the Northwest Ordinance of
1787. Still another cornerstone of national planning for the West, the Land Ordinance of
1785, derived from Jefferson's conception and revealed, once again, his passion for rational
order and precision. The effects of the rectilinear land survey projected by this legislation are
visible even today to anyone who flies over the prairies and plains and observes the linear
patchwork of the fields below. Throughout his life Jefferson showed remarkable vision
toward the West. As early as 1780 he spoke of the American experiment as an "empire of
liberty." The course of empire still ran westward; however, unlike European empires it
would rest not on colonial subservience but on the expansion of liberty and self-government
over a virgin continent.

For the next several years Jefferson would be primarily concerned with America's oceanic
frontier with Europe. In May 1784 Congress appointed him to a three-man commission to
negotiate commercial treaties with European states, and although the commission met with
indifferent success, Jefferson continued his efforts for American commerce when, a year
later, he succeeded Franklin as Minister to France. So often portrayed as a narrow
"agrarian" in his economic outlook, the Virginian was, in fact, an ardent commercial
expansionist. He perceived that the wealth and power of the new nation depended on the
growth of foreign navigation and commerce. The conditions for the development of a large

"home market" did not then exist. Until the Revolution the country had traded within the British Empire. Cut adrift in 1776, it had pursued a strategy of free trade to open new markets to American ships and productions. In its bearings for political economy – scarcely less important than in its bearings for political science – the American Revolution pitted the emerging liberal tenets of free trade and pacific intercourse among nations against the jealous mercantilist policies of European courts. Jefferson subscribed to these tenets not only as an American but as a philosopher of the Enlightenment. His continued hostility to Britain arose from his belief that the mother country, though she had lost her colonies, was determined to hold the United States in economic bondage. She was succeeding, too. The only solution, as Jefferson saw it, was commercial retaliation against Britain and the widening of American markets through liberal arrangements. He regarded France, already in treaty with the United States and, of course, the habitual enemy of Britain, as the key to the free commercial system so important to his country's future. Jefferson's diplomacy at Versailles won valuable concessions for American trade. Yet Britain maintained her economic ascendancy. Without abandoning the ambitious aim of throwing American commerce into a new orbit, Jefferson looked to the progress of reform in Europe and a strengthened national government at home to secure it.

The five years in France were among the happiest of Jefferson's life. He cared not a whit for the regal formalities of the court, and the tasks of diplomacy were often frustrating, but Paris was the acme of civilization, and such were its delights that Jefferson seemed to walk with an extra spring in his step and speak with a special lilt in his voice throughout his sojourn there. Paris showered him with the infinitely varied pleasures of the mind and spirit. He haunted the bookstores. He frequented the fashionable salons. He indulged his starved appetite for art and music and theater. He was excited by ingenious inventions – phosphorous matches, the copying press, the screw propeller – smitten by the beauties of architecture, and captivated by the French cuisine. He toured in the south of France and Italy, in England, and the Rhineland, not only for personal pleasure but that, from all his feverish activity, he might return home "charged, like a bee with the honey gathered on it," for the improvement of his own country. He interpreted the New World to the Old and presided over the two-way intercourse of science and thought. Some of this would have profound effects, as in his design for the Virginia Capitol, which inaugurated the Roman style in the architecture of the young Republic, and, of course, in his transmission of revolutionary ideas to the French. About France, and Europe generally, he expressed ambivalent feelings. On the one hand, taste and civility and artistic splendor; on the other hand, luxury, oppression, debauchery, and ignorance. On balance, the more he saw of Europe the dearer his own country became. "My God!" he exclaimed. "How little do my countrymen know what precious blessings they are in possession of, and which no other people on earth enjoy. I confess I had no idea of it myself...." In sum, like many of the countrymen who would follow him, he came into full possession of his Americanism on the shores of Europe.

Despite the restraints of his official position, Jefferson was a friend of the Revolution of 1789. Many Frenchmen, inspired by the American example, looked to him for advice, and some were surprised by its moderation. While he advocated liberal reform of the Bourbon monarchy, including the establishment of representative legislative bodies, guarantees of

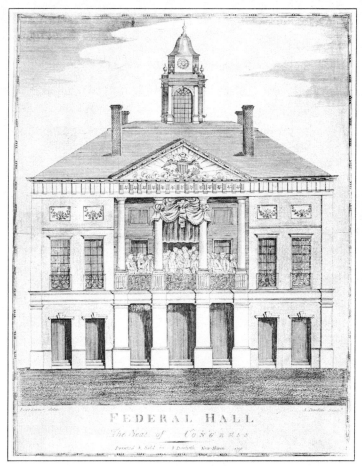

The Inauguration of George Washington in 1789 at
the Federal Hall in New York which was then the
capital of the United States.

certain individual liberties, and removal of the most objectionable feudal privileges, he did
not think the French people were prepared for democratic revolution on the American
model; and he cautioned his friends in Paris against pushing things too far lest they provoke
a conservative reaction such as had devastated the recent revolution in Holland. Yet as the
movement grew more radical, almost from month to month, so too did Jefferson. He went
with the Revolution, and at each critical juncture realigned his thinking with a swiftness that
would put a closet philosopher to shame. By the time he returned to the United States in the
fall of 1789 – after the ascendancy of the national assembly, the so-called abolition of
feudalism, and the adoption of the Declaration of the Rights of Man and Citizen – he looked
upon the French Revolution as an extension of the American and believed his own country

had a vital stake in its future. As France went, so would go Europe. "Here," he said, "is but the first chapter in the history of European liberty."

Jefferson came home on leave, fully expecting to return to Paris, but President Washington prevailed upon him to become Secretary of State in the new government. While he was away the United States had undergone a kind of revolution of its own. With the adoption of the Constitution of 1787, the country had established a national government to replace the feeble union of states under the Articles of Confederation. How feeble that union had been, especially when it came to dealing with foreign governments, Jefferson had learned from his own experience abroad. So he was cordial to the new experiment. At the same time, as he pondered the Constitution in Paris, he felt that it had been too much influenced by disenchantment with the democracy released in 1776. He objected, in particular, to the perpetual reeligibility of the chief magistrate, fearing that the office would degenerate into a monarchy with all the evils of the European prototype, and objected also to the omission of a bill of rights. He expressed these views to friends at home while the Constitution was in the course of ratification. Partly through his intervention, especially as it fell on his great friend James Madison, the advocates of the Constitution consented to the addition of the Bill of Rights by way of amendment. (Ultimately, by the Twenty-Second Amendment, he would prevail on the first point as well.) Anxious for the success of the new government, Jefferson took up his duties in New York, the temporary capital, in March 1790.

Although the State Department embraced a variety of domestic responsibilities, it was essentially the American foreign office. For this work the forty-six-year-old Virginian had impressive qualifications. Trained in Europe's leading school of diplomacy, Versailles, he had also won the respect of his countrymen without distinction of party or section. He had those qualities of quiet dignity, self-possession, adroitness, resourcefulness, and perseverance so much wanted in diplomacy. He had the talent of relating gracefully to any situation and the wit to slide around rough corners without losing sight of the object. He liked Franklin's rule: "never contradict anybody" – far better to tolerate differences of opinion, insinuate doubts, ask questions, and in this good-humored fashion discover grounds of cooperation. Above all, Jefferson had a clear conception of the national interest. But he would be sorely tried in his efforts to implement this conception, and the main objectives, while advanced, would seem as far from solution when he retired from office at the end of 1793 as when he began.

The main objectives were, first, the further liberation of American commerce, which Jefferson associated with a strengthened French alliance; second, the redemption of the West from European colonialism, the Spanish to the south, the British to the north, together with the pacification of the Indians; and third, the manipulation of American neutrality in any war involving European powers to advance the principles and interests of the United States. With Spain he sought to fix the southern boundary and to secure free navigation of the Mississippi River through Spanish territory to the Gulf. As long as Spain held the Floridas and New Orleans, in Jefferson's opinion they were America's for the taking; but he wished to obtain them peacefully and would have been quite patient but for the danger that they might again become sacrificial pawns on the chessboard of European politics and fall to Britain or France. These problems would not be resolved for many years.

Jefferson succeeded in 1791 in forcing negotiations with Britain. Removal of His Majesty's troops from below the Great Lakes and the settlement of other issues left over from the treaty of peace were the first aims. In any encounter with Britain, Jefferson believed the United States had a potent weapon, commercial discrimination, at its disposal. Britain could be made to pay for her virtual monopoly of the American market; and if this was not enough to extort concessions, then Britain's vulnerable dependence in war on American provisions, both at home and in the West Indian colonies, would be. But in his negotiations with Britain, Jefferson was thwarted by the Secretary of Treasury, Alexander Hamilton. Hamilton's fiscal system turned on the reality of British trade, credit, and power. The Treasury coffers were filled with the revenue of the British trade, revenue mortgaged to servicing the huge national debt, which in turn consolidated the creditor class to the government. The tendency of Hamilton's system as it affected foreign policy was to tie the country to Britain. Jefferson's system, on the other hand, looked to commercial expansion outside the British orbit, alliance with France, and the progress of democratic revolution in Europe. His commitment to the French Revolution was more than philosophical. He earnestly believed that its success was "necessary to stay up our own [revolution], and to prevent it from falling back into that kind of half-way house, the English constitution." The American experiment was still precarious; buffeted on treacherous seas with no other friend in sight but France, vulnerable to every "monarchical" crosscurrent, its future must ultimately depend on the outcome of the struggle for liberty in the Atlantic world.

Of course, the conflict between Jefferson and Hamilton – the archetypal conflict of American politics – went beyond foreign policy. The New Yorker's measures, mounted on the funded debt and bank stock, enriched the few at the expense of the many, excited speculation and fraud, corrupted even the Congress, and broke down the restraints of the Constitution. In Jefferson's opinion, the system was counter-revolutionary at home as well as abroad. To combat it he associated himself with the incipient opposition led by Madison in Congress. As the party division between Federalists and Republicans deepened, Jefferson was publicly denounced by Hamilton and company as the "generalissimo" of the Republicans and the real enemy of the administration he pretended to serve. His role was not an easy one – a Janus in the cabinet according to the Hamiltonians – but he endeavored to separate loyalty to President Washington from opposition to the ruling party, and he neither possessed nor coveted the Republican leadership at this stage.

When war erupted between France and Britain in 1793, the contrary dispositions of the parties toward these nations threatened American peace. Jefferson supported the neutrality declared by the President, but he attempted to use this policy to force concessions from Britain and consolidate the French alliance. Again checked by Hamilton, he was then embarrassed by the firebrand French minister, Edmond Genet. Arriving on a wave of victories by the revolutionary armies over the "conspiracy of kings," Genet aroused great popular enthusiasm for the new French Republic. Jefferson hoped that all this emotion might be converted into party capital with which to sink the anglophile Federalists. But Genet's warlike antics spoiled everything. To preserve peace, and to preserve the Republican party from the fallout of the threatened explosion, Jefferson was forced to destroy Genet. The rescue operation was successful. Indeed, Jefferson deftly restored Britain as the principal

enemy of American neutrality before he left the government at the year's end. Even so, the deterioration of Franco-American relations did irreparable damage to his political system.

Tired, disappointed, distressed by the drift of events, Jefferson had once again determined to quit the public stage forever. Return to the orange-red highlands of his native Albemarle – "the Eden of the United States" – was a return to the paradise of his soul. "My farm, my family and my books call me to them irresistibly." From his little mountain he portrayed himself as a plain farmer, a patriarch among his children, reading not a single newspaper, and while still capable of outraged ejaculations against the enemies of liberty, "preferring infinitely to contemplate the tranquil growth of my lucerne and potatoes." A touring Frenchman in 1796 found this American Cato in the midst of harvest under a scorching sun. "In private life," Duc de la Rochefoucauld-Liancourt wrote:

> Mr. Jefferson displays a mild, easy, and obliging temper, though he is somewhat cold and reserved. His conversation is of the most agreeable kind, and he possesses a stock of information not inferior to that of any other man. In Europe he would hold a distinguished rank among men of letters, and as such he has already appeared there; at present he is employed with activity and perseverance in the management of his farms and buildings; and he orders, directs, and pursues in the minutest detail every branch of the business relative to them.

Jefferson's estate was in excess of ten thousand acres, yet his debts ran to about that many pounds. By returning the farms to his personal management after so many years of neglect, he expected to reverse the course of fortune, get free of debt, and at the same time contribute to the improvement of the most useful of the sciences, agriculture. He really believed with Jonathan Swift "that whoever could make two ears of corn or two blades of grass to grow upon a spot of ground where only one grew before, would deserve better of mankind and do more essential service to his country than the whole race of politicians put together." And Jefferson did make such improvements, the best known of which was his moldboard of "least resistance" for the plow. But in practical farming he showed more science than skill. The payoff was marginal. Moreover, Jefferson could not curb his rather lavish tastes. He rebuilt Monticello – no small expense for fifteen years – the better to accommodate his children and grandchildren and the better to express his personal ideal.

As before, the pastoral idyl he imagined for himself at Monticello eluded his grasp, and in 1796 he yielded to pressures drawing him back into the politics he professed to hate. ("Wasn't it wonderful," John Adams cynically remarked, "how political plants grew in the shade!") Without a word of assent from him, the Republicans made Jefferson their presidential candidate against Adams, his old Massachusetts friend. Adams won in a close contest, and Jefferson succeeded him as Vice President, the post he actually preferred. "The second office ... is honorable and easy, the first is but splendid misery." In truth, it proved neither very honorable nor easy. The prolonged partisan controversy over Jay's treaty with Britain had, as Henry Adams later said, "plunged a sword into the body politic," and the wounds still festered. Angered by the treaty, which undercut the old alliance, France was in the diplomatic high ropes when Adams took office and his entire administration revolved around peace or war with France. Things came to a crisis with the XYZ Affair of 1798. This clumsy attempt by French officials to extort money from the United States as the price of

peace drove the administration toward war, made heroes of the Federalists, and villains of the Republicans, the Vice President at the head. In the enveloping hysteria Jefferson clung to the hope of peace, made the best excuses he could for France, and rallied the battered Republicans in opposition to the "war system." Enactment of the repressive Alien and Sedition Laws convinced him that the Federalists aimed under the smokescreen of war to annihilate the Republican party. Since the "war party" dominated all branches of the national government, it had the power, unchecked, to intimidate the press and clog the wheels of public opinion. The only salvation, Jefferson concluded, lay in the intervention of the state authorities.

Thus it was that he secretly drafted the Kentucky Resolutions of 1798. Enacted by the Kentucky legislature, these resolutions set forth the theory of the Union as a compact among the several states, declared the Alien and Sedition Laws unconstitutional, and prescribed the remedy of state "nullification" (Jefferson's word, omitted by Kentucky) for such usurpations by the national government. The Virginia assembly adopted similar resolutions drafted by Madison. The doctrine of the "Resolutions of '98" was complex. Professing to be expositions of the Constitution, they first needed exposition themselves. What is most important is that they joined the defense of civil and political liberty to the defense of state rights under the Constitution, and so it happened that the appeal to the revolutionary tradition became mixed up with the state rights issue on which the Civil War would be fought. But whatever the wayward tendencies of the doctrine, the Resolutions of '98 were born of a desperate struggle for political survival. As Jefferson said, they "pursued a political resistance for political effect." Without forcing a change of policy, they helped to throw the Adams administration on the defensive and to arouse the popular discontents that led to its defeat in 1800.

The election of 1800 was unusually bitter. Around the person of Jefferson the Republicans achieved a unity of action and feeling not known before. He was presented to the public as the "man of the people," while Adams was draped in the hideous garments of kings and nobles. The Federalists, sharply divided among themselves, united in sounding the tocsin about Jefferson, vilifying him as a Jacobin incendiary, infidel, visionary, demagogue, and the enemy of Washington, the Constitution, and the Union. For ten years Federalists pundits had been fashioning this ugly image of Jefferson. Now it became a diabolical obsession. Under him, surely, the churches would be destroyed and the nation laid waste by revolutionary fanaticism imported from France. "Murder, robbery, rape, adultery, and incest will be openly taught and practiced," wrote one pamphleteer, "the air will be rent with the cries of distress, and the soil will be soaked with blood, and the nation black with crimes." Jefferson, while personally hurt by the smear campaign, nursed his wounds in private. He had long since learned that for every libel put down another rose in its place; besides, he was committed philosophically to the widest latitude of public discussion on the principle he would state in his Inaugural Address: "that error of opinion may be tolerated where reason is left free to combat it."

By carrying New York, most of Pennsylvania, and all the southern states, Jefferson topped Adams in the electoral vote seventy-three to sixty-five. Unfortunately, his running mate, Aaron Burr, received an equal number of votes (the Twelfth Amendment had yet to be

A cartoon ridiculing the unpopular Embargo imposed
by Jefferson in 1807 which prohibited American ships
from going to foreign ports.

enacted), so the final decision went to the House of Representatives. There the "lame duck"
Federalist majority, defiant to the end, supported Burr. Only after thirty-six ballots was
Jefferson elected. Inaugurated in Washington, the embryo capital on the Potomac he had
himself helped to plan, Jefferson was anxious to quiet the political passions of the past decade
and to introduce into government that serene and noiseless course which, in his opinion, was
the mark of a society progressing in happiness. The Inaugural Address loftily appealed for
the restoration of harmony and affection. "We are all republicans: we are all federalists."
Although the defeated party monopolized the offices, Jefferson limited removals to excep-
tional cases, trusting that the mass of Federalists would become converts to Republicanism.
Even after partisan pressures forced him to revise this strategy, moderation characterized
his course.

Conciliation did not exclude reform, however. Jefferson viewed his victory as "the
revolution of 1800," by which he meant the overthrow of Tory politics, elitist, privileged,
distrustful of the people, centralizing and "monarchical" in tendency, and return to the
Whig principles of 1776. His Inaugural Address – a political touchstone for a century to
come – offered a brilliant summation of the Republican creed. Striking a balance between
reformation and reconciliation was not easy. But Jefferson and the new Republican
majority quickly restored freedom of the press, returned the law of naturalization to five
years (Federalists had raised it to fourteen), drastically reduced the army and navy (despite
war on Barbary piracy), repealed the partisan Judiciary Act of 1801 (thereby containing the
Federatism of the bench), abolished all internal taxes (together with a small army of col-

lectors), replaced courtly forms and ceremonies with "Jeffersonian simplicity," and began the planned retirement of the debt over a period of sixteen years. The reformation was founded on fiscal policy. By contracting the means with the powers of government, Jefferson sought to further peace, equality, and individual freedom. Of course, he did not tear down all the machinery the Federalists had built. He prudently tolerated Hamilton's bank, for example. "It mortifies me to be strengthening principles which I deem radically vicious, but the vice is entailed by the first error," he said, adding philosophically, "What is practicable must often control pure theory." Radical purists in his own party thought him too conciliatory, while hard-core Federalists found him as radical as they had feared. These political extremes proved troublesome, though powerless, throughout Jefferson's Presidency. The mass of the nation approved his pragmatic middle course, and he was overwhelmingly reelected in 1804, only two states, Connecticut and Delaware, voting against him.

The nation's prospects in foreign affairs were never brighter than at the beginning of Jefferson's administration. An uneasy *détente* prevailed with Britain; a new treaty with France removed the source of difficulty with that power; and after eight years of war, peace was in the offing in Europe. Almost immediately, however, the "embryo of a tornado" appeared on the western horizon. Spain's retrocession of Louisiana, with the great port of New Orleans, to France threatened American peace and the aspirations of the West. Under the terms of a six-year-old treaty with Spain, the United States enjoyed free navigation of the Mississippi and the privileges of the port. That was sufficient for the time being. But Louisiana, and possibly the Floridas also, in the hands of France was another matter, signaling the rebirth under Napoleonic auspices of French empire in the New World. The old Franco-American alliance was dead not only in law but in Jefferson's affections. From the time of the eighteenth *brumaire* of Napoleon Bonaparte, crushing Jefferson's last hopes for the French Revolution, France had become just another despotic empire in the European balance of power, to be used, like Britain, wherever possible for American advantage but not to be suffered as a force in the country's affairs.

Napoleon's designs on the Mississippi and the Gulf inevitably put France on a collision course with the United States. But these designs were beset by so many difficulties that Jefferson refused to take alarm in 1801. The new plan of empire centered on Santo Domingo, richest of the French colonies, then in control of rebel blacks led by Toussaint L'Ouverture; and the reconquest of Santo Domingo would not be easy. Unless the Floridas were included in the Spanish cession, Louisiana would be of doubtful value to France. Britain could not be indifferent to the revival of French power in North America. Nor could France be indifferent to confrontation with the United States on the Mississippi lest she find herself again at war in Europe. In Jefferson's jaundiced view, any peace, such as the forthcoming Peace of Amiens, must be only a truce, war being Europe's natural state; and on the first crack of the cannon, the United States might seize New Orleans and more as the price of neutrality or in reprisal for wrongs.

Considering all these imponderables, Jefferson made as little noise as possible and put Louisiana in the track of diplomacy. His strategy was one of delay and maneuver improvised to meet events as they unfolded. The American Minister, Robert Livingston, negotiated in

Paris, while Secretary of State Madison pressed the country's case on the French chargé d'affaires, who in turn transmitted every perturbation to his superiors at home. Jefferson exploited unofficial channels of diplomacy as well. In April 1802 he struck a bold new course. Through the good offices of his friend, Pierre Dupont de Nemours, Jefferson sternly warned Napoleon that from the day France took possession of New Orleans, the United States would have no alternative but to "marry ourselves to the British fleet and nation." While Jefferson flourished this thunderbolt, Madison worked up the purchase project, a project that could only have originated with an administration determined to settle international disputes without resort to force. Jefferson was still counting on time, which in this affair as in all things he believed to be on the American side. Napoleon had yet to make good his policy; his armies were decimated in Santo Domingo; no French expedition sailed for Louisiana; and war clouds again gathered in Europe. But the clock was turned ahead dramatically in October 1802 when the Spanish Intendant at New Orleans closed the river to the Americans. While quietly negotiating this crisis through the Spanish envoy, Jefferson magnified the clamor at home for maximum effect abroad and seized the occasion to appoint James Monroe Minister Extraordinary to join Livingston in treating for the purchase of New Orleans and the Floridas, supposing, wrongly, that the Floridas were France's to sell. If he failed Monroe was to take the problem to London.

But the problem was resolved before Monroe arrived in Paris. Napoleon, the dream of New World empire fading, turned his imperious gaze eastward and renounced Louisiana. The purchase treaty was quickly arranged. It was not exactly the bargain Jefferson had sought. It included the whole of Louisiana, together with New Orleans, but not the Floridas, for a price of approximately fifteen million dollars. Doubtless the Louisiana Purchase owed more to the vagaries of Napoleon's ambition than to Jefferson's lion-and-fox diplomacy. Jefferson never claimed that *he* bought Louisiana; still he resented the grumblers and doubters who from one side of their mouth denounced him for the acquisition and from the other denied him any credit for it. The entire proceeding was an impressive vindication of the ways of peace in American affairs. In the final analysis, Jefferson was saved by a European war; but this was not just a piece of dumb luck. The probability of war, like the probability of French disaster in Santo Domingo, entered into his calculations. He correctly weighed the imponderables in the European power balance, shrewdly threatened to throw his weight into the British scale, gauged the effect of renewed war on Napoleon's imperial design, and prepared to take advantage of the démarche when it came. It came sooner than he expected, and it brought the United States the great trans-Mississippi domain, which had not been an immediate object because the nation was not threatened there, though it would surely become American in good time. Instead it came all at once, which altered the timetable of American expansion but not its destination.

Jefferson had, in fact, already planned an expedition to the sources of the Missouri River and westward to the Pacific. By a happy coincidence the man he had chosen to lead this "voyage of discovery," Captain Meriwether Lewis, set forth from Washington on 4 July 1803, the acclaim of the Louisiana Purchase ringing in his ears. The Lewis and Clark expedition was a spectacular consummation of Jefferson's western vision. The addition of some 800,000 square miles to the American Union, almost doubling its size, presented some

Above: The small sketch is by Jefferson for red damask draperies for Monticello. The upper sketch is by John Rea who made the curtains.

Left: Sketches by Jefferson (c. 1798) of curtains for Monticello to be made of blue and red damask.

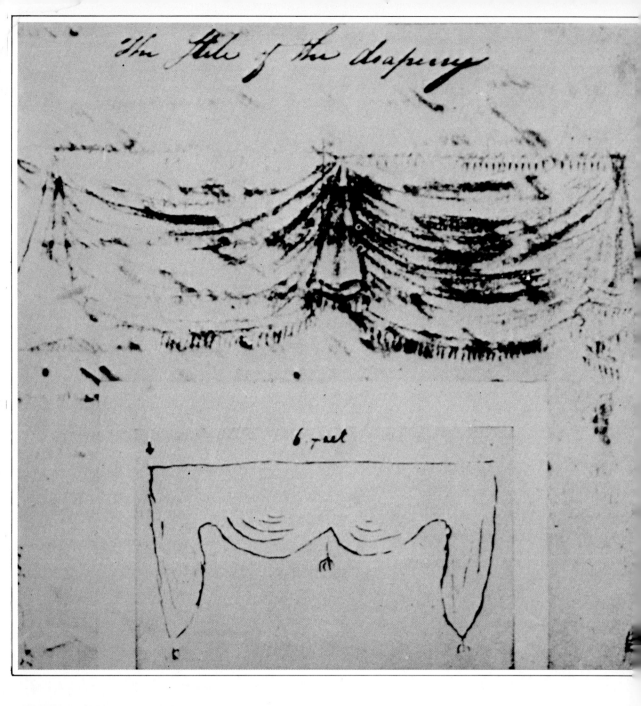

The Stile of the draperys

6 feet

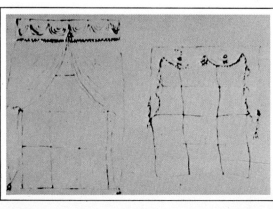

peculiar problems to the President. Did the Constitution allow it? Jefferson thought not and proposed an amendment to sanction the acquisition retroactively, but his friends in Congress and the cabinet dissuaded him from this course. How was the "foreign" populace of lower Louisiana, centered around New Orleans, to be governed? Jefferson believed the territory should be Americanized both in its demographic composition and in its laws and institutions before admission into the estate of freedom and self-government and partnership in the Union. There were many scrapes and perplexities along this road. Not until the western conspiracy of Aaron Burr was crushed in 1807 could Jefferson feel confident that the expanded Union would mature in common freedom and loyalty. Finally, there was the problem of boundaries. They were hopelessly obscure. Jefferson shiftily claimed West Florida as far as the Perdido River (the present western boundary of Florida) as part of the purchase, and he offered Spain two million dollars and half of Texas, also claimed, for East Florida. Spain disdained the overture, and Jefferson's relentless scheming for the Floridas vitiated his diplomacy abroad and exposed him to attack at home for the next five years.

It was ironic that the President who put a continent at the feet of his countrymen – an empire within itself – whose whole animus was to reject the wars and intrigues of European politics and turn the nation's energies inward, should have found himself embroiled during his second term in a struggle for American rights on the high seas. With the formation of the Third Coalition against Napoleon in 1805, all Europe was at war. The United States became the last neutral of consequence, in effect the entrepôt of Europe, and its commerce and navigation was not less profitable to the Americans than it was needful to the combatants. Each side demanded the trade on its own terms; adherence to one entailed conflict with the other. While Jefferson might try to play off one power against the other, little leverage was left for this game when they divided the land and the sea between them. Neither feared war with the United States, whose President prided himself on peace – "peace is my passion" – and who had neither army nor navy to speak of. So both Britain and France played fast and loose with American neutrality.

In Jefferson's eyes, however, Britain was the chief aggressor. Thousands of American seamen were cruelly impressed into His Majesty's service. Impressment assaulted the very existence of American nationality; it could not be tolerated. British privateers infested American waters and plundered American trade. The decision of a British admiralty court in July 1805 endangered the flourishing American re-export trade. On the previous rule of the "broken voyage," the insertion of an American port in the trade between enemy colonies and the continent had "neutralized" the cargoes: now this neutral trade was declared fraudulent and subject to seizure and condemnation. Why? Not, in Jefferson's opinion, to cut off supplies from Britain's enemies, but to force a dangerous commercial rival, the United States, from the colonial trade and to monopolize it for herself even to the length of actually supplying her enemies. American diplomatic initiative to settle these issues in 1806 produced a treaty, but it omitted the ultimatum on impressment and, failing in other respects as well, Jefferson angrily refused even to submit it to the Senate. This was followed in June 1807 by the inflammatory *Chesapeake-Leopard* Affair. The arrogance and brutality of this attack on an American frigate united the country in thunderous indignation against Britain. War only awaited the snap of Jefferson's fingers. Instead, he deliberately

View of windows at Monticello, designed by Jefferson.

cooled the crisis and attempted to make it a lever in negotiations with Britain, alas, to no avail. New orders in council in the fall closed the entire continent to American trade except on the monopolistic British terms. And Napoleon, viewing the neutral trade as British in disguise, extended his decrees to the Americans. Between the Emperor's tightening Continental System and the British orders, American commerce was caught in the jaws of a vise, a maniacal war of blockades, from which there seemed to be no appeal to reason or justice.

Thus it was that Jefferson recommended, and Congress enacted on 22 December 1807, the Embargo Law withdrawing American commerce and navigation from the oceans. More than an alternative to war, this most daring act of Jeffersonian statecraft was an experiment to test the effectiveness of "peaceable coercion" in international affairs. That the United States might, by withholding its commerce, force justice on the marauding powers of Europe, especially Britain, was an idea as old as the nation itself and one to which Jefferson had long been committed. He gave himself unstintingly to the enforcement of the embargo, a tedious business which stretched the administrative capacities of the government to the limit and, in time, over the constitutional limits Jefferson had long advocated. On the diplomatic front neither of the belligerents receded from its decrees, despite the tempting invitation thereby to force American hostilities with the other. As expected, the embargo gave rise to mounting discontents in Britain, among merchants and manufacturers and workers, but the discontents it produced at home proved more compelling. A storm of protest rolled over New England in the fall of 1808, then into the ensuing session of Congress. Finally, in the waning hours of Jefferson's Presidency, the embargo was repealed. The eventual sequel to this failure, three years later, was the War of 1812. In effect a second war of independence, Jefferson saw it as a deplorable necessity to preserve the American Revolution. He always believed that this inglorious outcome could have been avoided had the nation shown the unity and the courage to persevere in the embargo. If this estimate revealed a certain political blindness, if it suggests that Jefferson allowed himself to become the captive of an idea, seemingly insensitive to the harsh realities that opposed it, nevertheless all the angels of peace and goodwill must have shed a tear with him over the failure of so noble an experiment.

Jefferson went into retirement feeling like a prisoner released from his chains, eager to return at last to the things that he loved. His blessings were many: good health, a benign temperament, indefatigable industry, a loving family, pleasant country society, and the veneration of his countrymen. Monticello was not just a home; it was a monument. Visitors, both the great and the ordinary, came from far and near to see the Sage of Monticello. His daughter Martha (the younger daughter, Maria, had died in 1804) ran the household filled with adoring grandchildren. "My mornings are devoted to correspondence," he wrote in 1810. "From breakfast to dinner, I am in my shops, my garden, or on horseback among my farms; from dinner [mid-afternoon] to dark, I give to society and recreation with my neighbors and friends; and from candle light to early bed-time, I read." His favorite reading was in the ancient classics and in mathematics, though as always his intellectual pursuits spanned a broad front. For eighteen years, until 1815, he was President of the American Philosophical Society, the nation's premier scientific institution, to which he made important

contributions, especially in paleontology. Jefferson could not live without books. He sold his great library to Congress in 1815, where it became the nucleus of the Library of Congress, but at once commenced another. His correspondence was immense. Deluged by a hundred or more letters a month, he could not answer all of them; still he answered enough to make this daily drudgery an unfailing delight to posterity. Its best fruit was the correspondence with his old revolutionary comrade, John Adams, with whom he was reunited in friendship in 1812.

Although Jefferson wrote no books during these years, he sketched an autobiography of his early life, translated one or two books from the French, collected documents, compiled notes, essayed brief characterizations or lives of his contemporaries, and in various ways contributed to the writing of American history. Sometime before his death he completed a task begun in 1803 and which is now known as the Jefferson Bible. Through New Testament criticism, Jefferson attempted to isolate the *real* teachings of Jesus from the later corruptions of the priests and theologians. In his youth he had gone to the ancients, not to the Bible, for moral instruction; now, in the ripeness of years, he concluded that the plain, unsophisticated teachings of Jesus made the best of all moral systems. Jefferson's Bible was proof that he, whom the priests and pharisees called infidel, was "a true Christian" in the only sense that mattered, the love of man taught by Jesus. Of course, believing that religion belonged wholly to the private conscience, Jefferson disdained public defense and disapproved proselytization. The work was intended only for himself, his family, and his dearest friends. But clearly Jefferson was on the track of a unifying religion of humanity, morally earnest but stripped of supernaturalism, of which he saw anticipations in Unitarianism.

Several items of unfinished business from the Revolution claimed Jefferson's attention, among them reform of the Virginia constitution and gradual emancipation of the slaves. The former, however, would come only after his death (the Virginia oligarchs would not risk it while he lived); as for the latter, which would never come, he was disappointed when the younger generation, to whom he had committed this arduous cause, showed no more willingness to assume it than had their fathers. The great cause to which he gave himself was education. Jefferson's faith in freedom and self-government and the improvement of mankind was at bottom a faith in education. In 1814 he revived his general plan of public education. Apparently Virginia's leaders had learned nothing in thirty years, for the legislature again rejected the plan. However, shamed, cajoled, and outwitted by Jefferson and a little band of "Monticello men" in the assembly, it approved one part of the plan, the state university. Jefferson wondered at the folly of raising the apex without laying the foundations in the primary and secondary schools. Were it left to him he would abandon the university rather than the schools "because it is safer to have a whole people respectably enlightened than a few in a high state of science and the many in ignorance. This last is the most dangerous state in which a nation can be. The nations and governments of Europe are so many proofs of it." He rejoiced in the university none the less. It would be *his* university as well as the state's. In 1814 he had become associated with a local group seeking to found an academy in Charlottesville. Taking hold of the project, Jefferson at once escalated the academy into a college, chartered in 1816 at Charlottesville, and then the college into the University of Virginia, chartered in 1819. He was the master planner of the university in all

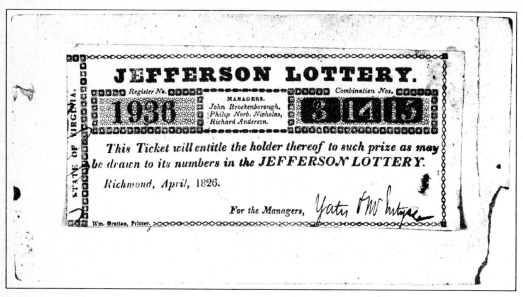

In severe financial trouble toward the end of his life,
Jefferson decided to dispose of his property by a
lottery. Funds were raised and the lottery was never
held.

its parts, from the grounds and buildings to the curriculum and faculty. Aggressively secular
and modern in conception, beyond any American counterpart, the University of Virginia
appeared the almost perfect case of Emerson's aphorism, "an institution is the lengthened
shadow of one man."

Jefferson's last years were full of anguish. For all his satisfaction with the university, he
often felt that he was "discharging the odious function of a physician pouring medicine
down the throat of a patient insensible of needing it." From the year 1819 he was deeply
troubled by the course of national politics. The Missouri Compromise "fanaticized" politics
on a sectional line dividing free and slave states; the Supreme Court became "a subtle corps
of sappers and miners" of the Constitution; and the drift toward consolidation – a new
national bank, national internal improvements, the protective tariff – threatened individual
liberty and the federal balance on which the future of the Union depended. Reeling from
these blows, Jefferson retreated to the "Resolutions of '98" and gave aid and comfort to the
revival of state rights politics in Virginia. At the same time, his personal fortune was
doomed. His estate, in sad repair when he left the Presidency, steadily deteriorated. Years of
embargo, non-intercourse, and war had injured all Virginia agriculture, and recovery had
only begun when the Panic of 1819 intervened. Jefferson, still struggling under the burden
of old debts, received his coup de grâce from a friend whose bank notes he had endorsed to
the amount of $20,000. When the panic sank the friend into bankruptcy, it almost sank
Jefferson as well. From then it was all downhill. In the end not even Monticello could be
saved from the wreckage.

Jefferson died at Monticello on the fiftieth anniversary of American independence, 4 July 1826. It almost seemed that he had arranged his death to embellish his legend. By his epitaph he chose to be remembered not for any honors his countrymen had rendered him but for what he believed were the most important services he had rendered them: Author of the Declaration of Independence and the Virginia Statute for Religious Freedom, and Father of the University of Virginia. For fifty years he had lived and worked in the faith born of the American Revolution. Death would not seal his influence. John Adams, who also died on that fateful day of jubilee, uttered a prophetic truth in his last words, "Thomas Jefferson still survives."

JEFFERSON AND THE ENLIGHTENMENT
Henry Steele Commager

It was some time during late September of 1780 that François Barbé-Marbois, newly appointed Secretary to the French Minister in Philadelphia (the Chevalier de la Luzerne), forwarded to governors and other dignitaries in each of the American states a list of twenty-two queries designed to provide him – or his government – with information about the new United States that might prove interesting and instructive. He was – as General John Sullivan observed – "one of those useful geniuses who is constantly in search of knowledge." Now it was America that he wanted to know about; he had, after all, married an American girl; and he planned to cast in his lot with this new Republic which fascinated him, as it fascinated so many of his fellow-countrymen. Only two of the many recipients of his inquiry bothered to answer him: General Sullivan, who eventually sent in a somewhat desultory response, and Thomas Jefferson, who had some claim to be considered the busiest man in the nation, but who found time to provide over three hundred pages of answers.

Marbois's questions covered geography, geology, natural resources, population, the native races, government, law, the economy, the military, religion, education and a miscellany of marginal matters such as commerce and money, weights and measures and even, for good measure, history. A big order this, comprehensive rather than searching, for it was information that Marbois wanted, rather than commentary, the kind of information that the *philosophes* soaked up like a sponge, and then organized in vast dictionaries and encyclopedias or, perhaps, in philosophical histories.

That was a pretty busy winter for Governor Jefferson, and an anxious one, too. In October an enemy fleet sailed into Cape Henry and debouched General Leslie, with several thousand redcoats on both shores of the James. The state seemed incapable of defending itself, and it was only good luck that took Leslie away from Virginia for more serious fighting in the Carolinas. The next month brought a more dangerous threat: the "parricide," Benedict Arnold, invaded Virginia, laying waste all the way to Richmond. Once again the state seemed helpless, and in December Arnold was back with further devastation. That spring of 1781 was one of the most difficult of Jefferson's life. His baby daughter, Lucy Elizabeth, died, and his beloved wife was dangerously ill; his private affairs were in disorder; his estates were in ruins. At the same time the people of Virginia, sorely beset by a series of invasions which culminated in the massive invasion by Cornwallis, were disorganized and desperate, and the government of the commonwealth was paralyzed, conscious no doubt,

Benjamin Franklin painted by Joseph Siffred Duplessis in 1778. Jefferson called Franklin, "the ornament of our country and . . . of the world."

of the sorry role it had played in these crises. The Assembly now sought a scapegoat in Governor Jefferson. In May it retired to Charlottesville, and Jefferson, his term drawing to an end, took up residence in his beloved Monticello, where he could contemplate the ruin of his estates, and of so many of his hopes. The first week in June, Cornwallis sent Colonel Tarleton on a lightning raid designed to capture Mr – no longer Governor – Jefferson, and the legislature. All escaped. After the Tarleton caper, Jefferson returned to his other home, Poplar Forest; on one of his daily rides around the farm, his horse threw him to the ground, and he was, for some weeks, incapacitated.

It is to that horse that we owe the early compilation of the *Notes on the State of Virginia*. For Jefferson, who never wasted a moment (his schedule for his daughter Patsy left no time for play, or even for meals), employed some of his enforced leisure by returning to what he had originally welcomed but put aside in the press of events: the inquiries of Marbois and the speculations they inspired. By Christmas 1781 he had finished what he considered to be merely desultory notes.

> This country [he wrote] affords to philosophic view an extensive, rich and unexplored field. It abounds in roots, plants, trees and minerals to the virtues and uses of which we are as yet stranger.... The mind of man is just awakening from a long stupor of many ages, to the discovery of useful arts and inventions. Our governments are yet unformed, and capable of great improvement. The history, manners, and customs of the aborigines are but little known....

"The philosophic view" is what Marbois's inquiries excited and what Jefferson – even then contemplating a shift from public life to the life of the mind – found irresistible.

Notes on Virginia – the informal title Jefferson gave to his book – was far more than Marbois had bargained for. It was, on one level, a guide book, even an encyclopedia; on a different and higher level it was a philosophical inquiry, an interpretation, and a platform. It discussed not only government but the nature of government, not only education but the purpose of education, not only the statistics of native races and the economy of Negro slavery, but sociological problems of uniformity or differentiation in mankind, and moral problems of race and of slavery. Like Crèvecoeur's *Letters of an American Farmer* it both probed and illuminated the American character. And – though only by implication – it presented more fully than any other treatise of its day what might be called the agenda of the American Enlightenment, an agenda which, though it drew its inspiration from the Old World Enlightenment, inevitably differed from it. It relied on reason, it rejoiced in freedom, it embraced humanitarianism, it was confident of progress, and – here the difference is dramatic – it was able, as the Old World was not, to translate these principles and faiths into practices and institutions.

This inquiry by Marbois was a typical Enlightenment inquiry. It was about the geography, the minerals, the cascades and caverns, the counties and townships and the weights and measures of Virginia, and mingled with these, questions about "all that can increase the progress of human knowledge," "the administration of justice," "the different religions," and "the customs and manners" of the people. It was, on the surface, direct and

unpretentious, but every philosopher on both sides of the water knew how to deal with this sort of thing: after all, just consider what the philosophers did with the innocuous and unambiguous subjects assigned them in the great *Encyclopédie*: Voltaire's long article on idols, for instance, was really an attack on the idolatry of the Christian church. *Notes on Virginia* takes its place, effortlessly, in the mainstream of Enlightenment literature: the literature that addressed itself to the exploration of climate, or the interaction of nature and man, and the literature that embraced civilization, or the social, political and moral institutions of man. All of these inquiries were scientific, all were sociological, all were, eventually, moral; for the philosophers were natural philosophers, they were social philosophers, they were moral philosophers and none more unequivocally than Jefferson.

Let us begin our study of Jefferson then with this matter of climate, what we call environment, one of the master ideas of the Enlightenment. The *Notes* open almost artlessly with "an exact description of the boundaries of Virginia" and with notices of "its rivers and mountains, its cascades and its caverns;" yet Jefferson manages to suffuse with poetry and to illuminate with philosophy even this prosaic record. Listen to his description of the passage of the Potomac through the Blue Ridge:

> The distant finishing which Nature has given to the picture ... is a true contrast to the foreground. It is as placid and delightful as that is wild and tremendous. For the Mountain being cloven asunder, she presents to your eye, through the cleft, a small catch of smooth blue horizon, at an infinite distance in the plain country, inviting you, from the riot and tumult roaring around, to pass through the breach and participate of the calm below.

From *Robinson Crusoe* of 1719 and Haller's epic poem, *The Alps* of 1728, to the poems of Ossian and the *Sorrows of Werther* of 1774, the Enlightenment carried with it so much of the romantic that we must conclude that some infusion of romanticism is essential; nowhere – not even in Goethe – is the admixture more pronounced than in the Jefferson who planted his Palladian Monticello on the brow of a hill looking westward across a limitless wilderness, sat up all night with the Marquis de Chastellux reciting the *Odes* of Ossian – (Ossian fradulent, but not the enthusiasm he inspired) – confessed that music was the "dearest passion" of his life, and combined reason and romance in the *Notes on Virginia*.

It is when Jefferson turns to the description of quadrupeds and man in the New World that the argument of climate gathers force, and more than force – that it becomes part of the great Enlightenment controversy over the role of climate in civilization – to what extent climate was responsible for the apparent backwardness of civilization in the New World. Here, as in so many of his speculations, Jefferson gave a new dimension to the Enlightenment theory of climate, one at that time unexplored by Old World naturalists or philosophers. For in presenting the native races of Virginia, Jefferson was fairly confronted by that curious theory of New World degeneracy which had the support not only of malicious scribblers like the notorious Corneille de Pauw ("a mere compiler who read the writings of travelers only to repeat their lies," said Jefferson), but of a formidable galaxy of historians, sociologists, and naturalists, among them the crusading pamphleteer, the Abbé Raynal, the distinguished historian, William Robertson of Edinburgh, and the lord of all creation, the Comte de

NOTES on the ſtate of VIRGINIA;

written in the year 1781, ſomewhat cor-
rected and enlarged in the winter of 1782,
for the uſe of a Foreigner of diſtinction, in
anſwer to certain queries propoſed by him
reſpecting

MDCCLXXXII.

The title page of the first edition of *Notes on the State
of Virginia*, published in Paris in 1785.

Buffon. These, and others, accepted for a time the argument that America had been doomed,
by nature itself, to degeneracy. For it was, in very truth, a New World, one which had
emerged later from the flood than had the other continents, which was still afflicted with
dismal swamps, impenetrable forests, and desperate extremes of heat and cold; a melancholy
region where, according to Buffon:

nature remains concealed under her old garment and never exhibits herself in fresh attire. Being neither cherished nor cultivated by man, she never opens her beneficent womb. In this abandoned condition everything languishes, corrupts and proves abortive. The air and the earth, overloaded with humid and noxious vapors, are unable to purify themselves or to profit by the influence of the sun, which darts in vain his most enlivening rays upon this frigid mass.

Not only animals and plants, but man himself degenerated in this inhospitable clime, for the noxious air and the poisonous soil did not sustain more than a sparse and miserable population! "The least vigorous European," wrote de Pauw, "is more than a match for the strongest American." Feeble, indolent, sluggish, without strength or courage, without ardor for the female, unable to reproduce themselves, the natives of America scarcely deserved the name of men!

One might have supposed that a theory so palpably false would not require refutation. Not at all. It had, after all, for its basis the elementary fact that the vast area from the Rio Grande to the Hudson's Bay did not support a population as large as that of Ireland; it had for its incentive the risk that the same climate that condemned the natives of America to degeneracy would work havoc on European immigrants; it had for its animus fear of the loss of population to the New World and fear of rivalry by the New World.

All Americans rallied to refute these canards, but first and last it was Jefferson who formulated the grand strategy of the campaign and directed the tactics, and whose *Notes on Virginia* delivered the decisive counter-stroke. His method was the one he had used in the Declaration of Independence, a combination of rhetoric and inductive reasoning; here as in the Declaration Jefferson established a philosophical position, and then submitted "facts ... to a candid world." Here are the facts, exact, comprehensive, and conclusive. Are American animals enfeebled and degenerate? Let us measure them. Let us weigh the European and the American bear, the first a mere 153 pounds, the second 410 pounds. In Europe the beaver grew to a maximum of eighteen pounds, in America to over forty pounds. Or look at the European deer, or renne, a mere three feet high; why, we will show you a moose from the forest of Maine that stands seven feet, and the spread of his magnificent antlers is twice that of his European cousins. Or contemplate the American bison of almost two thousand shaggy pounds, or the bullock, of over two and one-half thousand pounds, or the hog – why Jefferson himself had seen one that weighed a thousand pounds! What has Europe to compare with this? And because Jefferson knew that visible evidence was more persuasive than verbal, he followed up his arguments with demonstrations. Soon he was in Paris, inundating the Comte de Buffon with specimens of the American beaver, the American eagle, a brace of pheasants, the skin of a panther, the horns of a caribou, an elk and a roebuck. The search for a moose with which to confound Buffon reached epic proportions, with General Sullivan leading a mid-winter expedition into the Maine wilderness to track down a bull moose whose majestic size would forever silence all aspersions on nature in America. It was successful, too: the moose which Sullivan shipped over to the *Jardin de Roi* – at Jefferson's expense of course – converted even the reluctant count.

Even more eloquent was Jefferson's vindication of the native races – more eloquent and more far-reaching in its implications. How the primitive fascinated the Enlightenment: cultural anthropology was in a sense an invention of the eighteenth-century philosophers and explorers.... Men were after all everywhere the same; the youthful Benjamin West spoke for all of them when, on first seeing the Apollo Belvedere, he exclaimed, "My God, how like a Mohawk Indian!" Undress them, literally and figuratively, and the similarity was palpable – in the courts of Europe or on the shores of the Huron, in civilized China or on an island paradise in the South Pacific; if there was nobility, it was to be found not at Versailles or Vienna, but among the savages. There were differences, to be sure, but they were differences imposed not by nature, but by social and cultural conditions. Back then to original man, sail to Tahiti or find some Omai who could be transported to England to titillate the ladies of the court; penetrate the forests of Canada and find some Adario running wild in the woods, just as Dryden had described him; recover him among the remnants of the once proud Incas in some remote mountain fastness in Peru; or resurrect him from the ruins of the ancient world "so full of beautiful and godlike and youthful forms."

This was mostly moonshine, as every American knew; the truth was somewhere between the mendacities of a De Pauw and the romantic imaginings of the Baron Lahontan, who had invented Adario, or Father Lafitau who was sure that the Hurons were the descendants of the Trojans and the Greeks. The truth was indeed to be found in America, and among the Indians with whom Europeans had been familiar for two centuries. Formally, or informally – and mostly the latter – all the American philosophers were ethnologists: Franklin, who had made treaties with the Indians; Governor Cadwallader Colden of New York, who wrote on the Five Civilized Tribes; Washington, who had fought them; John Bartram, who had lived with them; Charles Thomson, Secretary to the Philosophical Society, who was adopted into the Delaware tribe; Dr Rush, who speculated so audaciously about their physical and mental characteristics; and Crèvecoeur, who saw their best and their worst qualities. None knew them better than Jefferson, or had studied more assiduously their character and their history; over the years he had collected some fifty Indian vocabularies, a priceless collection since lost to vandalism. No one contributed more to our knowledge of them, directly through the *Notes on Virginia*, indirectly through sponsoring such explorers as the Yankee John Ledyard, whom Jefferson launched on his astonishing pedestrian expedition from Paris to Kamchatka, and who was prepared to prove, from personal experience, the unity of the natives of Siberia and of the American West, or André Michaux, who combined botanizing with ethnology, and a bit of diplomacy too, or Meriwether Lewis and William Clark, whose famous expedition was one of the glories of the Jefferson administration.

In the *Notes*, Jefferson seized the opportunity to demonstrate that the Old World animadversions on the Indian were as misguided as those on nature. The Indian was a product of climate, and, over the ages, had adapted himself perfectly to that climate. He was ardent and brave, strong and agile, resourceful and sagacious, perfectly adapted to the nature which produced him. As for ardor and virility, the Indians had the passions and the powers that the circumstances of their lives dictated, neither more nor less, and their bodies and minds were as well adapted to their environment as were the bodies and minds of Europeans to the environment of civilization. And with this went eloquence, and nobility

of character. To demonstrate these qualities, Jefferson reproduced the speech of Chief Logan of the Mingoes, a flight of eloquence worthy of Demosthenes himself – or perhaps we should say of Jefferson, for we cannot wholly resist the suspicion that it was more Jefferson than Logan.

If climate was decisive, then logically the animadversions of Buffon and Raynal and de Pauw extended to all who were the victims of that climate, Europeans as well as natives; de Pauw embraced this logic, as did many others, and wrote:

> The Creoles, though educated at the Universities of Mexico and Lima, have never produced a single book, and through the whole length of America, from Cape Horn to the Hudson Bay, there has never appeared a philosopher, an artist, a man of learning whose name has found a place in the history of science or whose talents have been of any use to others.

You might ignore de Pauw, but what do you say to the learned Dr Robertson, Rector of the University of Edinburgh, and author of a famous *History of the Americas*: "The same qualities in the climate of America which stunted the growth ... of its native animals proved pernicious to such as have migrated into it voluntarily." What do you say to the Abbé Raynal? "How astonishing it is that America has not yet produced a single good poet, or able mathematician, or a man of genius in any one of the arts or the sciences." The charge – which was to resound again and again in the next half-century – was absurd on the face of it, and Jefferson might well have disdained it. Instead he disposed of it with two characteristic thrusts. First – indulging his passion for calculating – he pointed out that America, "though but a child of yesterday," had produced, in a single generation, a Washington, a Franklin, a Rittenhouse (and, he might have added, a Jefferson). "We calculate thus," he wrote: "The United States contains three millions of inhabitants; France twenty millions, and the British islands ten. France then should have produced half a dozen of each, and Great Britain half that number, equally eminent." Clearly neither had done so. More interesting was Jefferson's second argument: that Americans had not only made striking contributions to government, philosophy and war, but had "given hopeful proofs of genius of the nobler kinds, which arouse the best feelings of man, which call him into action, which substantiate his freedom, and conduct him to happiness." Here is the Jeffersonian test of civilization – not power, not even philosophy and culture – but freedom, and happiness.

All of this was a stunning refutation of the denigrations of a Buffon, a Raynal, of all those who argued the natural inferiority of the New World to the Old. Far from being degenerate, feeble, enervated, without talent or genius, the inhabitants of the New World were the most fortunate of men, and the New World environment was the most favorable of any in the western world. It was one blessed by every climate and every soil, where nature produced the most abundant of crops, the tallest of trees, the most numerous, largest, and most varied forms of bird and animal life of all climates. It was most favorable to the health and happiness of men. It was a theme to which Jefferson returned again and again for half a century – the infinite superiority, natural as well as social, of the New World to the Old.

What was the test of a successful civilization that was universally acknowledged in the

eighteenth-century world, what but the test of population? It was a subject that fascinated all the philosophers. The Abbé Raynal himself had made clear the central significance of population:

> But it will be asked, whether a great degree of population is of use to promote the happiness of mankind. This is an idle question. In fact the point is not to multiply men in order to make them happy; but it is sufficient to make them happy, that they should multiply.

By this test – and none had any misgivings about it – few Old World peoples could claim to be happy. Here and there to be sure, and increasingly in the second half of the century when the harvests were good, when small pox and malaria and typhus withheld their ravages, and when there was an interlude of peace, countries could show a modest increase in population – Britain, Ireland, Finland, Hungary, Prussia. But mostly the nations of Europe barely held their own, and large areas of Europe – Spain, Portugal, and some of the German and the Italian states – actually lost population. But look at America: everywhere, from Massachusetts to Georgia, in countryside and in towns, among whites and blacks, Americans obeyed the biblical injunction to multiply and replenish the earth. At the beginning of the century the English colonies counted less than 400,000 inhabitants; sixty years later their numbers had increased five-fold, and when they took the first census in 1790 they counted four million. Nor was this the product of immigration, though that, too, was a tribute to the attraction of the New World. It was, as Benjamin Franklin had pointed out, "the salubrity of the air, the healthiness of the Climate, the Plenty of good provisions, the Encouragement of early Marriages by the certainty of Subsistence in cultivating the Earth."

Soon everyone was a demographer, estimating the rate of increase of population and correlating it with the happiness and welfare of man. And how impressive the agreement among them: all came to the same conclusion – Franklin, Jefferson, Dr Rush, Dr Currie, William Smith Barton, all of them members of the Philosophical Society circle – that in America population doubled every twenty or twenty-five years. What a prospect for the future: soon the Reverend Edward Wigglesworth was confidently predicting a population of 1,280,000,000 by the year 2000! Jefferson himself predicted a population of four and one-half million for Virginia by the year 1860, even without immigration which, oddly enough, he thought dangerous to the republican experiment.

As Dr Barton concluded, "Must not the mind of every American citizen be impressed with gratitude and glow with emotions of a virtuous pride, when he reflects on the blessings his country enjoys?" That was, indeed, the Jeffersonian thesis: that a population which flourished and increased was both a product of and a tribute to the blessings which America enjoyed – blessings not only of nature, but of government, economy, and society.

Oddly enough – for Marbois was familiar with, and not unsympathetic to, the teachings of Oesnay and Turgot and Du Pont and the Abbé Morellet, and the other economists who made up what Du Pont called the Physiocratic School – not one of the twenty-two queries which were submitted to Jefferson concerned agriculture. But Jefferson did not feel himself bound by the letter or the order of the queries. He used them as points of departure for what

he wished to say. And here was Query XIX: "The Present State of Manufactures, Commerce, Interior and Exterior Trade?" After all Virginia had no manufactures, and precious little commerce or trade except for trade in tobacco. Jefferson seized upon the question to discuss what was central to his philosophy and close to his heart – agriculture.

Just as in the vocabulary of the eighteenth century "natural philosophy" stood for the whole of science, and "climate" for the total environment, to men of the Enlightenment "agriculture" was more than farming, it was a way of life. This was the truth that the Physiocrats had caught and made central to their philosophy – that an agricultural economy was the only one that conformed to the dictates of nature and nature's God, avoided the evils of colonies, wars, and exorbitant taxes that plagued governments, the misery, luxury, and vice that were the concomitants of great cities, added real wealth to the commonwealth, and nourished and safeguarded the virtue of men and society.

One of the great issues of the day was the debate between mercantilism and physiocracy. Like the controversies between reason and faith, the ancients and the moderns, civilization and the primitive, progress and happiness, the controversy between mercantilism and physiocracy connected itself with almost every aspect of life and spread out from its economic center to embrace great questions of politics, sociology and morals. The debate went to the very heart of the issue that divided most of the philosophers from the rulers: what was the center of gravity, the power and prosperity of the state or the happiness and liberty of man? The mercantilists and their allies the Cameralists, such as Frederick the Great in the Old World and Hamilton in the New, were prepared to subordinate everything to the prosperity of the state; this was the policy followed by the rulers of France, Spain, Russia, Denmark, and (though Joseph II was dazzled by the Physiocrats) by the Empire. These men strove to be self-sufficient, which meant control of the economy at home and abroad, a ceaseless struggle for colonies and for the mastery of trade to the far corners of the globe, armies, navies, merchant shipping, and taxation to support all this – all the things that the Abbé Raynal had exposed in his great *History of the European Establishments in the East and West Indies*. The Physiocrats and their allies – and they had allies everywhere, Joseph in Vienna, Charles in Baden, Gustavus in Sweden and Struensee in Denmark, Adam Smith in Edinburgh and Filangieri down in Naples – thought that wealth, like virtue and happiness, was rooted in conformity with nature and that, in the last analysis, it was only the cultivation of the soil that was truly natural. They abjured great cities, colonies, the search for exotic products which led to slavery and all its evils, the panoply of armies and navies, courts and palaces, with their inevitable accompaniment of luxury and extravagance. They celebrated the simple life.

Morally the Physiocrats had the best of the argument; Raynal made that quite clear in his vast *History* which was a moral as well as an economic tract, tracing most of the evils of the age, such as slavery and the slave trade, to the insensate search for wealth by individuals and for power by governments. But in the Old World, alas, the Physiocrats came too late; history had baked their cake. They came too late to alter the pattern of politics, too late to reverse the tides of history, too late to change the minds of men. The great cities were there, draining off the best of the countryside, spreading social and moral ruin, just as Hogarth depicted, just as Fielding made clear; the kings and princes were there, determined to

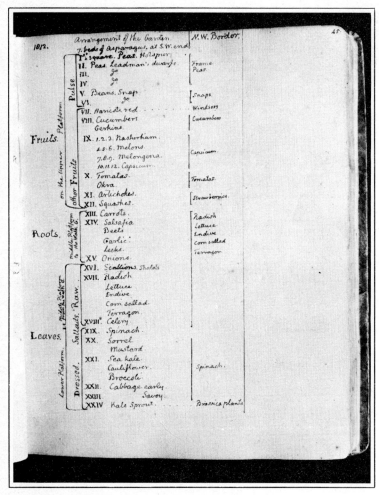

A page from the Garden Book, which Jefferson kept from 1766 to 1824, which shows his arrangement of the vegetable garden in 1812.

strengthen the state, and themselves, at all hazards, greedy for territory, colonies, and markets; the great merchant companies were there, exploiting backward peoples, draining the wealth from distant lands to fatten the fortunes of princes and nabobs; the armies and the navies were there, eager for glory, and spoils, and spreading devastation where they went; the courts and the palaces were there, breeding places for luxury and vice; the remnants of feudalism were there too.

But America presented a very different scene and one which offered the most exhilarating prospect to all those who believed in the moral superiority of agriculture and the rural life.

There everything was precisely what the Physiocrats prescribed: a boundless territory with, as Jefferson said in his first Inaugural Address, "room enough for our descendants to the thousandth and thousandth generation," and land, too, of unrivaled fecundity; a staunch yeomanry (aside from slavery, a curse which all American *philosophes* were determined to root out) every one, according to Crèvecoeur, independent and happy. With Jefferson leading the way, the new nation rid itself of feudal remnants; no great cities; no manufacturers; no colonies – for the territories west of the mountains were not to be territories but commonwealths; no great military to eat up the substance of the people or to subvert their government; no ecclesiastical establishment to claim tithes or aggrandize land. And, on top of all this, Americans were "kindly separated by Nature and a wide ocean from the exterminating havoc of one quarter of the globe" and "too high-minded to endure the degradations of others." It is of course Jefferson who is speaking, Jefferson who all his life counseled isolation from the political and moral contamination of the Old World.

The New World was an experimental laboratory for physiocracy; nowhere was the laboratory more nearly ideal than in Virginia. It was, after all, the most populous of American states, and the largest, stretching as it did from the ocean to the Mississippi: no Old World nation outside Russia had so imperial a domain! All of its people were farmers, slaves as well as masters, drawing their sustenance from the virtuous soil. It was ruled not by princes or absentee nabobs but by planters who lived on their farms and busied themselves with the welfare of the communities, every one a Cincinnatus, a Fabius or a Cato or, better yet, a Washington, a Madison, or a Jefferson. And those who were not planters were even more independent, for they were independent of the curse of slavery. Where was there a fairer prospect for the evolution of an agrarian republic? Where, not even excluding France, was there a spokesman more eloquent, a practitioner more skilful, or a statesman more effective than Jefferson?

Let us return to the *Notes* and listen to Jefferson weighing the issue of agriculture versus manufacturers.

> We have an immensity of land courting the industry of the husbandman. Is it best that all our citizens should be employed in its improvement, or that one half should be called off from that to exercise manufactures and handicraft arts for the other? Those who labor in the earth are the chosen people of God, if ever He had a chosen people, whose breasts He has made his peculiar deposit for substantial and genuine virtue. It is the focus in which He keeps alive that sacred fire, which otherwise might escape from the face of the earth. Corruption of morals in the mass of cultivators is a phenomenon of which no age nor nation has furnished an example. It is the mark set on those who, not looking up to heaven ... for their subsistence, depend for it on casualties and caprice of customers.... Generally speaking, the proportion which the aggregate of the other classes of citizens bears in any state to that of its husbandmen, is the proportion of its unsound to its healthy parts.

Jefferson spent his life in public service, but he always counted himself a husbandman. He had inherited many acres, and acquired more through marriage; at the time he wrote the *Notes* he was owner of thirteen farms including his favorites, Monticello and Poplar Forest;

and to the cultivation and improvement of these he gave his unflagging attention. Again and again, in his long life, he sought to abandon that public career which threatened to absorb all of his energies, and devote himself to that occupation which promised such rich rewards of contentment and the assurance of usefulness, but always, until 1809, in vain.

> I have often thought [he wrote to the painter Charles Wilson Peale] that if Heaven had given me choice of my position and calling, it should have been on a rich spot of earth, well watered, and near a good market for the productions of the garden. No occupation is so delightful to me as the culture of the earth, and no culture comparable to that of the garden.

His passion for the garden is lovingly recorded in the *Garden Book* which he kept faithfully through much of his life. The greatest service which anyone can render his country, he asserted in his autobiography, is to add a new plant to its culture, and this he himself did in ample measure. He was indefatigable in his search for different varieties of rice and obtained seed from the Piedmont, Egypt, and even Sumatra. From Italy he imported the Lombardy poplar, soon to be as familiar in America as in France and Italy. In an effort to encourage the cultivation of the olive ("of all the gifts of Heaven to man it is, next to [bread] the most precious"), he shipped over more than five hundred olive trees – alas, in vain. He experimented with figs from France, vetch from England, grapes and strawberries from Italy, endives from France, and silk trees from China and Constantinople. He visited the vineyards of the Loire, Bordeaux, the Moselle and the Rhine, and encouraged viniculture in Virginia; he instructed his old friend Philip Mazzei (who had lived for some years at Monticello) to send him from Italy four vignerons each of whom could play a different musical instrument. Fascinated as he was with inventions and contrivances, he experimented with spinning machines, and with a new seed-box for sowing clover (which reduced the cost from six shillings to two shillings an acre), built and perfected a hemp-breaking machine, and was the first Virginian to import one of the new Scottish threshing machines, which, as usual, he improved. Most important of his inventions was the moldboard plow, specifically designed for the soil of Virginia. Jefferson thought it "the finest plow ever constructed in America;" the Agricultural Society of Paris agreed with this verdict, and awarded it a gold medal. In all this, as he himself put it, he combined "a *theory* which may satisfy the learned, with a *practice* intelligible to the most unlettered laborer."

All these were, in a sense, private contributions, which Jefferson made simply as a farmer cooperating with other farmers. Far more important were the public contributions. Jefferson was, in a sense, an American Turgot, able to carry through on a most favorable theater the kind of program that Turgot was unable to carry through in France. But Jeffersonian agrarianism was very different from the physiocracy of a Turgot, or of his disciple, Du Pont de Nemours; it was pragmatic not doctrinaire, democratic not exclusive. To Jefferson an air of unreality hung over much of the thinking of the *économistes* – an unreality which was a product, in part, of their own abstract thinking and, in part, of the circumstances of French society and economy. Du Pont, who of all the *économistes* was the closest to Jefferson, persuaded himself that, as only those who labor in the earth are real members of the community, all others – he called them "inhabitants" rather than citizens –

should be excluded from the suffrage. But Jefferson's belief that those who labor in the earth are the peculiarly beloved of God did not lead him to exclude all those who were not farmers or landowners from God's favor, or from the American agrarian paradise. His common sense and his commitment to the principle that society was a contract which embraced all its members equally prevented that.

Common sense characterized Jefferson's thinking in almost all political and economic matters. He had little more interest in or patience with doctrinaire philosophers such as La Mettrie or Holbach or Mably than did John Adams, although he was far more discriminating than that irascible Yankee. It was, in the end, the *idéologues* whom Jefferson most admired – Condillac, Cabanis, Destutt de Tracy, and the other members of that fascinating school who most vigorously carried on the traditions of Lockean sensationalism, rooted them firmly in biology and zoology, and applied them, somewhat less firmly, to politics, economics, education and morals.

Once again we are in the presence of the most pervasive pattern of the American Enlightenment, and one which Jefferson represented better than did any of his countrymen: the pattern of Old World formulation, and New World actualization of Enlightenment principles. Nowhere, except in the realm of religion and the church, is this pattern more ostentatious than in the realm of what was coming to be called "political economy" – a concept which embraced such diverse interests as agriculture, commerce, finance, politics (domestic and imperial), demography and sociology. To the philosophical foundations of political economy, the Americans made but meager contributions. They felt no need for philosophy; what they did was, quite simply, "to realize the theories of the wisest writers." Here, as elsewhere in the American Enlightenment, philosophy was the product of circumstances rather than the other way around; a recognition of an existing condition. The more formal and sophisticated rationalization of agrarianism – as with Jefferson's disciple, John Taylor of Carolina – came only in response to the Hamiltonian challenge, and even then it was argued rather as the common sense of the matter than as a body of scientific principles.

Almost alone of the great agrarians of that era, Jefferson stood not in the shadow of power but at the center of power. As a member of the Virginia legislature he took the lead in abolishing those remnants of feudalism, primogeniture and entail, and his program of disestablishment carried with it the ultimate forfeiture of the glebe lands of the church. His proposal to grant fifty acres to every adult male who was landless was rejected, but where he failed in Virginia he succeeded on a vastly larger theater: the purchase of Louisiana doubled the agricultural domain and, together with the liberal provisions of the Ordinances for organizing the transmontane West, guaranteed (for at least another generation) a flourishing agrarian republic. Jefferson had sought to link that guarantee with one prohibiting slavery in all the new western domain, but in this, too, he was frustrated. It was one of the ironies of Jefferson's career that the policies which contributed so richly to nourish agrarian democracy nourished too that institution of slavery which he regarded as the gravest evil and the gravest danger facing the Republic. To its eradication Jefferson devoted much of his thought, his energies, and his emotions. He succeeded in ameliorating slavery, but not in ending it, and this failure he came to regard as irreparable. It was, needless to say, more than a personal failure; it was the most conspicuous failure of American democracy, it was the

most conspicuous failure of the American Enlightenment.

Marbois had not inquired directly about slavery – was that an example of Gallic tact? – but Jefferson made room for a consideration of the tragic subject in replies to two marginal queries, one long, detailed, and analytical, the other short, general, and philosophical. Let us listen as Jefferson elaborates on "the particular customs and manners that may happen to be received" in Virginia:

> There must doubtless be an unhappy influence on the manners of our people produced by the existence of slavery among us. The whole commerce between master and slave is a perpetual exercise of the most boisterous passions, the most unremitting despotism on the one part, and degrading submissions on the other. Our children see this and learn to imitate it.... The parent storms, the child looks on, catches the lineaments of wrath, puts on the same airs in the circle of smaller slaves, gives a loose to the worst of passions, and thus nursed, educated, and daily exercised in tyranny, cannot but be stamped by it with odious peculiarities. The man must be a prodigy who can retain his manners and morals undepraved by such circumstances. And with what execration should the statesman be loaded who, permitting one-half the citizens to trample on the rights of the other, trans-forms those into despots, and these into enemies, destroys the morals of the one part and the *amor patriae* of the other.... With the morals of the people, their industry is also destroyed. For in a warm climate no man will labor for himself who can make another labor for him.... And can the liberties of a nation be thought secure when we have removed their only firm basis, a conviction in the minds of the people that these liberties are of the gift of God? That they are not to be violated but with His wrath? Indeed I tremble for my country when I reflect that God is just; that his justice cannot sleep for-ever.

Here was the voice of the Enlightenment which, after Montesquieu, turned more and more against slavery and the slave trade. Though Denmark was the first nation to abolish the slave trade, it was the French who, more than any other, formulated the argument against slavery itself. Nowhere was the moral argument stated more eloquently than in the *Encyclopédie* – almost the official organ of the *philosophes*:

> There is not a single one of these hapless souls [wrote the Chevalier de Jaucourt of Negro slaves] who does not have the right to be declared free, since he has never lost his freedom; since it was impossible for him to lose it; and since neither his ruler nor his father nor any one else had the right to dispose of his freedom; consequently the sale of his person is null and void in and of itself. This Negro does not divest himself, indeed cannot under any condition divest himself, of his natural rights. He carries them every-where with him, and has the right to demand that others permit him to enjoy these rights. It is therefore a clear case of inhumanity by judges in free countries to which the slave is shipped, not to free the slave instantly by legal declaration, since he is their brother, having a soul like theirs.

Jefferson's "mold-board" plow for which the
Agricultural Society of Paris awarded him a gold medal.

Slavery troubled not only the conscience of the Enlightenment, but its philosophy and its logic. For in the eyes of the philosophers slavery was not merely a moral wrong; it was, as Jefferson made clear with his references to the attitude of the Almighty, a violation of the natural order of things. For it was one of the basic convictions of the Enlightenment that men were everywhere fundamentally the same, a conviction which implied equality *in esse* or *in posse*. That was why it was so easy for the philosophers to draw so casually but so confidently on China and Peru, the Greeks and the Trojans, the Vikings and the Hurons, the nomads of Arabia Felix and the Gaelic bards of Ossian. That was why political philosophers assumed that men everywhere displayed the same passions, ambitions, zeal for power and for glory, and for tyranny, too, and that the conclusions to be drawn from the histories of Athens and Sparta and Rome were valid for France and England and America. That is why the hundreds of Utopias depicted men responding everywhere to the same persuasions of reason and morality and self-interest. So if nature had made all men the same, to exalt some as masters and condemn others as slaves was quite simply to violate the laws of nature.

Nor was there any room for the notion of the permanent inferiority of the Negro in the conception of the universe as a "great chain of being." That concept assumed an infinite hierarchy of beings, and in this hierarchy man – "a little less than angels, a little more than apes" – was one.

Everywhere the Enlightenment exalted freedom – not that convulsive freedom of conduct for the individual that animated a Werther indulging his sorrows, a Beckford his eccentricities, an Alfieri his passions, a Gustavus his vanities – but that larger freedom which a Voltaire, a Condorcet, a Priestley, a Jefferson celebrated: freedom to resist and overcome the pretentions of authority, the audacities of government, the fanaticism of the church, the superstitions of ignorance, the burdens of poverty, the paralysis of impotence; freedom from slavery in every form. And what form more ostentatious than that which flourished so incongruously in that new Republic which purported to vindicate the right to life, liberty and the pursuit of happiness?

At the time he published the *Notes on Virginia* no one had contributed more to the struggle against slavery in his own state, and perhaps even in the nation, than Jefferson, who was himself a large slaveholder, and whose private relationship to the peculiar institution was marked by those ambiguities almost inescapable in a southerner. As early as 1770, in his argument in the obscure case of Howell *v.* Netherland, which involved the freedom or enslavement of a third-generation mulatto, Jefferson had pled that "we are all born free" and that slavery was contrary to nature – an argument which the court dismissed out of hand. Time did not reconcile Jefferson to the paradox of a society proclaiming freedom and perpetuating slavery, and six years later he tried, in vain, to identify the political rights of the Americans with the personal rights of Negro slaves.

> He has waged cruel war against human nature [so went Jefferson's original draft of the Declaration], violating the most sacred rights of life and liberty in the persons of a distant people who never offended him, captivating them and carrying them into slavery in another hemisphere.... Determined to keep open a market where *men* could be bought and sold, he has prostituted his negative for suppressing every legislative attempt to prohibit or restrain this execrable commerce.

The Continental Congress was not ready for either the sentiment or the rhetoric, and the passage was omitted. That fall Jefferson returned to the Virginia assembly, where he promptly introduced a bill ending the importation of slaves, and two years later Virginia enacted the prohibition. Nor should we forget that it was President Jefferson who urged, and signed, the bill which at the earliest moment permitted under the Constitution, permanently outlawed the importation of slaves to the United States.

That same fall of 1776 Jefferson introduced a bill for the complete revisal of the laws of Virginia; he was appointed to the committee responsible for the revisal and promptly seized the laboring oar. His proposed revisions – one hundred and twenty-six bills altogether – embraced the whole of the legal code: citizenship, land, crime, religion, education, and, inevitably, slavery. Here Jefferson submitted a bold proposal of emancipation for all Negroes born after 1800, with the provision that those born of slaves, "should be brought up, at the public expense, to tillage, arts, or sciences according to their geniuses" and, when they reached maturity, colonized "to such place as circumstances should render most proper." This proposal rested on two assumptions: that "nothing is more certainly written in the book of Fate than that these people are to be free," and that it is not less certain "that the two races, equally free, cannot live in the same government." The first of these assumptions was

characteristically optimistic; it was not fate but war that brought freedom to the slave. The second was not only uncharacteristically pessimistic, but inconsistent with Enlightenment principles which emphasized how much men had in common as members of the human race, rather than how they could be divided by race or color. The proposal was, in any event, so radical that it was unacceptable and died in committee.

What a stupendous, what an incomprehensible, machine is man [wrote Jefferson to Demeusnier, whose article on America for the *Encyclopédie Methodique* Jefferson largely rewrote], who can endure toil, famine, stripes, imprisonment and death itself in vindication of his own liberty, and the next moment be deaf to all those motives whose power supported him through his trial, and inflict on his fellow-men a bondage, one hour of which is fraught with more misery than ages of that which he rose in rebellion to oppose.

By now Jefferson had moved back from the state to the national arena, and had transferred to that arena the campaign against slavery, and it was here that he may have made his most significant contribution. As chairman of the Congressional Committee to provide government for the vast hinterland west of the Allegheny Mountains, he tried to write into the Ordinance a clause prohibiting slavery in any of the territory after the year 1800. The proposal was lost by one vote; as Jefferson wrote to Demeusnier, "the voice of a single individual ... would have prevented this abominable crime from spreading itself over the new country. Thus we see the fate of millions unborn hanging on the tongue of one man, and Heaven was silent in that awful moment." All was not lost; three years later the Northwest Ordinance incorporated for all the territory north of the Ohio the principle that Jefferson had attempted to apply to the entire West. And we should not forget that until the crisis of the 1850s, which (as Jefferson had foreseen) rent the Union apart, that principle applied to most of the vast Louisiana Territory which Jefferson had acquired for the nation in 1803.

Slavery resisted all pressures of the Enlightenment. But in other areas the familiar pattern was vindicated: Old World theories became New World realities, Old World philosophies were translated into New World institutions. Clearly this was not because American philosophers were more effective, or more ingenious, than their Old World colleagues, but because their task was incomparably easier.

If the deepest and most pervasive commitment of the Enlightenment on both sides of the water was to freedom Jefferson spoke for them all – certainly for all his fellow countrymen – when he dedicated himself to the "illimitible freedom of the human mind." Though Americans did not win freedom for slaves, elsewhere they were more successful, and nowhere more than in that realm which was to the Old World what slavery was to the New – religion. Voltaire's great rallying cry, *Ecrasez l'Infâme*, was the cri de cœur of the *philosophes* everywhere, even in liberal Britain where Catholics and Nonconformists were far from free. From London to St Petersburg, from Stockholm to Naples, the church was imperial, powerful, formidable, magisterial, and established; everywhere it shared with the crown power over the minds and the souls of men and – except in Holland – regarded the slightest rent in the web of conformity as not only morally, but politically pernicious. It controlled the education of children, and guarded the portals of universities; it censored scholarship and literature, forcing Buffon to retract his estimate of one million years since the creation,

stopping the *Encyclopédie* for seven years, sending luckless writers to the Bastille and printers to the galleys. It dispensed justice and injustice, broke dissenters on the wheel or burned them at the stake. Its domains were imperial, it owned two-thirds the land of Portugal, half the lands of Belgium and Tuscany, and was the largest landowner in a dozen other states. In Russia it exploited the labor of one million serfs, and in Poland one peasant out of every seven was a serf on church lands. It tore Protestant children from their parents, expelled eighteen thousand Hernhütters from Salzburg and twice that number of Moravians from the Germanies. Even in enlightened England, which Voltaire admired, it penalized all forms of nonconformity. Unitarians were required to take the Test Act oath: Edmund Burke asserted that they were disciples of Tom Paine and against all religion; and Justice Sir William Scott insisted that the Quakers were so dangerous that they were "unworthy of legislative indulgence" of any kind. Nor was the power of the church confined to the Old World: it dominated the political, economic, and intellectual life of Spanish America from Santiago to San Francisco, and even after the fall of Canada, the British, while they extended their own establishment to their new province, allowed the Catholic church to retain most of its ancient authority.

Nowhere in the American states was there an established church that enjoyed anything remotely like the power exercised by the Establishments of the Old World. But five of the American states did inherit Anglican Establishments, and though these were mild enough in their pretentions and harmless enough in their conduct, they were – or to the American *philosophes* they seemed – pernicious in principle.

Here as elsewhere Jefferson seized the lead in the struggle not merely to overthrow the Anglican Establishments, but to build something scarcely dreamed of in the philosophy of Old World radicals: "a wall of separation between Church and State."

It is hard for us now to appreciate the audacity of this proposal, or the radicalism of the philosophy which dictated it. The *philosophes* of the Old World did not really want to wipe the religious slate clean. It was not the Establishment they assailed, but the conduct of the Establishment; not the power of the church, but the abuse of that power. They were prepared, most of them, to settle for a well-behaved Establishment – for ending the Inquisition, expelling the Jesuits, confiscating some of the church lands, lifting ecclesiastical censorship. Most of the Utopias which they constructed – and every *philosophe* had a Utopia in his pocket – provided for a state religion. Rousseau, who drew up model constitutions for Poland and Corsica, proposed that every citizen subscribe to his state religion or suffer exile or even death. The Abbé Mably in *Phocion* called for a state religion and the outlawing of all new religions. The Abbé Robin, who had fought in America, called upon the United States to impose a common faith on all its people in order to insure national unity. And when Sebastian Mercier imagined his Utopia of *The Year 2440* he arranged for an established church, ecclesiastical censorship, and the expulsion of atheists! It is against this background that we should view Jefferson's campaign which culminated in the enactment of the Statute for Religious Freedom of 1786.

Marbois's Query XVII provided Jefferson with the opportunity to rehearse the story of his own assault on the established church and to elaborate on the philosophy not only of religious freedom, but of the "illimitable" freedom of the mind in every area. It is one of the

most illuminating of all the passages of the *Notes*.

In his Revisal of the Laws, Jefferson had already prepared a bill calling for the complete equality of all churches, and the divorce of church and state. When Jefferson wrote the *Notes*, the fate of that bill was still uncertain, and he seized the opportunity to make his answer to the Query "on The Different Religions Received in the State" an eloquent plea for religious freedom. When, a few years later, the *Notes* were published the bill had triumphantly weathered all opposition and become law, and Jefferson could include it as an appendix in the *Notes.*

> The error [so runs Jefferson's reply to Query XVII] seems not sufficiently eradicated, that the operations of the mind as well as the acts of the body, are subject to the coercion of the laws. But our rulers can have no authority over such natural rights, only as we have submitted to them. The rights of conscience we never submitted, we could not submit. We are answerable for them to our God.... Reason and free inquiry are the only effectual agents against error. Give a loose to them, they will support the true religion by bringing every false one to their tribunal, to the test of their investigation. They are the natural enemies of error, and of error only.

This was directed to the threat of church authority and religious superstition. Jefferson was not, however, content with this; after all there was little likelihood of either in America. To Jefferson the issue was broader: it was the fundamental issue of freedom of the mind from authority of any kind. His argument can stand with *Areopagitica*:

> Reason and experiment have been indulged, and error has fled before them. It is error alone which needs the support of government. Truth can stand by itself. Subject opinion to coercion, whom will you make your inquisitors? Fallible men, men governed by bad passions, by private as well as public reasons. And why subject it to coercion? To produce uniformity. But is uniformity desirable? No more than of face and stature. Reason and persuasion are the only practicable instruments. To make way for these, free inquiry must be indulged, and how can we wish others to indulge in it while we refuse it ourselves?

Nothing that he ever did gave Jefferson greater satisfaction than this act which, as Madison somewhat optimistically assured him, "extinguished forever the ambitious hope of making laws for the human mind," and he included it in his epitaph as one of the three achievements for which he wished to be remembered. Nothing that he ever wrote brought him greater acclaim, in his own lifetime, than the preamble to the act, not even the Declaration of Independence; it was, as he wrote,

> received with infinite approbation in Europe, and propagated with enthusiasm.... It is comfortable [he continued, with transparent gratification] to see the standard of Reason at length erected, after so many ages, during which the human mind has been held in vassalage by kings, priests and nobles, and it is honorable for us to have produced the first legislature who had the courage to declare that the Reason of man may be trusted with the formation of its own opinions.

The tyranny of kings and of priests was ostentatious and formidable, but in the last analysis

Maria Cosway whom Jefferson admired when he lived
in Paris. The engraving was done in London in 1785
after a miniature by Maria's husband, Richard.

it rested on a tyranny still more intractable: the tyranny of ignorance. How revealing (and
how appropriate) that the third accomplishment which Jefferson thought might entitle him
to immortality was another of his contributions to overthrowing that tyranny: the establish-

ment of the University of Virginia. Important as that was in itself (and no *philosophe* elsewhere in the world had to his credit the creation of a university) its importance is symbolic as well as real, for education, which played little part in the Old World Enlightenment, was central to the American. How interesting that to the *philosophes* of the Old World such terms as *Aufklärung, éclaircissement, illuminismo*, encompassed the whole of the Enlightenment, but in America Enlightenment meant, quite simply, education. And how suggestive that while the Old World made science and scholarship the primary instruments of the Enlightenment, in the New it was rather popular education that was thought to be fundamental.

In Europe education had long been the prerogative of the rich and the well born. In some of the German states, in parts of Holland, Switzerland and Sweden, there were changes under way – or gestures toward changes – but almost everywhere it was taken for granted that the vast majority of the people – peasants, workers, servants, soldiers, and sailors – would languish in ignorance; such statistics of literacy as we have testify to the triumph of this policy, for over vast areas of Europe not ten per cent of the adult population could read or write. The third edition of the *Encyclopaedia Britannica* justified this philosophy in its article on "education" which distinguished between the education proper for gentlemen and that suitable for the "lower ranks."

> Let the youth who is born to pass his days in this humble station be carefully taught to consider honest, patient industry as one of the first of virtues. Teach him contentment with his lot by letting him know that wealth and honor seldom confer superior happiness.

Nor did the *philosophes* challenge this view. Urging Frederick the Great to extirpate "the infamous superstition" of orthodox Christianity, Voltaire added that, "I do not say among the rabble, who are not worthy of being enlightened, and who are apt for every yoke."

That was the point, and that was why America required a very different educational philosophy from that which obtained everywhere in the Old World. There was no "rabble" in America, "apt for every yoke," except the unfortunate blacks – quite an exception. In America all citizens were expected to be apt for self-government, apt for freedom, apt for progress, apt for happiness. In part because the European class system was not transferred to America; in part because a new society in a new land desperately needed whatever talent was available to meet the challenges which confronted it; in part because the success of self-government depended so palpably on the intelligence and virtue of the people, education speedily assumed a central place in American thought and society.

This development was implicit in the thinking and explicit in the public conduct of most of the American *philosophes*. Well they knew that the experiment in self government would work only if conducted by a people intelligent, well informed, and reasonable, for, as Madison put it, "a popular government without popular information or the means of acquiring it is but a prologue to a farce or a tragedy." They realized, too, that they were constructing political mechanisms of unprecedented complexity whose operation required a degree of sophistication which no previous political system had called for. They looked to

education to provide the moral foundation for an enduring political system, ameliorate religious antipathies, bridge racial and class misunderstandings, give reality to the principle of equality, justify the logic of freedom, and provide the common denominators of national unity. They depended on it to vindicate the new principle of progress – progress which would raise the general well-being of men rather than enhance the culture of an elite. No one put this better than Jefferson in a letter to his old mentor, Chancellor Wythe, written from Paris in 1786:

> If all the sovereigns of Europe were to set themselves to work, to emancipate the minds of their subjects from their present ignorance and prejudices, and that as zealously as they now endeavor the contrary, a thousand years would not place them on that high ground, on which our common people are now setting out.... I think by far the most important bill in our whole code, is that for the diffusion of knowledge among the people. No other sure foundation can be devised, for the preservation of freedom and happiness. If anybody thinks that kings, nobles, or priests are good conservators of the public happiness, send him here. It is the best school in the universe to cure him of that folly.... Preach, my dear sir, a crusade against ignorance; establish and improve the law for educating the common people.

"A crusade against ignorance!:" that was the crusade upon which so many of the founding fathers embarked with all the boldness of Jason seeking the Golden Fleece, and none more boldly or more hopefully than Jefferson. "I have sworn upon the altar of God eternal hostility against every form of tyranny over the mind of man," he wrote to his friend Dr Rush in 1800, and he kept his vow to the end. "Enlighten the people generally, and tyranny and oppression of body and mind will vanish like spirits at the dawn of day," he wrote when he was already in his seventies, and towards the close of his life he confessed that he still looked "to the diffusion of light and education as the resource most to be relied on for ameliorating the condition, promoting the virtue, and advancing the happiness of man." He had launched his own crusade against ignorance as early as 1779 when he introduced his three-part plan "to diffuse knowledge more generally through the mass of the people:" a system of elementary schools (to be maintained at local expense) in every ward of the state, feeding into grammar schools, and eventually into a university; a sweeping reform of the almost moribund College of William and Mary including new chairs of law, medicine, and modern languages; and the creation of a state library. None of this materialized at the time, but Jefferson was tenacious. He never did get a system of public education which was to bring Virginia abreast with Massachusetts and Connecticut, but what he got was, in the end, more important. He was chairman of the committee which drafted the Land Ordinance of 1785 with its enlightened provisions establishing the policy of setting aside public lands for the support of schools and universities, a policy extended, eventually, to all the territories acquired by the United States. In 1816 he drew up plans for ward schools in Virginia, and the following year launched another and more ambitious plan for general education which included the astonishing provision of a literacy test for citizenship – a provision all the more astonishing in that it was drawn from the proposed constitution for Spain.

The Virginia Assembly did not accept Jefferson's far-sighted proposal for the creation of

a state library, but here once again Jefferson had his way. As President of the United States he was responsible for the creation of the Library of Congress, and that responsibility became a very personal one when his own private library – one of the best in the country – provided the basis for what was eventually to be the largest and richest of all national libraries.

Jefferson did not succeed in reforming the College of William and Mary – his plan to bring over the faculty of the University of Geneva failed – but for a quarter-century he labored to create a university which would hold its own with the most eminent in the Old World and, unlike them, would be a bastion of freedom too. When in 1825 the University of Virginia at Charlottesville opened its doors to its first class of students, it was, more than any other institution of its kind in history, the lengthened shadow of one man. It was Jefferson who had drawn up the charter and steered it through the legislature; Jefferson who was chairman of the Board of Trustees, and the first Rector of the University. It was Jefferson who designed every building, every column, every window, every door, every mantelpiece; planted every tree and shrub and flower, laid out every path and built every wall, Jefferson who provided the library, chose the professors, and the students too, and drew up the curriculum. And it was Jefferson who dedicated the institution "to the illimitable freedom of the human mind." Not bad that, for a man in his eighties! The University was, at its birth, not only "the most eminent in the United States" as Jefferson said, but the most enlightened and the most liberal, the most nearly like some of the great universities of the Old World.

All in all it was a record of educational achievement which no other American has ever equalled. If Jefferson was not, like Rousseau or Pestalozzi or Grundtvig, an original educational thinker, he was, with Lord Brougham and Wilhelm von Humboldt, the greatest educational statesman of his day.

In education, as in religion, we see once again the familiar pattern of the New World institutionalization of Old World theories. In France, Germany and the Italian states ideas boiled to the surface, then subsided and cooled off; in America – and perhaps only in America – they boiled over and enriched the soil around them.

To three other areas of Enlightenment thought Americans made original contributions: the concept of happiness, the concept of progress, and the concept of history. Each of these concepts is part of the pattern of Jeffersonian thought; to each he made a distinguished contribution. Happiness was a preoccupation, almost an obsession, of the Enlightenment. Americans of all sections and all faiths shared the preoccupation. George Mason wrote happiness into the Virginia Bill of Rights and dour John Adams inserted it five times into the Constitution of Massachusetts; Washington invoked it again and again in his moving *Circular Letter to the States* of 1783, and returned to it with equal frequency in his Inaugural and his Farewell Addresses; and Crèvecoeur intoned it thirteen times in his famous Third Letter of an American Farmer. Tom Paine argued that it was the responsibility of America "to make the world happy;" Joel Barlow wrote an epic poem of ten thousand lines (*The Vision of Columbus*) on the dual theme of happiness and progress; and orthodox theologians like President Timothy Dwight of Yale and President Samuel Johnson of King's College found a moral obligation to happiness which was wholly compatible with their ideas of religion.

As so often, the most memorable invocation came from the gifted pen of Jefferson: the assertion that "life, liberty, and the pursuit of happiness" are among the unalienable rights of man. It was a theme to which he returned again and again throughout his long life, but we must content ourselves with two illustrations. The most familiar is doubtless that moving passage in the first Inaugural Address invoking the blessings of "an over-ruling Providence which, by all its dispensations, proves that it delights in the happiness of man here, and his greater happiness hereafter." Most felicitious of all is the letter congratulating his beloved Maria Cosway on the birth of a daughter: "They tell me *que vouz faire un enfant*. . . . You may make children there, but this is the country to transplant them to. There is no comparison between the sum of happiness enjoyed here and there."

The point of this, and of a hundred similar observations, is that in America happiness was not just a dream, it was a reality. It was rooted in material abundance: as the Marquis de Chastellux wrote "America has no poor." It was nourished by a benign political order: as Crèvecoeur wrote, "we are strangers to feudal institutions; our laws are simple and just." It was sustained by an almost universal enlightenment: as Jefferson wrote of education, "no other sure foundation can be devised for the preservation of our freedom and happiness." It was vindicated, as it were, by the continuous migration from the Old World to the New; who, after all, except loyalists, went the other way? And finally, as if to dramatize the practice of institutionalizing Enlightenment ideas, it was written as a formal guarantee into one state constitution after another, until it can be said with confidence that in the United States happiness is not only a moral, but a constitutional right.

Nowhere does the American emphasis, nay, concentration, on the practical emerge more clearly than in American concepts of progress. It was an ideal of the Old World, that reason and science in alliance could eradicate the evils and miseries that had so long afflicted mankind, and set man on the road to progressive improvement in every area – an improvement which, by conforming more and more surely to the laws of nature, would lead in time to perfection. To the philosophers of the Old World progress meant, for the most part, improvement in the arts and sciences; in the refinement of manners, and of morals; it was aristocratic, intellectual, and aesthetic. Thus D'Alembert's *Preliminary Discourse* refers hopefully to "progress of the mind," to "erudition, philosophy, and belles lettres;" thus Immanuel Kant, in his *Strife of the Faculties*, observed of progress that "if it is to come, it must come from above, not by the movement of things from the bottom to the top but by the movement from the top to the bottom.... To expect to train men to improve themselves by means of the education of the youth in moral and intellectual culture is hardly to be hoped for."

How different the American concept of progress. What it meant in America to a Franklin, a Dr Rush, a Tom Paine, a Crèvecoeur, a Jefferson was something immediate, practical, and universal. It meant material abundance, good health, large families; it meant freedom to move from place to place, from church to church, from one work or profession to any other; and, in so far as there were social divisions (and by Old World standards there were none) from class to class. It meant milk for the children, meat on the table, a well-built house, a well-filled woodshed, a well-tilled farm with cattle in the pasture and hay in the barn. It meant self-government, religious freedom, schools and colleges. It was not an elitist but a

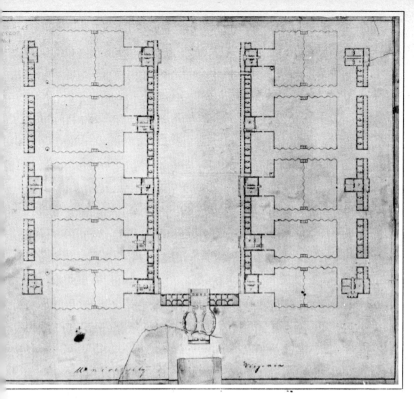

an of the University of Virginia: a study for Peter
erick's engraving published in 1822. The drawing
ws the Rotunda at the head, and ten pavilions
dormitories between them.

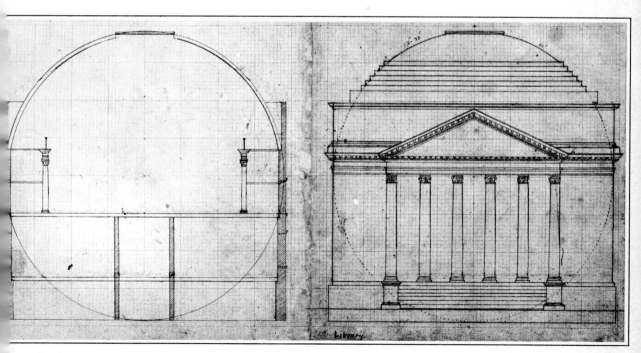

Rotunda of the University of Virginia: section
levation. The exterior of the Rotunda was
led after the Pantheon in Rome.

democratic concept, not an aesthetic but a material one and it was, for most Americans, not something in the distant future but in the present.

Old World philosophers, all but despairing of progress in these terms, tended to conjure up progress in terms of a golden age, an island paradise inhabited by noble savages, a Utopia in some exotic part of the globe, or an imagined world, and usually in some distant day. Virtue, reason, well-being were to be found in Arcadia, in China, in Tahiti. Americans had no need to go to the South Seas, the ancient world, or some imaginary Utopia, past or future. After all, *here* was the true "happy valley," not in Abyssinia; *here* was innocence, not in Tahiti; *here* was virtue, not in Plato's Greece or Morelley's "floating island." *Here* was freedom and justice, *here* was abundance, prosperity, and happiness.

There was still another dimension to progress, as understood by Americans, and one which we associate peculiarly with Jefferson: that is what we may call historical, or even evolutionary, progress. In the Old World it was not the historians who were confident of progress, not Montesquieu or Raynal, Voltaire, Rollin, Gibbon or Hume. Quite the contrary. They took, on the whole, a dour view of the prospects of mankind. The chief use of history, as Hume asserted, was "to discover the constant and universal principles of human nature" and of these the most nearly constant and universal was that men and governments were everywhere the same: that men were creatures of interest, vanity, greed, passion and ambition, that the rich and the powerful everywhere exploited the poor and the feeble, and that governments everywhere abused their powers. A good many Americans accepted this view uncritically, notably John Adams, whose monumental *Defense of the Constitution of the United States* was built entirely out of materials dredged up from these historical quarries.

It was here that Jefferson made perhaps his most original contribution to Enlightenment philosophy, one deeply rooted in the American soil. He was not, to be sure, alone: Franklin had anticipated him; Tom Paine and Dr Rush and Joseph Priestley associated themselves with him, but it was Jefferson alone who was in a position to vindicate the new historical philosophy. His position was, quite simply, that though men in the Old World might be the prisoners of history, Americans were not; they could triumph over it. Human nature was not always and everywhere the same; in a new and favorable environment human nature itself would change. History is not exhausted and here in America it is prospective rather than retrospective.

This is the note that resounds in Jefferson's exultant letter to his friend Dr Priestly, written just after his accession to the Presidency in March 1801:

> We can no longer say there is nothing new under the sun. This whole chapter in the history of man is new. The great extent of our republic is new. Its sparse habitation is new. The mighty wave of public opinion which has rolled over it is new.... The order and good sense displayed in [the] recovery from delusion and in the momentous crisis which lately arose bespeak a strength of character in our new nation which argues well for the duration of the republic.

Never before, in fact, had man been vouchsafed so favorable an opportunity to achieve the

good life; everywhere the auspices were favorable. Nature was not only abundant but beneficent; and where it was not, science stood ready to improve it. Government was benign, and society flourished in freedom as it could not under tyranny, and flourished in peace as it could not in war. Learning and science, now to be the universal possession of the people, could be counted on to teach wisdom and advance happiness. In such a country, with such a society, under such a government, the lessons of the past were irrelevant, and all that could be hoped for the future of man might come to pass. That was a characteristic Enlightenment faith, but even as Jefferson's accession to the Presidency dramatized the triumph of the Enlightenment in the New World by the choice of a philosopher as king, the dark clouds of reaction were sweeping across the skies of the Old World. Most of the ardent hopes of the French Revolution had been betrayed, and though Jefferson still explained that gigantic upheaval as "infuriated man seeking through blood and slaughter his long lost liberties," it was pretty clear that Napoleon had other purposes in mind. Britain was in the throes of a black reaction which would not loosen its grip until after the massacre at Peterloo; the papacy had recovered much of its former power, the Inquisition returned to Spain, and the Jesuits were given a new lease on life. Now the Empress Catherine sweeps away all the busts of Voltaire and Diderot, and puts all her pet philosophers in jail or ships them off to Siberia, and her successor, Paul, dismantles what is left of the Russian Enlightenment. Karl Theodore expels Count Rumford from Bavaria; in Tuscany, Milan, and Naples the reformers are in disgrace, or in chains, and the Venetian Republic is no more. And in Vienna the reforms of Joseph and Leopold have gone by the board. Only America is free from reaction: the priests declaim and the Federalists bluster, but it is Jefferson who is in the new White House, and whose disciples will keep the faith for another quarter-century.

For Jefferson had lost none of his faith in those truths which he had once called self-evident. Well might he rejoice that the Enlightenment, driven out of the Old World, had found refuge in the New, and that Providence had placed him in a position where he might vindicate all its claims: vindicate the claims of freedom, the claims of reason and of the cultivation of reason through science and education, the claims of agrarian democracy, the claims of peace, and of the supremacy of the civil over the military authority; vindicate the claims of the commonwealth of law and of the commonwealth of learning. In the Old World the philosophers had formulated such ideas but had been wholly unable to realize them, for the kings, who did have the power to realize them, had not the will. In America alone the idea and the act could be one, as in America alone the philosopher and the king were one – more triumphantly in Jefferson than in any other figure in the history of the Enlightenment.

Certainly Jefferson's commitment to the Enlightenment was tenacious and unqualified. What he said at the dawn of his career in Philadelphia and Virginia, he said and did at high noon as Secretary of State and Vice President and President, and in retirement at Monticello as the evening shadows fell. The faith he declared, the convictions he professed, the hopes he nourished, lived on as ardently in the quarter-century after his election to the Presidency as in the quarter-century before. No other Enlightenment figure on either side of the Atlantic was as consistent, as active, or as effective: not Tom Paine who, after his imprisonment in France, declined into ineffectiveness, not Bentham who increasingly took refuge in his own

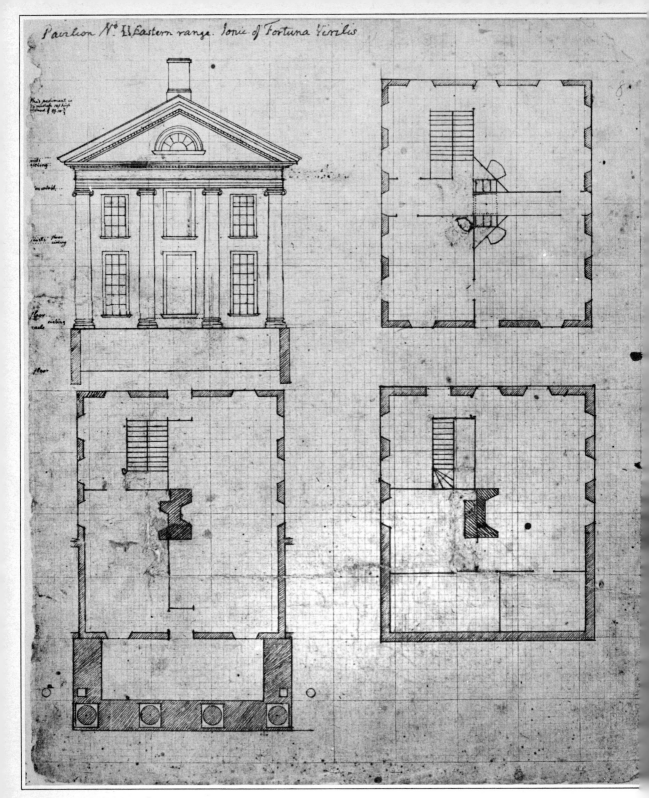

One of the pavilions that Jefferson designed for the
University; each pavilion had a classroom on the first
floor and living quarters for a professor on the second
floor. Jefferson varied the architecture of each pavilion.

A German print of the University of Virginia.

private world, nor Miranda who laid waste his powers in military and amorous adventures, not Lafayette who never really understood the intellectual implications of the Enlightenment, nor Goethe whose commitment to the Enlightenment was always ambiguous. Jefferson alone of the great galaxy of the *philosophes* embraced the whole of Enlightenment philosophy, interpreted it with matchless eloquence, added to it from his own well-stored mind, and translated it into law and practice on one of the great theaters of history. Alone of them he kept his faith and played his part well into the new century: perhaps that was merely because he lived long after most of his associates had gone to such heavens as their philosophy permitted them to enter. Let us take leave of him now. It is 24 June 1826. He is eighty-three years old, and feeble, but his mind is still clear and his spirit undaunted. He is explaining to Mayor Weightman of Washington why he cannot participate in the celebration of the fiftieth anniversary of the Declaration of Independence, and making a reaffirmation of the faith of the great Declaration which has sustained him to the end:

May it be to the world what I believe it will be, the signal of arousing men to burst the chains under which monkish ignorance and superstition had persuaded them to bind themselves, and to assume the blessings and security of self-government. That form which we have substituted, restores the free right to the unbounded exercise of reason and freedom of opinion. All eyes are opened, or opening, to the rights of man. The general spread of the light of science has already laid open to every view the palpable truth that the mass of mankind has not been born with saddles on their backs, nor a favored few booted and spurred, ready to ride them legitimately by the grace of God. These are grounds for hope for others. For ourselves let the annual return of this day forever refresh our recollections of these rights, and an undiminished devotion to them.

HERE WAS BURIED
THOMAS JEFFERSON,
AUTHOR,
OF THE DECLARATION OF
AMERICAN INDEPENDENCE.
OF
THE STATUTE OF VIRGINIA
FOR RELIGIOUS FREEDOM, AND
FATHER OF THE UNIVERSITY
OF VIRGINIA.

PROLEGOMENA TO A READING OF THE DECLARATION

Garry Wills

The glittering and sounding generalities of the Declaration of Independence.

Rufus Choate (1856)

Enlightenment taste ran much toward epitaphs, which neatly mix permanence and demise, monumentality and concision – the final public gesture, a whole life in an epigram. As the dying Roman emperor feared he soon would be a god, famous men of Jefferson's time aged almost perceptibly toward marble. Tomb inscriptions were among their authors' most famous compositions. Swift's was shapely, and justly admired. Franklin's was, characteristically, a sermon inside a joke – and was circulated ahead of time so he could hear the laughter. Some men, indeed, spent a good deal of their lives trying to die well in verse. Judgement day had been moved up into time, with posterity sitting at the bar; and each man's stone was his plea for the defense.

Dr Johnson, as usual, cauterized with wit this lapidary fever – his suggestion that the eulogist is not on oath was meant to put the audience on guard. By his own wish, Johnson's grave announced just the bare dates of his life. Yet even modesty can look affected, once ostentation has become a bore. Feigned humility is as common as the discreet boast on these headstones, a fact that casts its shadow on Jefferson's self-designed grave obelisk. Passing over trifles like his Presidency, he chose from a vast range of achievements only three for lasting mention – the Declaration of Independence, a statute of religious freedom for his native state, and the University of Virginia. Was this simplicity "composed," as for a Houdon study in the basic virtues? One wonders, as – time after time – this sophisticate describes himself as a farmer. Dr Franklin, after all, did not describe himself as a kite flyer – true, he called himself simply "a printer" on his tombstone; but he was always joking, and Jefferson never was. Our suspicion deepens when we learn that Jefferson, elegant in France and *simplex* in Monticello's *munditiis*, was almost shabby in the White House, greeting visitors in worn "democratic" slippers, as if it were a President's job to be a walking sermon, a statue not yet entirely marble.

Just before entering the White House, Jefferson listed the reasons "my country is better off for my having lived here." He had a mania for these surprising lists; and prominent in this short account are his importations of the olive (which took no lasting root) and of "heavy upland rice" into Virginia – which he regularly called "my country." At the very top

Jefferson's tombstone listing the three achievements
for which he wished "most to be remembered."

of the list is his opening of Monticello's Rivanna River to commercial navigation. Is this concentration on things that appear almost trivial the product of a posed humility, or of an obscure piety, or merely of misjudgement in his own case?

Take another example. Jefferson published only one book in his life, but it made him internationally famous. In a time passionate for numbers, his *Notes on the State of Virginia* supplied men with a verbal map of the largest American state, replete with argued statistics – yet he said this whole exacting labor was less valuable than the plate he prefixed to the book, a map drawn up thirty-seven years before by Joshua Fry and Peter Jefferson (his father). Here humility seems to link hands with piety, warning us no man is on oath when praising his ancestors. Jefferson maintained most of the time, that men's piety for preceding generations is a blindness.

Still, Jefferson could, when he wanted to, be boastful. Indeed, when he was not exaggerating in one direction, toward diffidence and shy self-appraisal, he seemed to be overstating his own claims or the case at hand. He called his election as President the country's second revolution. He resented the improvements made in his draft of the Declaration, and for half a century tried to keep alive the memory of his pristine version. He knew, in his own quiet way, his worth; at times, even overestimated it. When he told John Quincy Adams that he had taught himself Spanish in nineteen days, Adams dryly observed that "Mr Jefferson tells large stories."

Even the Declaration is a large tale of sorts, or a set of very large claims. The language does not, perhaps, outreach the occasion in its solemn final words: "We mutually pledge to each other our lives, our fortunes, and our sacred honor." Nor is it surprising that Jefferson should already be groping toward this cadence, two years earlier, when he defended "the lives, the labors, and the fortunes" of Americans. But to grasp that century's high serious-ness, we must read an earlier statement still – in which Jefferson and five other men (including Patrick Henry), forming a league to collect delinquent legal fees from their clients, conclude with these words: "for the invariable Observance of which we mutually plight our Honor to each other."

We may expect a declaration of rights to appeal, in that time, to "the laws of Nature and of Nature's God." But Jefferson just as quickly adduced the laws of nature as underwriting Americans' desire to have a port in Spanish New Orleans. This was, he argued, "written in the hearts of men" (and in the river's currents). One cannot read far in Jefferson without a growing hunch that any case he felt called on to plead would end up "self-evident," based on nature's everlasting writ. Though he held "metaphysics" in contempt, he speaks almost always from some abstract proposition – even in his early courtroom business. This in-flationary tendency affects even his judgement of men and books and buildings. He invariably found some category in which the latest one he praised must rank first, or among the first. Rittenhouse is the best of living astronomers, as Priestley of divines. M. Flourens wrote "the most extraordinary of all books." The Norriton "orrery" is the modern world's *first* wonder. The Virginians must model their capitol after the *finest* extant relic of antiquity.

It is not unusual to say that Jefferson's high phrases have the ring of emptiness. Rufus Choate's contribution to the language – "glittering generalities" – was coined to describe the most revered terms of the Declaration. And a member of the Continental Congress,

looking over one of Jefferson's replies to the King, thought it typical Virginian's fustian, with all "the faults common to our Southern gentlemen:" Robert Livingston, who disassociated himself from Congress, had already sized up Jefferson's style in this way:

> Much fault-finding and declamation, with little sense or dignity. They seem to think a reiteration of tyranny, despotism, bloody, &c. all that is needed to unite us at home and to convince the bribed voters of the North of the justice of our cause.

Most historians agree that Jefferson's list of the King's offenses falls too readily into a rant of "despotism, bloody, &c." And few could think its grand first assertions self-evident any more.

How to judge a writer who seems, alternately, too modest and too proud? It is often best to work one's way toward a man through such thickets of apparent contradiction. Obviously his words, on different occasions, did not seem contradictory to him; and if we can reach the state where they seem reconcilable to us, we have a chance of seeing the man "from within," as he saw himself. For that kind of understanding it will not do to say that Jefferson compensated for an almost painful restraint in his personal bearing by long-range hyperbole in using his pen. It is true that Jefferson's audacity shows up most in his writings; nor is this an unusual thing in history – one often looks through or around bombastic writings to find a timorous author. But such an explanation does not meet our test. For one thing, the modesties we looked at were also put down in writing. For another, this view of the author's double standard is taken from outside; it does not reconcile contradictions in the man's own terms. Jefferson did not think of his own life as divided between an understated truth of bearing and overstated truths in writing. He must have felt one truth running through all his efforts at enunciation, whether in person or with his pen.

If we could argue with him now and say he took a different tack in his two modes of self-expression, immediate and remote, I think he might grant the point, without considering either mode a departure from the truth. The difference, in his mind, would not arise from private psychic needs, but from convention. When he finally met George III ten years after the Declaration, he was polite (though George was not); yet this was the man his pages had thundered against. Of course, circumstances had changed in the interval – Jefferson was, by 1786, the emissary of a realm separated from the King. But one suspects that Jefferson (as opposed, say, to Patrick Henry) would have been just as polite had he been ushered into the royal presence on 5 July 1776. There was a procedural nicety in eighteenth-century men that sharpened, rather than fuzzed, the point of their disputings – grand courtesy in serving up grand insult. Pope's deadliest lines would lose much of their edge if they were not urged home with ironic little bows and curtsies:

> Yes, I am proud; I must be proud to see
> Men not afraid of God, afraid of me.

It is true that Jefferson, when he appeared wild in print but mild in person, was reflecting the conventions of his time. We see that in his chivalrous treatment of war prisoners, as Virginia's revolutionary Governor, by contrast with his written execrations of the foe. He was one of the rare men who truly do hate ideas, who wish error could be killed without harming the men who profess it.

Yet even to speak of "convention" in our day – to speak of it conventionally – is to risk misunderstanding. The word suggests to us formality, a matter of empty forms – yet the "forms" of society were ceremonies then. "Convention" was a lively matter, as lively as the constitutional convention in Philadelphia. It is not mere punning to link such uses of a word. The active note of con-vening still animated words that seem placid to us – as when John Adams called a good wine and his constitution "convenient."

Men of the time, schooled by classical grammarians, liked to take words apart as they did their clocks, and then to see what new combinations could be made. Thus Jefferson was not content to support the principle of "neology;" he also wanted the word. And, along with that, he wanted all the things he could do with it:

> I am a friend to *neology*.... And given the word neologism to our language, as a root, and it should give us it's fellow substantives, neology, neologist, neologization; it's adjectives neologous, neological, neologistical, it's verb neologize, and adverb neologically.

By reactivating the root sense of words, men were led to think in etymological clusters – like convening, convenience, convention. To accept a convention was to come together in conscious agreement on its observation and significance. It was a great time of congress and convenings; of public business, carried on in public by conferrings and consent. "Convention" was just consent put in more lasting form – the word still meant certain kinds of written laws, as well as unwritten usage. Locke took men's agreement on the conventional worth of money as a sign that parties to the social contract were tacitly renewing their assent. We cannot take seriously enough Jefferson's fear of the first President's "monarchical" manners until we see how vital were manners and "mere" social usage in his day. If we call Jefferson's ups and downs of stylistic wrath and restraint "conventional," we risk saying that he did not mean them; he would have felt their "conventional" nature demonstrated his intent. Did the constitutional convention not *mean* to form a government?

If we do not solve the problem of Jefferson's "exaggerations" by calling on convention, at least we shift it toward ground recognizably his. If critics seek the "real" Jefferson in terms of private quirks or psychic mystery, they neglect the way that public discourse mattered to him. One vast difference between our time and his is that we think of the "real" self as hidden, but they thought man *becomes* man only in "congress" with his fellows, in the marketplace, in contracting for human "conventions," including speech and thought. Even their myths, like the hypothetical "nature" of Locke, are explanations of society, of the public fact. That is why men of the period felt so urgently that *authority* – that vast center of all lifegiving convention – must live up to itself, be authenticated. The age of definition was the age of revolution; it remade the compacts by which men deal with each other – a task that called, equally, for new dictionaries and new governments. For Jefferson, to seek a private man, unengaged in this great commerce of the mind, would be a drastic diminution of purview. And we must try to make those things matter to us which mattered to him. To understand "from within" is to share the man's concerns.

One barrier to this congruence of concerns is language. Jefferson deceives by speaking our tongue – or what we think is ours. But he not only spoke English. He spoke eighteenth-century. Even when he used his halting French abroad, Lafayette understood him, because

Jefferson's instructions for his tombstone and epitaph.

could the dead feel any interest in Monu-
-ments or other remembrances of them; when, as
Anacreon says: Ολιγη δε κεισομεσθα
                    Κονις, οςεων λυθεντων
the following would be to my Manes the most
gratifying.
On the grave
            a plain die or cube of 3.f without any
mouldings, surmounted by an Obelisk
of 6.f. height, each of a single stone:
on the faces of the Obelisk the following
inscription, & not a word more

                    Here was buried
                Thomas Jefferson
    Author of the Declaration of American Independance
            of the Statute of Virginia for religious freedom
        & Father of the University of Virginia.

because by these, as testimonials that I have lived, I wish most to
be remembered. ~~to be~~ to be of the coarse stone of which
my columns are made, that no one might be tempted
hereafter to destroy it for the value of the materials.
my bust by Ciracchi, with the pedestal and truncated
column on which it stands, might be given to the University
if they would place it in the Dome room of the Rotunda.
on the Die, of the Obelisk, might be engraved
            Born Apr. 2. 1743. O.S.
            Died ——   ,

the two men shared a world. There was an international vocabulary of the Enlightenment which only partly meshes with surviving English words from that great conversation.

The inconcinnity shows in thousands of little ways. An intelligent modern author suspects a coolness between Jefferson and his principal teacher of classical languages, because the Autobiography refers to Dr Maury as merely "correct" in his scholarship. Looking back across intervening romanticisms, we stress ardor and inspiration in the teaching of literature as well as in its writing. And even back in the eighteenth century, Pope could write that poets should be "Correct *with spirit*." But first of all, correct – even for poets. And, for scholars, correct first and last. When Jefferson calls a scholar correct, it is not a bored half-compliment, but simply the accurate word. Jefferson used it of the Rev. Maury's teaching as he used it of Mr Rittenhouse's clocks, or of his father's map. In that context, there is no higher praise. Jefferson did not want an enthusiastic grammarian any more than he wanted an enthusiastic clock-maker. Indeed, the difference between our language and his is summed up in the fact that he would have been insulted if called an enthusiast.

Perhaps, then, Jefferson seems to take up contradictory attitudes because we have not taken pains enough to understand him well. If he seems inexact, that may be our fault, as when the man read a slight into "correct" where Jefferson meant only praise. We understand as merely vague – vaguely modest, or vaguely boastful – terms he meant to be exact. It is what we should have expected. Look at his blueprints and maps, his mathematical formulae. They aim with great rigor at being correct. Is it likely he drew up verbal plans for his country with less care than he used on the ratios for his plow?

Assume, then, that he really *meant* he was a farmer above all other things. That is, of course, literal economic fact – his income (which always seemed insufficient) was mainly drawn from his plantation, whose returns he labored intensely to improve. But even on this basic economic level, the word had a different ring for men of Jefferson's Virginia. We expect a farmer to farm, to labor behind the plow – at least occasionally, or at one managerial remove. But that was slave work in Jefferson's time. The farmer *owned* land – and slaves. Farming often retained its first sense, of "leasing out." Men like A. Whitney Griswold have written long discussions of Jefferson's "agrarianism" without once mentioning slaves – which shows they are talking about a quite different fact of life than he was. Jefferson's very disaste for slavery discouraged him from engaging in idyllic tasks out of Vergil. The closest he came to working with a plow was the set of equations he worked out for its moldboard's curve. And he studied crop rotation and climate just as he studied the proper angle of a furrow. Farming was not just a source of income for him, but an object of the mind's inquiry – indeed, the nexus of many sciences: "Agriculture is a science of the very first order. It counts among its handmaids the most respectable sciences such as chemistry, natural philosophy, mechanics, mathematics generally, natural history, botany." At this point, where economic necessity gets etherialized into "respectable" science, there is nothing self-deprecating – or even democratic – about calling oneself a farmer. The very King attacked in the Declaration, who had read Arthur Young's agricultural books and written up some experiments, liked to be called Farmer George, and there was no question of false modesty in him. John Dickinson, in his *Letters From a Farmer*, called this a learned life, since it gave more leisure for books than would trade or litigation. No wonder Jefferson said gentlemen's sons should be

"closing their academical education with this, as the crown of all other sciences, fascinated with its solid charms."

Finally, the economic and scientific importance of farming converge on its political meaning for Jefferson. He defended the small farmer, and thought of him as the common man; but he did this with an aristocrat's distaste for "low" merchants – they must fawn and haggle, which undermines a virile independence. He had almost as low an opinion of lawyers (George Wythe excepted) and doctors (Benjamin Rush excepted). He entered the lawyer's state reluctantly, loitering five years amid Wythe's books to squeeze out another and another last master–pupil conversation; and, despite heavy business (almost as good as Patrick Henry's, when the latter was a juror's Perry Mason), he gave up practice even before the Revolution summoned, to go back to Monticello. He had a fastidious dislike for cities; when abroad, he tramped through fields whenever he could, instead of towns. Jefferson preferred to meet and be met by means of a ride into a man's own territory, his "moral space," the sign of his separate and equal station among men. Since manners were so important to him, and a free uncrouching manner was best instilled on land one owned, the promotion of virtue in others meant giving them land, as the preservation of one's own virtue meant returning to the land.

For men like Jefferson, no legislature could be less desirable than the kind we have now in Congress, made up mainly of lawyers. As Henry Adams realized, Jefferson could not understand New England states which kept sending lawyers and merchants to the seat of national government. The only good politician, in his eyes, was the amateur, the reluctant one. Despite all his misgivings over George Washington, this tie remained between them – Washington, also, wanted to go home; and had a home to go to. Men like Hamilton, whose whole life was politics, would eventually do anything for the sake of politics.

This attitude does not conflict with what I said earlier about Jefferson's insistence on public duty and discourse. At Monticello, he was a citizen of the world. In Philadelphia (as Secretary of State) or Washington (as President) he was merely an American. It is often said that holding office forced him to scan wider – indeed, imperial – horizons. But that is not what he felt. Politics had to *contract* his mind to a national outlook. He was cramped in the White House. At home, he moved on a larger stage.

So "farming" meant something complex but definite to Jefferson – and something quite different from what it means to us. Where men suspect that he demeans or ingratiates himself, he is actually boasting. Were he not one in fact, he would almost have to pretend he was a farmer. After all, some people made that pretense. Crèvecoeur back in Paris, Dickinson gouty in Philadelphia, or Cobbett feeding endless copy to the presses – they all faked up rural episodes into epistolary "lives" of themselves as farmers. "Letters of an American farmer" was just the genre for aspiring moralists.

If Jefferson was only being correct where we thought him modest, perhaps the same is true where he seems too expansive in his claims – as in his frequent use of superlatives. He described men and books *too* regularly as the first or best? But Jefferson lived amid pro-liferating categories. Studies now safely named, gradually tamed, were struggling out of old "metaphysical" straitjackets – some with names as new as themselves, and some without. Lacking terms that would later grow up – demography, sociology, macroeconomics – men

spoke of things like "political mathematics." A term like "mechanics" covered fields as disparate as meteorology and hydrodynamics. Jefferson rejoiced in all these ramifyings from the tree of knowledge. Appealing to Diderot's *arbor scientiae*, he indulged his love of classification:

> Naval architecture teaches the best form and construction of vessels; for which best form it has recourse to the question of the Solid of least resistance, a problem of transcendental geometry. And its appurtenant projectiles belong to the same branch, as in the preceding case. It is true that so far as respects the action of the water on the rudder and oars, and of the wind on the sails, it may be placed in the department of mechanics, as Diderot and Dalambert have done; but belonging quite as much to geometry, allied in its military character, to military architecture, it simplified our plan to place both under the same head [of pure mathematics].

It is with this taxonomic nicety that Jefferson distinguishes De Tracy as the first author in *civil* government and *political* economy, or Rittenhouse as the leading *descriptive* astronomer. Priestley is best of the divines because the first to take a scientific approach to the Gospels. Flourens replaces psychology with neurology. New fields were being opened in a new world, and they called for new words. Above all, they demanded an assertion that "modern" men were not doing the same *kind* of things as their predecessors. One of Jefferson's conflicts with Adams arose over just this issue. Adams had written that "the longest liver of you all, will find no Principles, Institutions, or Systems of Education, more fit, in general to be transmitted to your Posterity, than those you have received from your Ancestors." Jefferson wrote to Priestley that this was evidence of surviving bigotry: progress demanded that men look forward, not backward. When this letter reached the public, Adams complained of it to Jefferson, but the latter held his ground: "You possess, yourself, too much science, not to see how much is still ahead of you, unexplained and unexplored. Your own consciousness must place you as far before our ancestors, as in the rear of our posterity." A false piety to ancestors kept men from recognizing progress – "for I am sure they had no words which could have conveyed the ideas of Oxigen, cotyledons, zoophytes, magnetism, electricity, hyaline, and thousands of others expressing ideas not then existing." He called a thing "first" as he called it "correct," because that is what it was – and he never used numbers loosely. His world was full of untagged specimens and infant sciences. It was a labor of scientific recognition to call men first in fields no others had trod, and to achieve for them fresh terminology: "Dictionaries are but the depositories of words already legitimated by usage. Society is the work-shop in which new ones are elaborated."

Jefferson always admired explorers – men like his father, or like George Rogers Clark. And he felt the same awe for men who moved into new areas of science. The activities were not only cognate; they were almost identical. Along with Priestley, Jefferson denied any distinction between mind and matter; all "exploration" was literally spatial to him. The model was in every case Newton, the supreme genius, charting the universe as surely as Peter Jefferson traced the previously undiscovered boundaries of his huge native state. Peter's son tried to imitate this kind of discovery, searching always for the new, and for new language to distinguish it when found. He spent years tracking rumors of a giant American

Watch paper, probably French, owned and used
by Jefferson.

sloth; the obsession was rewarded when this phantom got the name *Megatherium Jeffersonii.*
He tried to map out the Northwest Territory systematically, like a man arranging scientific
categories: Metropotamia, Polypotamia, Assinisipia, Pelisipia, etc. In the same way he
carved up his own farm into mathematical segments, seven fields of forty acres each on a
seven-year rotating scheme. Unfortunately, his crops did not flourish as effortlessly as the
arbor scientiae he drew up for them, and an imbalance in a single year was enough to throw off
the whole scheme.

Jefferson's fault is not vagueness; if anything, he was too precise, his categories too fine-
drawn, his distinctions gauged to hairbreadth boundaries. The specifics were too fascinating
for him to be dazzled by generalities. As a working hypothesis, then, it is reasonable to hold
that his most famous axioms were exactly stated. His own words may at times suggest the
opposite – as when he said the Declaration was meant only "to place before mankind the
common sense of the subject." And he went on, in the same passage, to call his work "an
expression of the American mind." That proves, we are told, that Jefferson deliberately
generalized, trying to include the views of everybody at the Philadelphia Convention. But
we should remember the occasion of his words. He had been accused of plagiarism – of
writing in such a definite fashion that definite sources could be named. John Adams, it is
true, called his phrases "hackneyed;" but still traced them first to James Otis and then to the
Mecklenburg Resolution. Richard Henry Lee claimed Jefferson's finest words had been
cribbed from Locke. One does not steal everyone's common air, but some one person's
well-filled purse.

Jefferson's answer was that he stated the common sense – which, later readers assume,
means the common sense *of the assembly* (i.e., what all agreed to in general, despite particular
differences). But that is not what Jefferson wrote: he said he put down the common sense *of
the subject.* "Common sense" was a technical term in the philosophy of Jefferson's day; and by
the time he wrote this sentence he was a good friend of its main surviving spokesman
(Dugald Stewart). This philosophy – aimed mainly at Hume, but partly at Locke – argued

77

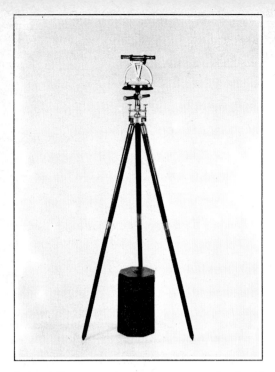

A theodolite, a surveying instrument, owned and used
by Jefferson at Monticello.

with Thomas Reid that "To judge of first principles, requires no more than a sound mind
free from prejudice, and a distinct conception of the question." In this view, to state the
common sense of a subject is to cast it in terms that make its truth immediately perceptible
(self-evident). If we continue the quotation from Jefferson, we see that this is precisely what
he had in mind: "to place before mankind the common sense of the subject, *in terms so plain
and firm as to command their assent.*"

He meant "self-evident" in a very strict sense. In fact, that sense was sharpened (probably
at Benjamin Franklin's suggestion) when self-evident was substituted for "undeniable" in
the Declaration. The perverse can deny anything. That is why Reid said that "a sound mind
free from prejudice" is the second thing needed for perceiving the common sense of a subject.
So we have another case of words being read as a mild disclaimer (I only phrased what
everyone was thinking) when they actually make a harder, more specific, higher claim (I
supplied the distinct terms for minds unprejudiced enough to grasp them as self-evident).

The pattern is recurrent, and leads us to face a question that will make all the difference in
our reading of the Declaration. If we have often erred in reading Jefferson's language as dim
and general – vaguely deferential or superlative – have we missed a narrower, more
challenging sense in the opening axioms of the Declaration (which have been thought to
glitter with generality even by their defenders)? Are these inspirational trumpet calls, whose
music matters more than the words, or precise claims meant to be understood precisely?

The very form of the document suggests a preliminary answer to that question. Later
generations, less interested in the origins of the dispute than in its glorious outcome, have
dwelt on the opening passages as the main "argument," treating the appended list of grievances as mere occasion for this grand opening statement. But the opening paragraphs state
the *basis* of the argument, which is conducted in ensuing accusations. The first sentences
state agreed-on things, against which the King's conduct is to be tested. And the historical

charges, which resemble a lawyer's brief, necessarily one-sided, would lose all effect if the norms appealed to were not accepted. Jefferson says that America is submitting to standards of judgement shared by all men but the perverse; that is why he addresses "a candid world" (Reid's unprejudiced minds). And he claims he can cast this address in terms that bring out its "self evidence." Jefferson was not speaking to Congress, trying to make it agree – its members had already taken the momentous step that was incorporated into Jefferson's peroration. He was not informing the King of the colonies' separation – that declaration of independence (the "real" one) was Richard Henry Lee's, debated and passed before Jefferson's text was taken off the table. He was addressing mankind, out of a decent respect for its opinions, explaining the step already taken. It was an expression *of* the American mind *to* mankind's candor, in terms that unite the two.

From this very function of the Declaration, some men have argued to a necessary vagueness in it. Jefferson was writing war propaganda, with all the license that gives men who are locked in a life-and-death battle. But Jefferson himself did not limit its application. He recurred to it as equally relevant, sometimes as more relevant, long after the war had been decided. He urged the document's celebration and use in later struggles, foreign and domestic. It is given prominent, disproportionate, space in his Autobiography. When he ordered it placed first on his monument, he was making a very conscious choice, based on a firm belief that it was his most important contribution to America – not to its war with England, not even to its subsequent history but to history *tout court*. To History. Men of his time did not choose their epitaphs lightly, but with posterity in mind.

Did Jefferson literally *mean* that all these "truths" were obvious? It seems exaggerated to say so. But we should suspect our suspicions of exaggeration. No one ever aimed to be more accurate, more "correct," in manner, in word, in deed; in his drawings and plans; in his beliefs, so meticulously dissected through letter after letter of his correspondence. A man with these standards would hardly commend to posterity, as his main claim upon it, an effusion of enthusiasm. When he used words like inalienable, or self-evident, or happiness, he drew on meanings sharpened by debate in his day, though dulled by use in ours. To understand him we have to re-enter those debates – the debates over common sense, over alienable property, over the pain-pleasure calculus – all of them debates he took part in, along with his friends.

Furthermore, we must read with more care than we have in the past his own original draft. The Autobiography thrusts that task upon us with almost unbecoming urgency. Men have argued convincingly that Congress made the Declaration a better piece of propaganda by its emendations. Why, then, should Jefferson still be distressed, late in his seventies, at all the alterations and omissions? Was it mere vanity? I think the answer lies in his high standard of accuracy. The idea he meant to express is dimmed by the omissions – not only the famous deletion of all reference to slavery, but less-known ones as well (like that on "agonizing affection"). We may be surprised by some of the meanings turned up through strict attention to the language in its historical context. But we have no excuse for our surprise. It was to be expected, after all, that he would give as much careful attention to his "finding" of America, to the clearest statement of its Idea, as he gave to his other inventions. Or as he gave to the epitaph where that Idea holds pride of place.

THE POLITICAL ECONOMY
OF THOMAS JEFFERSON
Richard E. Ellis

Thomas Jefferson is a figure of monumental importance in American history. No one really denies this. Yet if we are willing to admit that Jefferson's impact on the American way of life has been great, the exact nature of that impact still has not been adequately explained. This is particularly true when one tries to come to terms with the elusive subject of Jefferson's theories on economic matters and his effects on the course of America's economic growth. This is unfortunate, for it is a subject of great significance, not simply because it sheds so much light on Jefferson's long public career but also because it helps explain the particular direction in which he helped to channel America after the Revolution. Indeed, so successful was Jefferson in this endeavor and so fundamental were his ideas on economic problems that they still remain at the heart of the basic values of most Americans today.

There are certain difficulties in coming to terms with Jefferson's economic thought. Save for the *Notes on the State of Virginia*, written very early in his career and mainly for foreign consumption, he never wrote up his ideas in systematic form. He also was a public figure for an unusually long period of time, for over half a century. This is important to keep in mind because what Jefferson said shortly after 1776, when he was caught up in the idealism of the Revolution, or in the 1820s, when old age began to show and he was stunned by the Panic of 1819, are not good indications of what he was thinking during the cabinet battles with Alexander Hamilton in the early 1790s or when as President of the United States during the heady prosperity of the first years of the nineteenth century he articulated his program of internal improvements. Moreover, Jefferson had a strong tendency toward a kind of verbal extremism, so that much of what he said made him appear to be a good deal more radical and revolutionary than he actually was. This was particularly true when he was not restrained by the responsibilities of political office and power. James Madison excused his good friend in these terms: "Allowances ought to be made for a habit in Mr Jefferson as in others of great genius of expressing in strong and round terms, impressions of the moment." John Quincy Adams was less generous but he described Jefferson similarly: "He was a mixture of profound and sagacious observation, with strong prejudices and irritated passions." In short, Jefferson said and wrote a lot of things that he probably did not really mean or that did not fully reflect his mature judgement on a subject. It is this that helps explain many of Jefferson's more extreme utterances of hostility toward cities, commerce, manufacturing and the laboring classes. In truth, Jefferson was seriously concerned with the problem of

America's economic growth, and at crucial times in his public career made an important constructive political compromise to try to obtain an urban center for Virginia; deliberately did more than any other statesman of the early national period to encourage the development of manufactures; and successfully helped formulate a blueprint for his country's economic development.

Although economic policy was a subject to which he gave considerable attention throughout his life he never really thought about it in specifically economic categories. To be sure, he occasionally used such terms as value, distribution, allocation, exchange, capital, and productive and unproductive labor, but, like most public figures of his time, he thought about economic affairs in the broader but less precise categories of political economy which emphasized the interrelationship between the political and economic processes. The American Revolution was the seminal event of Jefferson's life, and his concern with economic matters had to do mainly with translating the ideas of that event, which he so deeply believed in, into the realities of a viable political system.

At the time he drafted the Declaration of Independence, Jefferson was above all else a Virginian. As a member of the Old Dominion's ruling class he had received enormous benefits: a place in society, a good education, and a position of political leadership. With these benefits, however, also came obligations and some real problems. For despite its political and intellectual prominence in the new nation, Virginia faced very serious economic difficulties. By the eve of the Revolution a long tradition of wasteful agricultural methods, extravagant living and widespread debt, together with declining tobacco prices and land values, and the lack of an adequate specie supply, had combined to create a crisis mentality in Virginia where economic matters were concerned. Like the rest of the planter class Jefferson placed most of the blame for Virginia's economic problems upon the British imperial system which had prevented the colony from issuing paper money, had closed the fertile lands of the West to settlement, and most important of all, through the Navigation Acts, had given English and Scottish merchants a monopoly of the tobacco trade which they used to force planters to sell their crops cheaply and to pay high prices for manufactured goods, services, and loans, thus keeping them in a position of perpetual debt. While Jefferson's support for the Revolution cannot be explained exclusively or even primarily in economic terms there is no question but that he hoped for and tried to embrace the opportunities that independence offered for alleviating his state's economic difficulties.

Whatever else Jefferson was, he was not the self-sufficient yeoman farmer that he frequently idealized. A planter and businessman in private life, he was constantly hard-pressed and in debt until, during the Panic of 1819, his estate finally collapsed when he secured the note of a close friend who failed. Perhaps it was for this reason that Jefferson throughout his life paid an inordinate amount of attention to the finding of new crops and fertilizers to revive worn-out soils, to the development of more effective farming implements, to the making of numerous efficiency studies, and to the keeping of careful financial accounts. Although his political opponents often denounced him for being abstract and visionary in his thinking, there was an important practical dimension to the man. Jefferson had considerable first-hand experience with the problems of commercial agriculture, and this greatly influenced his thoughts on his country's political economy.

But Jefferson was not simply a Virginia planter, he was a revolutionist as well. He fervently believed in America's great republican experiment in liberty. Moreover, for him the Revolution was only just beginning in 1776, and he immediately turned his attention to his home state where he hoped to implement needed reforms. Although he was engaging in his usual hyperbole when he later claimed that his numerous reform proposals, many of which were enacted, actually "laid the axe" to the Old Dominion's aristocracy, they were none the less significant. Compared to the Old World, as Jefferson was so fond to point out, Virginia was a land of opportunity, but this was not so in absolute terms, or if conditions in the Old Dominion were compared to those in most of the other states in the Union at that time. In Virginia the ruling class had begun to consolidate its political power in the late seventeenth century and this, combined with economic stagnation in the eighteenth century, had saddled the state with one of the largest disfranchised and landless classes in the new nation. Jefferson's reforms did not annihilate the local elite, but they did help to bring to a halt a distressingly accelerating tendency to the creation of a closed society. This was important to Jefferson because while he embraced the numerous benefits of his high social status he was unsympathetic to the exclusiveness of his state's ruling class. His unsuccessful Bill for the More General Diffusion of Knowledge clearly revealed this. Its purpose was "to illuminate, as far as practicable, the minds of the people at large," and to make sure

> that those persons, whom nature had endowed with genius and virtue, should be rendered by liberal education worthy to receive, and able to receive the sacred deposit of the rights and liberties of their fellow citizens, and that they should be called to that charge without regard to wealth, birth or other accidental conditions or circumstance.

It provided for a rigid selection system that recognized that not everyone was capable of education at the highest levels. Its elitist overtones ("the best geniuses will be raked from the rubbish annually," he noted at one point) reflected his belief in a "natural aristocracy," and its stress upon the concept of equality of opportunity as opposed to equality of final result gives an important insight into what he felt the role of the government should be in economic matters.

Underlying Jefferson's preoccupation with the problem of widening opportunities was his recognition that America had an enormous asset at its disposal: physical land, which most people of his time considered the most important form of wealth. In Europe the existing real estate was of a known and fixed dimension and most of it was owned by a select few. But in America a broader distribution of landed property already existed and much of the country remained unexplored and uninhabited. This greatly influenced Jefferson's political thinking, for in his draft of a constitution for Virginia in 1776 he required a property qualification to be able to vote, but significantly also proposed that the state, through grants of land, should make sure that every adult white had at least fifty acres, which in effect would have meant universal suffrage. As Richard Hofstadter perceptively observed, Jefferson was "more democratic in his conception of the economic *base* of government than in his conception of the *structure* of government." In his home state Jefferson worked assiduously to protect the interests of small farmers against those of large land companies and profiteering adventurers. On the national level, under the Articles of Con-

federation, he helped establish a land policy that would ensure a republic of freeholders, and formulated a territorial system of government that stressed the importance of new states coming into the union as equal partners. The West, with its enormous quantity of un-inhabited land, was fundamental to all of Jefferson's thinking on political economy; it made it possible, as he later put it, for America to become an "Empire of Liberty."

What of Jefferson's agrarianism? His belief in the moral superiority of the yeomen as "the chosen people of God, if ever he had a chosen people"? This has been exaggerated as a dimension of his early thinking. Its main source was the anxiety that gripped most thought-ful Americans after 1776: that their republican experiment in liberty would end in disaster. Cynical European critics pointed with considerable effect to the record of history and argued that a large country with a republican form of government had never succeeded. In refutation of these criticisms Jefferson emphasized America's physical blessings, the social base the country created for a republic, and the singularly virtuous citizenry produced by it. Exaggerating the difference between a corrupt Old and pure New World was part of the rhetoric that had made the Revolution, and also a useful way of assuaging one's own self-doubts.

And his hostility to commerce? It was real enough in the sense that, despite his supposed irreligion and his taste for extravagant living, Jefferson subscribed to a form of the puritan ethic that condemned avariciousness and preoccupation with moneymaking and had only an imperfect understanding of the mechanisms of the market place which were beginning to sweep the western world. But he did not carry this hostility very far, certainly not as far as many of his contemporaries did. Another source was his fear of the Old World's influence on American values. To a friend he observed, "Were I to indulge my own theory I should wish them [the Americans] to practice neither commerce nor navigation, but to stand with respect to Europe precisely on the footing of China. We should thus avoid wars, and all our citizens would be husbandmen." Yet he was quick to add in the same letter: "But this is theory only, and a theory which the servants of America are not at liberty to follow." Beginning when Jefferson was a member of the Continental Congress and continuing on through the time he was Minister to France, where he did more than comment on the miseries of Europe and await the coming of the French Revolution, he worked long and hard to obtain favorable trading privileges for Americans throughout the continent, wrote a treatise on the whaling industry in hopes of getting France to purchase American whale oil, and tried to build a Franco-American commercial system to counterbalance Britain's control of American trade. Even during his most idealistic phase Jefferson's actions belied his anti-commercial rhetoric.

As the 1780s wore on whatever there actually was of Jefferson's agrarianism dwindled rapidly. The idealistic fervor of the Revolution was giving way to the realities of imple-menting a positive program of economic growth both for Virginia and the nation. In politics on the state level Jefferson and his friends opposed the policies of Patrick Henry who at this time was the true spokesman of the small farmer interests. And although he was in Europe when the Constitution was written and adopted in 1787–8, and had reservations about its lack of a bill of rights, he warmly endorsed it, and in 1789 assumed the position of Secretary of State. The underlying social and economic division in the ratifying struggle

James Madison, the fourth President of the United
States, by Asher B. Durand.

was between the country's commercial interests – merchants, artisans, and market-oriented
farmers and planters – who supported the Constitution because they wanted a strong and
active government capable of encouraging economic development, and the subsistence
farming interests who had only a minimum of contact with the commercial nexus and who
desired a frugal, weak, and inactive government that would for the most part leave
them alone.

The adoption of the Constitution with its various restraints upon the political and
economic activities of the state governments, which many believed had been too responsive
to small farmer and agrarian pressures during the 1780s, was a significant victory for the
American commercial community. But it was only a frame of government, and it still
remained for an actual national program of economic growth to be implemented under it.
It soon became clear that real differences existed among the founding fathers over the
particular kinds of economic policies which the national government should adopt. The
earliest skirmish took place on Alexander Hamilton's proposals to fund the national debt at
face value for its current holders and to assume all the state debts. Hamilton's program
stressed the importance of welding the mercantile and financial classes to the federal
government and implied a trickle-down conception of economic development toward both
the small farmer interests and commercial–agricultural interests of the country which would
bear the major portion of the tax burden. Jefferson and Madison opposed these measures

A view of the Capitol in Washington, D.C. as it was
when first occupied by Congress in 1800.

because they failed to discriminate between the original holders (for the most part farmers
and planters) and the speculators (mainly to be found in the financial centers of the northeast)
who had bought most of the national debt at a greatly depreciated value, and because the
great agricultural states of Virginia and North Carolina had already used their landed assets
to pay off much of their own debts while the great mercantile states of New York and
Massachusetts had not made much progress in this area. If all the state debts were assumed
by the national government it would mean that Virginians and North Carolinians would be
further taxed to pay off the debts of their sister states.

Hamilton's proposal for the funding of the national debt was adopted by Congress, but
Jefferson and Madison managed to temporarily block the assumption measure. It is
significant that in his opposition to Hamilton's funding scheme Jefferson never favored the
agrarian solution, that of repudiating a part of the national debt as unnecessarily bloated, but
supported Madison's plan for discrimination between the original holders and the
speculators who currently held the various government promises to pay. This proposal
would have given the speculator the highest market value for his holdings with the balance
going to the original holder. It would not have reduced the amount of the national debt
(which is what the agrarians wanted), but would only have redistributed it. It is also
revealing that, when Jefferson and Madison finally compromised the assumption question in
Hamilton's favor in 1790, their chief reward was the permanent location of the nation's

86

capital at Washington, D.C. This was something they both wanted because they believed that the city would develop into a major commercial center which would infuse some vigor into their state's sagging economy.

Much more fundamental, and thus less easily open to compromise, was the question raised by the relationship of differing concepts of economic growth as to what the new nation's foreign policy should be. On one side were the great majority of American merchants, who, as a result of their experience during the 1780s, when a whole series of generally unsuccessful attempts to find markets outside of the British empire had been made, had come to believe that their self-interest and the future of American economic growth lay in the restoration and maintenance of close commercial ties with England. Led by Alexander Hamilton, this group believed that nothing should be done to disrupt American ties with the former mother country, even if it meant allowing economic domination by Great Britain. On the other side was a very small portion of the American mercantile community that did not have the close financial ties with England, and commercial farming interests, particularly planters, led by Jefferson and Madison, who were opposed to having the American economy controlled by a single country. Jefferson's attitude on this question originated from his view of Virginia's colonial experience under the Navigation Acts, a condition which seemed to be rapidly returning during the 1780s. As Madison observed in the First Congress, Great Britain "has bound us in commercial mannacles, and very nearly defeated the object of our independence." What Jefferson wanted was to see America's commercial ties extended to as many nations in addition to England as possible in order to raise prices through competitive bidding for America's marketable crops. His views were not simply limited to agricultural staples, however. As Secretary of State in his Report on the Cod and Whale Fisheries he complained that British restrictions had also depressed prices in those areas. To rectify this Jefferson believed that America had to build up its merchant marine and place discriminatory duties on English ships in order to force Great Britain to grant the United States trading concessions. The idea of commercial pressure was crucial to all his thinking about economics and foreign policy. "War," he wrote in 1797, "is not the best engine for us to resort to, nature has given us one *in our commerce*, which if properly managed, will be a better instrument for obliging the interested nations of Europe to treat us with justice."

It has become fashionable to describe Hamilton as a "realist" and a "nationalist," but these terms become very ambiguous when one compares the economic basis of his foreign policy with that of Jefferson. Hamilton's foreign policy worked to the interest of only a very small minority of the country and led the Federalists to a political defeat from which they never recovered. How realistic can it have been? Although he was not an agrarian, Jefferson's foreign policy was founded on the wise recognition that America was essentially an agricultural nation. Being more in touch with the economic realities of their day, he and Madison remained consistently on the political winning side throughout their careers. Hamilton, to be sure, was a great nationalist on domestic issues, but his foreign policy predicated a kind of economic vassalage to Great Britain. In this sense Jefferson, who was always much more anti-British than he was pro-French, was much purer in his concern for the rights of his country on the international scene.

Of course there was much more than simply economic issues at stake in the political battles of the 1790s. Republicans and Federalists differed over a host of constitutional and ideological questions: the meaning of the American Revolution, the proper way to interpret the Constitution, the significance of the French Revolution, and the right to criticize the government, to name a few of the most important areas. But a basic economic division did exist in these battles, and it was between the agricultural and mercantile–financial interests of the country. This, however, changed sharply after Jefferson's accession to the Presidency in 1801. For it soon became clear that the Republican victory was so complete (they captured permanent control of both Houses of Congress and Jefferson carried every state except Delaware and Connecticut when he was re-elected in 1804) that the Federalists were no longer a real threat. After 1800, therefore, the most important political divisions occurred within the Republican party and they too had a definite economic basis, though it was different from the one that had existed in the 1790s. On one side were the commercial interests of the Republican party: most planters, market-oriented farmers, and artisans, merchants, and bankers, many of whom at one time had been Federalists. The other side was primarily composed of subsistence farmers who did not really participate in the market economy and basically were non-commercial in their thinking, and of a small but very significant group of Old Republican planters from eastern Maryland, Virginia, and North Carolina, areas that did not participate in the entrepreneurial spirit that began to sweep the country in the early nineteenth century, and whose spokesmen therefore had a strong anti-commercial bias. Although Jefferson liked to view himself as President of all the people and generally tried to stay aloof from partisan politics, he basically was sympathetic to the commercial wing of the Republican party. "It is material," he asserted, "to the safety of Republicanism to detach the mercantile interests from its enemies and incorporate them into the body of its friends. A merchant is naturally a Republican, and can be otherwise only from a vitiated state of things."

In addition to his own strong appreciation of the value and need for commerce, political factors also led him in the direction of compromise. He fully appreciated that his inauguration represented the first peaceful change of government under the Constitution. With no precedents to emulate, he realized that the course he chose to follow would influence the success and nature of future peaceful changes in administrations. He was especially concerned that Federalist fears of Republican excesses would lead to internal disorder and possibly even anarchy and an end to the Republic. To a close friend he wrote, shortly after becoming President, that while desirous of "effecting all the reformation which reason would suggest, and experience approve, we see the wisdom of Solon's remark, that no more good must be attempted than the nation can bear." Although no evidence exists to indicate that Jefferson engaged in any outright political deals to emerge victorious over Aaron Burr in the disputed election of 1800, it was generally understood that he had no plans for a wholesale assault on the Hamiltonian system.

Because he was essentially a moderate and so openly concerned with conciliating the Federalists, Jefferson's severest critics both among the Federalists and within the Republican party, for example, Josiah Quincy and John Randolph, denounced his administrations as simply a series of compromises with Federalism. There is enough truth in this claim to give it

some merit, and it has been picked up by numerous historians who argue that what Jefferson did in power was to out-Federalize the Federalists. But to argue in this manner is to ignore both the deep divisions that existed in the Republican party over policy questions and the very real differences that existed between the Hamiltonian and Jeffersonian economic programs. For example, on the question of a national debt: Hamilton believed that a national debt was a national blessing in that it wedded the moneyed interests of the country to the national government; the agrarian-Old Republican wing of the party denounced it as an immoral concentration of power in a small group and favored cancelling it on the grounds that it had been corruptly acquired; while Jefferson, if the policies of his administration and the writings of his Secretary of the Treasury, Albert Gallatin, are any indication, believed a permanent national debt created an unnecessary tax burden and was counterproductive because it took active capital out of the private sector of the economy, and he therefore worked out a system to pay it off completely as quickly as possible.

Banking was another issue: Hamilton created the First Bank of the United States because it could be used to provide valuable financial services to the national government, because its note-issuing powers were an effective way of converting the national debt, which was used to buy stock in the Bank, into a useful medium of exchange, and because, along with the existing state chartered banks, it had the added political benefit of being an important source of short-term loans to the credit-starved Federalist-oriented American mercantile community; the agrarian-old Republican wing of the Republican party was fundamentally hard money and disliked all banks, whatever their purpose; whereas Jefferson, though he had opposed the adoption of the First Bank of the United States in 1791 for constitutional reasons, had, as President, with Gallatin's help, come to appreciate the useful functions it played in servicing the government's financial operations and was more than willing to go along with its existence as long as it stopped operating as a partisan Federalist institution. "I am decidedly in favor of making all the banks Republican," he wrote early in his first administration. Also, while Jefferson occasionally expressed uneasiness about the proliferation of state-chartered banks under Republican auspices, he did not oppose them because they would make long-term agricultural loans for the purchases of land and slaves and the raising of new crops.

Jefferson's program of economic growth differed from Hamilton's in a number of other key areas. Land policy and the development of the West are cases in point. The Federalists, unhappy about the steady stream of settlers who moved westward after the Revolution, feared the consequences, for as new states entered the Union they invariably became Republican strongholds. While in power, therefore, the Federalists worked to retard the settlement of the West: they sold land only in large lots and charged high prices; they also moved very reluctantly to open the Mississippi to American navigation. In contrast, Jefferson, in his first Inaugural Address, praised America as a "chosen country with room enough for our descendants to the hundredth and thousandth generation." During his administrations he encouraged the growth and development of the West: by reducing the size of tracts of land needed for a minimum purchase and selling much of the national domain to settlers on credit; by treating the Indians in the old northwest and southwest harshly and forcing a great many to be removed beyond the Mississippi River; by adopting a

very aggressive stance toward the New World possessions of France and Spain which led to the Louisiana Purchase, an event which doubled the size of the country; and by supporting various expeditions, such as Lewis and Clark's, to explore the continent. On the question of the West, Jefferson was a decided expansionist.

> However our present interests may restrain us within our limits [he observed] it is impossible not to look forward to distant times, when our rapid multiplication will expand itself beyond those limits, and cover the whole northern, if not the southern continent, with a people speaking the same language, governed in similar forms, and by similar laws.

Jefferson's concern with the problem of how the West should be settled was also revealing. Always critical of the disorganized and unsystematic way that Virginia had parcelled out its western lands, he much preferred the orderly township system developed in seventeenth-century New England. It emphasized the importance of contiguous settlement, and with Jefferson's support had been adopted by the Continental Congress in the 1780s as the way to administer the national domain. As President, Jefferson worked hard to bring about an orderly development of the West. His administration was particularly harsh on the large number of squatters who settled on the unsurveyed part of the public domain. The reason for this, as many people in post-revolutionary America recognized, was that if an indiscriminate and haphazard settlement of the West were allowed it would increase the number of subsistence farmers outside of the cash nexus. This would retard economic development and create dangerous political tension over the question of the kind of country America should become.

Very closely related to the problem of how the West should be settled, and central to the Jeffersonian concern with economic development, was the subject of internal improvements. When in 1803 an act to enable Ohio to become a state was passed by Congress, Jefferson arranged that Congress provide for part of the proceeds from the sale of the state's public lands to be used to build a national road. By 1805 so much progress had been made in reducing the national debt that Jefferson requested, in his second Inaugural Address, that an amendment to the Constitution be adopted which would allow the federal government to apply part of its surplus revenue *"in time of peace* to rivers, canals, roads, arts, manufactures, education and other great objects within each state." He repeated the request even more strongly in his sixth annual address to Congress because "by these operations new channels of communication will be opened between the states; the lines of separation will disappear, their interests will be identified, and their union cemented by new and indisoluble ties." And in 1808 the administration presented an elaborate plan, authored by Gallatin, for a national system of internal improvements which provided for a series of roads and canals to link the country together. By this means it would be possible to ensure the West's participation in the eventual development of a national market economy.

Although Jefferson placed primary emphasis upon the development of marketable crops he was by no means indifferent to the other sectors of the economy. The main thrust of his economic program was to make the United States as self-sufficient as possible, and he recognized that to accomplish this meant achieving "a due balance between agriculture,

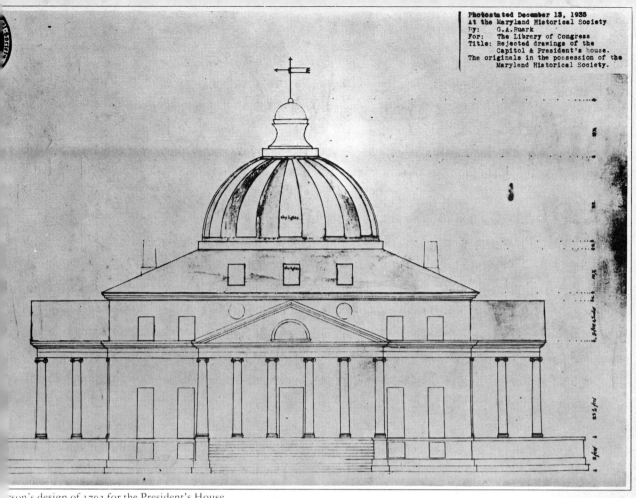

son's design of 1792 for the President's House
l on Palladio's Villa Rotunda.

manufactures and commerce." Under his auspices as President the United States Coastal Survey was begun. He and his closest friends took considerable interest in the work of Robert Fulton whose development of the steamboat was to do so much for the spread of commerce throughout the country. And defending the controversial embargo policy which dominated his last year of office he argued that the various measures "will have hastened the day when an equilibrium between the occupation of agriculture, manufactures and commerce shall simplify our foreign concerns to the exchange only of that surplus which we cannot consume for those articles of reasonable comfort or convenience which we cannot produce." Here then is another significant difference between Hamilton and Jefferson. The former believed that American economic growth was dependent upon close ties with England, while the latter stressed American self-sufficiency through the development of an internal market. Jacob Crowninshield, an important Massachusetts merchant and Republican, knew whereof he spoke when in 1805 he observed, "you may be assured not a man in the administration is an enemy to commerce ... surely Mr Jefferson has done enough to show that he has no hostile views to the commercial interest."

What is so important about Jefferson's beliefs on economic matters is that, despite some tough going in certain areas, they realistically reflected and in many ways laid the groundwork for the economic growth that was actually to take place in the United States in the early nineteenth century. It is true that Gallatin's internal improvements plan was never brought to fruition by the federal government because of political differences over its constitutionality, but it was implemented in piecemeal fashion through an alliance of public and private enterprise at the state and national level. The nation may have floundered politically and economically between 1808 and 1812, and suffered a great deal during the War of 1812, but the economy, despite the boom-bust cycle it entered, developed vigorously after 1816, and much in the way that Jefferson and his advisers envisioned when he was President: American agricultural staples brought in foreign capital; American industries fostered by a protective tariff slowly provided cheap manufactured goods and a domestic market for agricultural surpluses; the economic system thus generated was made possible by a series of roads and canals, and by the steamboat; and the domestic economy was lubricated by means of the paper money issued by the Second Bank of the United States and the various state banks.

Perhaps the most significant thing about Jefferson's theories on political economy is that they helped to bridge the gap of the enormous division created by the Revolution. This difference had not played an especially important role during the coming of independence but it emerged quickly after 1776 as Americans began to debate among themselves the question of what kind of country the United States should become. On one side were the agrarian-minded who thought of issues in highly emotional, absolutist, and moral terms. They were ignorant of the complexities in economic development and tended to be provincial and superstitious, distrusting change, cities, impersonal economic organizations such as banks and corporations, as well as people who were worldly and had learning. Most of them also tended to be democratic in their political thought, emphasizing in particular the tendency of the ruling class toward corruption and misrule. Because of this they favored a popularistic type of democracy with devices such as broad suffrage, annual elections, rota-

tion of office, legislative supremacy, and the diffusion of political power through de-centralization in order to prevent its consolidation in a few hands, as the best way to keep the government directly and immediately responsible to the people. They believed that economic development and political democracy were incompatible and they pursued the latter at the expense of the former. On the other side were the commercial-minded. Many of them were educated and cosmopolitan, but above all else they were involved in business in some way. They were enthusiastic about the Revolution, viewing it mainly as an opportunity to develop their country's economic possibilities. Indeed, some of them had a sophisticated (for the eighteenth century) understanding of how economic development took place, the role of banks and credit, and the importance of a system of jurisprudence in affording opportunity and security to a business community. After 1776 they thought increasingly in the categories of political economy, stressing the importance of growth, stability, harmony, efficiency, uniformity, and order. Although still committed to a republican form of govern-ment their experiences during the 1780s made them fearful of the dangers inherent in a political system too susceptible to the whims and caprices of the people. Moreover, the fact that a large, perhaps even dominant, portion of the population viewed their way of life as contemptible and even immoral made them extremely wary of the democratic process. As a consequence of this many of them came to believe that business enterprise and democracy were incompatible, and were willing to sacrifice the latter to the former.

It would be simplistic to say that all Americans during the 1780s were either agrarian-minded or commercial-minded, but those who were not were so disparate in point of view and were so disorganized that they were incapable of becoming a third force and therefore were forced to choose between the agrarian-minded and commercial-minded points of view instead of creating their own alternatives. This is why Jefferson's thoughts on political economy are so important. The Jeffersonian economic system, beginning slowly during the early 1790s when he opposed Hamilton and coming to fruition during the early years of his second administration, successfully forged a new political and economic synthesis from the old dichotomies of the Revolution. Recognizing the vast richness and potential in the American economy, Jefferson moved to develop it in such a way that everyone could partici-pate in the market revolution that was to transform American life in the nineteenth century. What the Jeffersonian economic system did was to democratize business enterprise and sub-stitute for the fear and pessimism prevalent in so much post-revolutionary thought that spirit of infectious optimism in America's future that was to fructify into the American System under the initial leadership of Henry Clay and John C. Calhoun.

The effect of all this on the development of American democracy has been profound. Because Jefferson was such a central figure in the early years of the Republic and because he was always on the winning side politically, it was his view of the meaning of the Revolution that has come to dominate the American creed. And it is hardly possible to overemphasize the impact of the Revolution on American values, for even today the United States in many ways continues to be an eighteenth-century nation: what there is of a national philosophy is to be found in the second paragraph of the Declaration of Independence, and the Constitu-tion, which Jefferson as President did so much to preserve against Republicans, such as John Randolph, who wanted to dismantle it, is still the basic form of government. What is ironic

is that the popular view of Jefferson, despite the efforts of a number of distinguished historians, continues to be that of a crusading radical. Nothing could be further from the truth. He tended always to be a political and constitutional moderate. His political thought, in the context of his times, was always much more whiggish than it was democratic. His Presidency was predicated on the need to avoid ideological strife and to achieve a political consensus, and he was delighted with the general lack of concern with politics that characterized the opening part of the "era of good feeling." Jefferson did not really think about the problem of democracy in political terms. He believed that the country should be ruled by a "natural aristocracy," that is, by people who had earned and deserved their positions of leadership and had not obtained them merely by the accident of wealth or birth; that they should lead and educate the country rather than simply react to popular demands; and that political leaders should be ultimately rather than immediately and directly responsible to their constituents. Moreover, he deeply believed in the concept of private property. Writing in 1816 when the American System was actually beginning to be implemented, he stated:

> To take from one, because it is thought his own industry and that of his fathers has acquired too much, in order to spare to others who, or whose fathers have not exercised equal industry and skill, is to violate arbitrarily the first principle of association, "the *guarantee* to everyone a free exercise of his industry and the fruits acquired by it."

For Jefferson, democracy mainly meant an equal opportunity for everyone to advance himself socially and economically.

This is not to say that Jefferson's concept of democracy is the only one that has been advocated by Americans. There have been others, but Jefferson's concept has invariably dominated. The desire to have a politically popularistic form of democracy established in the United States had a great many supporters immediately following independence, and also found strong expression in the agrarian rhetoric of the Jacksonians; in some of the demands for reform by the Popularists and Progressives; and more recently in a number of the political movements of the 1960s. But while certain limited successes have been achieved, actual political democracy in America still remains very elusive, whereas for most people social and economic democracy, in terms of the improvement of their material wealth and of their relative position in society, have been very real and continuing phenomena. These have been the areas where American democracy has been most successful, and their basic tenet, that the immense wealth of the country, whether it be dispensed by the government or the private sector, is capable of solving almost all problems, is still fundamental to the way most people in the United States think about solving their country's problems, wherever they fall on the political spectrum.

Nor is it meant to argue that the Jeffersonian solution created a trouble-free country, for it did not. It failed to grapple with some of the problems facing the new nation and it created others. Jefferson, alert to the very end, recognized this from the confines of his retirement at Monticello. The avariciousness, which a central concern with the market place created in many people, bothered him a great deal. He was also concerned that the enormous growth of wealth in his country was becoming unevenly distributed. And he seemed to realize that his

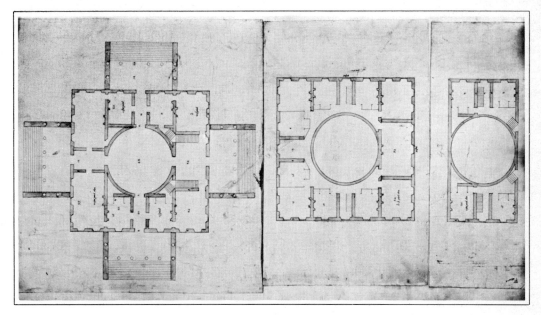

Jefferson's floor plan of the President's House.

economic system had not done anything about the race question and had in fact, by its emphasis on the importance of agricultural staple crops, inadvertently contributed to the expansion and profitability of slavery. In his declining years Jefferson became unhappy over these developments. Further, old age, sickness, bitterness over what he called the coup de grâce to his fortunes inflicted by the Panic of 1819, and disappointment about Virginia's failure to participate effectively in the nation's economic growth, caused him during the 1820s to align himself politically with Old Republican, anti-commercial types like John Taylor and John Randolph, and he vigorously denounced banks, speculators and the Supreme Court. Yet for all his crabbiness, Jefferson in his declining years remained fundamentally optimistic about his country's ability to devise, just as he had done during the years of his Presidency, viable and original solutions to its most difficult problems. Although he had not been as systematic as some of his contemporaries in his thoughts on political economy, he had been more flexible and realistic than most. Never an absolutist or ideologue, he realized that "no one axiom can be laid down as expedient for all times and circumstances."

THOMAS JEFFERSON AND THE ITALIAN RENAISSANCE
Kenneth Clark

Thomas Jefferson has been my hero ever since my schooldays, when an intelligent school-teacher gave us a term off from Tudors and Plantagenets and introduced us to the study of American history. At almost the same time – I suppose it was in about 1918 – I read for the first time that masterpiece of compressed and imaginative learning, Jacob Burckhardt's *Civilization of the Renaissance in Italy*, a book which in some ways has influenced my life more than any other; and it set working in my mind the concept of the universal man, the man for whom all branches of knowledge and experience could be related and used for the advancement of human happiness. It is from this point of view that I shall venture to speak about Thomas Jefferson.

Jefferson was a man of insatiable curiosity. He wanted to master every branch of knowledge so that he himself could use it for the good of others. First of all agriculture, for that was the basis of life: he never tired of studying new methods and discovering new seeds and plants. But his interest was not solely material, because he was also a resourceful botanist, introducing many new species of flowers. Closely connected with agriculture, the weather. For years Jefferson noted the weather each day, and one of his first instructions given to any traveler or emissary was to do the same. Then irrigation, and, from that, the study of canals, not only for irrigation but for transport. What else? Philology: he made a vast comparative study of Indian dialects, which was lost or stolen in a packing case. Paleontology: he reconstructed the first mammoth. Archeology: I am told that his unearthing of mounds in Virginia was amongst the first pieces of scientific excavation ever achieved. He was, how-ever, not interested in geology, not foreseeing how it could be made of use to man. What else? Meteorology, astronomy, chemistry, anatomy, mechanics, civil engineering. And, of course, architecture, of which I shall have more to say.

Such achievements were made possible by a rare combination of will power, industry, and intelligence. He can seldom have spent an idle moment. But he had two sources of pleasure which can, in a sense, be called relaxations, music and horsemanship, in both of which he excelled.

This character of the universal man was hardly known in antiquity, perhaps because the disciplines of rhetoric and philosophy were too demanding; and it was certainly not admitted in the Middle Ages, with the possible exception of Roger Bacon, because all intellectual activities were directed towards the love and knowledge of God. The idea that one man

Bust of Thomas Jefferson by Jean Antoine Houdon, done in Paris in 1789.

should master all knowledge and put his knowledge into practice was an invention – if you like, a fantasy – of the early Italian Renaissance. It was part of what Burckhardt called "the Discovery of Man." It grew out of a state of society that existed above all in the Florentine Republic from about 1400 onwards, and was recommended by several thinkers of the time: but only one man achieved it, Leon Battista Alberti.

It is possible to know a lot about Alberti, because, although his papers do not fill eighteen volumes (and more to come), he left over a dozen dialogues on morals and society in which he and his family are the chief speakers; he left a book on the theory of painting (the first ever written), a book on sculpture, a book on the moving of weights, a book on mathematics, a book on excavating a Roman galley, an immense book on the art of architecture, the first since Vitruvius, and an autobiography, the first since St Augustine. In this autobiography he tells us how he questioned everyone he met about the mysteries of his craft, scholars and artisans, down to the very cobblers, and in this way acquired every sort of accomplishment, the knowledge of which he imparted freely to others. His only two relaxations were music and horsemanship.

I do not think one can fail to be struck with the resemblance to Thomas Jefferson, and it is confirmed when we look at their portraits: Alberti's bronze relief of his own profile, which he executed himself, and Houdon's bust of Jefferson. We see the same proud, wilful heads – taut, determined, self-confident. The poet Blake wrote a famous aphorism: "Damn braces; bless relaxes." It sometimes comes to our minds when we study these two extraordinary men.

Since Alberti's life is not very familiar, and his writings are relatively inaccessible, I want to speak about him in a little more detail, because I believe that his character and achievements may throw a little more light on the already brilliantly illuminated figure of Jefferson.

Alberti was born in the year 1404. He learned Greek and Latin at the University of Padua, and throughout his life had a remarkable facility in languages. He then moved to Bologna, where he studied law. Evidently he overworked, and suffered some kind of breakdown. Letters, he tells us, which had once seemed to him like vigorous and sweet-smelling buds, now swarmed beneath his eyes like scorpions. But he conquered this breakdown, as he conquered all physical weakness; for, as he said, "A man can do all things with himself if he will." And he developed an almost morbid industry.

> Although at no hour of the day could you see him idle, yet that he might win for himself still more of the fruits of life and time, every evening before going to bed he would set beside himself a wax candle of a certain measure and, sitting half undressed, he would read history or poetry until the candle was burnt up. The followers of Pythagoras used, before they slept, to compose their minds with some harmonious music. Now our friend finds his reading no less soothing than was the sound of music to them; but it is more useful. They fall into a profound sleep in which the mind is motionless; but he, even when asleep, has noble and life-giving thoughts revolving in his mind; and often things of great worth become clear to him, which, when awake, he had sought with unavailing effort.

He had only two recreations, riding and music. He was an outstanding performer on the viol, and so great was the power of music on his spirits that when he underwent an operation music allayed his pain.

After the law he turned to mathematics, and received instruction from the leading mathematician of his day. But as a typical humanist, Alberti did not practice mathematics for its own sake, but in order to secure control over the forces of nature, in particular how to use the powers of wind and water. He invented a means of measuring the depths of the sea, a hygrometer for measuring damp, and various devices for raising weights. He was interested only in the practical application of his studies, for, as he said, "Man is born to be of use to man. What is the point of all human arts? Simply to benefit humanity. So the wise will blame those who studiously devote themselves to complicated and unimportant subjects."

With his outstanding abilities as a writer and a classical scholar it was almost certain, in humanist Italy, that Alberti should enter the public service. He became a civil servant in the Roman curia. But here my parallel with Thomas Jefferson must be suspended because Alberti had no gift for politics. His love of action was subordinate to his love of order. What can a supremely intelligent man do who is distressed by the imperfections of society, whose sense of human needs prevents him from retiring into pure science and mathematics, but enjoins him to put his technical knowledge to human use? There is really only one answer. Become an architect. And what is an architect? Alberti put his definition into the first chapter of his book:

> Him I call an architect who by sure and admirable method is able with mind to advise and in execution to complete all those works which, by the movement of weights and the conjunction of bodies can, with the greatest beauty, be adapted to the uses of mankind: to which end he must understand all noble and excellent sciences.

Here the parallel may be resumed. Alberti, like Jefferson – and for that matter Christopher Wren – began as an amateur architect; that is to say he did not learn his art in a stonemason's yard, but in a library. This charge of amateurishness was leveled against him by nineteenth-century critics, although anything less amateurish than his two churches in Mantua it would be hard to imagine. But his efforts to recreate the architecture of antiquity were largely dependent on literary sources. He never executed an exact copy, as the Virginian Capitol in Richmond is a copy of the Maison Carrée in Nîmes, but he did use out of context certain Greco-Roman motifs derived from the triumphal arch. To the creation of architecture he brought all his knowledge of forces, weights, and materials, and all his experience of human needs.

Alberti did not build very much – three churches, one palace, one renovated façade. But he did write the first book on architecture since antiquity. It is a great book. Several times in the text Alberti admits to feeling that he has bitten off more than he can chew; and in consequence there are a certain number of digressions, and, as in all humanist writing, down to Montaigne, the number of classical examples quoted is exasperating. But it is all there. Amongst other things he describes pieces of architecture that he did not build: a country villa and a small ideal city. Let me quote from the description of the country house:

> It must be near the city upon an open, airy road; it must make a cheerful appearance to those who go a little way out of town to take the air, and for this reason I would have it stand pretty high, but upon so easy ascent that it should be hardly perceptible to those that go to it till they find themselves at the top and a large prospect opens itself to their views.

Nor should there be any want of pleasant landscapes, flowery meads, open champains, shady groves and clear streams. . . . I would have the whole body of the house perfectly well lighted that it be open to receive a great deal of light and sun. Let all things smile and seem to welcome the arrival of your guests. Let those who enter be led from square rooms into round ones and again from round into square, and so into others of mixed lines, neither all round, nor all square. And let the passage to the bedroom be, if possible, all on one floor.

Well, that was written in 1444 – in what we call the late Middle Ages. It was realized in the United States of America in the 1770s, in Monticello, Jefferson's beautiful and lovable house.

I will not take up time with Alberti's descriptions of an ideal city, which are scattered throughout his ten books of architecture. It consists of a series of straight streets leading to piazzas. He gives the width of the streets and the sizes of the piazzas, and by a curious coincidence both plans and proportions are practically the same as Thomas Jefferson's first plan for Washington. As is well known, this was superseded by the radial plan of l'Enfant. But one Albertian idea was actually realized in the state of Virginia. I mean the piazza with colonnaded buildings on two sides, and a domed temple at the end. Nothing, I am sure, would have given Alberti greater pleasure than that the colonnaded buildings should present in succession the orders of architecture, and that the temple should be a perfect sphere, and in fact be used as a library. I doubt if there is a more Albertian concept in existence than what Jefferson called his "academical village."

The correspondence between Jefferson's architectural ideas and those of Alberti can be explained in concrete terms. Jefferson's architectural mentor, Palladio, had drawn very freely on Alberti's *Ten Books*, sometimes using the same phrases, and this is particularly true of the passages on the planning of ideal cities. But why should there be so many other points of resemblance between the *uomo universale* of early fifteenth-century Florence and the universal man of late eighteenth-century Virginia? Thomas Jefferson had spent five years in France, and one would have supposed that a parallel with the French Enlightenment would have been more apropos. The answer is twofold: first that the Encyclopedists of the eighteenth century were themselves heirs to the humanists of the fifteenth century, and secondly that the eighteenth-century Enlightenment came at the end of a period of sophistication. In fact, by the time Jefferson reached Paris the great age of the Encyclopedists was over. From 1784 to 1789 French society was on the brink of collapse – and knew it. The Florentine Republic, on the other hand, was on the way up. Its founders, Salutati, Traversi, and Bruni, were confidently reconstructing a political system and a society that had broken down in the aftermath of the Black Death and the wars of rival factions. Just as the Republic seemed to be reaching a point of stability it was attacked by a tyrant, Giangaleazzo Visconti of Milan. Bruni writes of him in words that Jefferson might have applied to George III:

I would not think this serious if our struggle was with other people, for then conditions would be the same on both sides. But now our struggle is not with another people, but with a tyrant who watches continually over his own affairs, who has no fear of cavillers, who is not hampered by petty laws, who does not wait for the desires of the masses or the deliberation of the people.

I might add that Giangaleazzo was also a great deal more intelligent than George III.

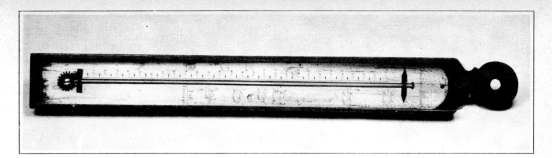

A thermometer thought to have been Jefferson's.

A table of thermometrical observations, made at Monticello, from January 1, 1810, to December 31, 1816.

	1810.			1811.			1812.			1813.			1814.			1815.			1816.			mean of each month.
	max.	mean	min.	max.	mean	min.	max.	mean	min.	max.	mean	min.	max.	mean	min.	max.	mean	min.	max.	mean	min.	
Jan.	5½	38	66	20	39	68	5½	34	53	13	35	59	16½	36	55	8½	35	60	16	34	51	36
Feb.	12	43	73				21	40	75	19	38	65	14	42	65	16	36	57	15½	41	62	40
Mar.	20	41	61	28	44	78	31½	46	70	28	48	71	13½	43	73	31	54	80	25	48	75	46
April	42	55	81	36	58	86	31	56	86	40	59	80	35	59	82	41	60	82	30	49	71	56½
May	43	64	88	46	62	79	39	60	86	46	62	81	47	65	91	37	58	77	43	60	79	61½
June	53	70	87	58	73	89	58	74	92½	54	75	93	57	69	87	54	71	88	51	70	86	72
July	60	75	88	60	76	89½	57	75	91	61	75	94½	60	74	89	63	77	89	51	71	86	75
Aug.	55	71	90	59	75	85	61	71	87	62	74	92	56	75	88	58	72	84	51	73	90	73
Sep.	50	70	81	50	67	81	47	68	75	54	69	83	52	70	89	45	61	82	54	63	90½	67
Oct.	32	57	82	35	62	85	39	55	80	32	53	70	37	58	83	38½	59	76	37	57	73	57
Nov.	27	44	69	32	45	62	18	43	76	20	48	71	23	47	71	20	46	70	24	46	71	45½
Dec.	14	32	62	20	38	49	13	35	63	18	37	53	18	38	59	12	36	57	23	43	69	37
mean of clear weather.	55			58			55			56			56⅓			55½			54½			55½

Meteorological records maintained by Jefferson from
1 January 1810 to 31 December 1816.

These early humanist chancellors, at the turn of the fourteenth century, ascribed the success of their cause to the republican inheritance and constitution of their city. They believed earnestly that free men could achieve anything. But they were not pure idealists. They had no patience with elaborate philosophical theories. They subscribed to a philosophy of common sense.

This was the climate of opinion which survived in Florence up to about 1440. There was about it an earnestness and a certain naïvety, very different from the society of Diderot and D'Alembert. It must be admitted that the humanists had a Voltairean side. Alberti himself wrote a satire called *Momus*, which in its destructive impudence is remarkably similar to *Candide*, and Lorenzo Valla's *De Voluptate* has been justly compared to the *Dictionnaire philosophique*. What a subject to appear in the late Middle Ages! I don't suppose that Jefferson had ever heard of Valla, but without *De Voluptate* the pursuit of happiness might never have appeared among the "self-evident truths."

On the other hand, one discovers in the early Florentine Republic a kind of democratic puritanism and a distrust of pomp and rank that are entirely Jeffersonian. "A man's a man for a' that" appears in many variations in the speeches and dialogues of the time; for example, in Poggio's dialogue *(On Nobility)*, where it is put rather incongruously into the mouth of that exquisite scholar and arbiter of taste, Niccolo Niccoli. "Eminence," he says, "conferred on individuals by social and political distinctions is a hollow sham and people are distinguished only by their personal virtues that they activate in private." This legend of the unassuming frugality of early humanists was still alive a hundred years later when Vasari wrote his *Lives of the Painters*. He records how Donatello, the greatest artist of the early humanist group, had refused to accept the scarlet cloak that Cosimo de Medici had sent him as a present.

Another point of likeness, which has a direct bearing on the concept of the universal man: the Florentine humanists and the founding fathers of the American Republic were both working in an untilled field. Things had to be thought out afresh. Constitutions and political morality had to be deduced from Plutarch and Cicero. In both his book on the *Art of Painting* and in his *Ten Books of Architecture* Alberti claims emphatically that he is the first to write on these subjects and has nothing to support him except the texts and ruins of antiquity. One must remember (although it is always difficult to do so) that these books were written before the invention of printing. The oppressive sequence of classical examples that they contain were all drawn from manuscripts which had to be sought for in the uncatalogued libraries of Rome and Florence. A manuscript of Vitruvius had existed in the twelfth century in the library of Cluny; no doubt several were available to Alberti. But they had not acquired those elaborate commentaries on the obscure text that became available almost a hundred years later in the edition printed in Como in 1521. Alberti had to work it out for himself.

Do it yourself. That could have been the motto of the founding fathers, from Benjamin Franklin downwards, and it was certainly the motto of Thomas Jefferson when he built Monticello with (as we are told, but I am not sure if it is correct) the help of the only copies of Vitruvius and Palladio in America. Of course, this independence led to what I may call, with respect, a kind of experimental crankiness. Alberti may have had to work out the laws of classical architecture for himself, but behind him lay a great tradition of fine building, so that he could give plans, elevations, and measurements, without those curious adjustments and

displays of ingenuity which one finds in Monticello and even in the University of Virginia.

I hope I have persuaded you that the resemblance between Thomas Jefferson and the Florentine humanists of the early fifteenth century, Alberti in particular, is not a matter of fancy or coincidence but the result of similar personalities, placed in similar circumstances. I must now consider the great differences that lie between them. To take first the circumstances. Fifteenth-century Florence was an urban culture, based on a long tradition of commerce and banking. Jefferson believed passionately and almost exclusively in an agrarian community. "The people," in whom he so often said that he placed his trust, were in fact the yeoman farmers and agricultural laborers of Virginia, together with a few craftsmen necessary to maintain the life of a small town. This is a type of citizen not represented at all in the dialogues of Poggio and Alberti.

It is true that Gianozzo, the representative of the plain but honest man in Alberti's most famous dialogue, *Della Famiglia*, recommends the pleasures of living in a villa surrounded by one's own farms. But he also advises his young hearers to avoid public life, and he makes a speech on making money which has been quoted as the first apologia of bourgeois capitalism:

> A man cannot set his mind to greater or more liberal work than making money. Business consists of buying and selling and no one of any sense can consider this a base occupation, because when you sell it is not only a mercenary affair; you have been of use to the buyer, and what he pays you for is your labor.

It might be any enlightened manufacturer of the mid-nineteenth century, but not Thomas Jefferson. In fairness to Alberti one must remember that this was a semi-fictional character being used for dramatic effect. In another dialogue, speaking for himself, Alberti says:

> I would have been certain to make money if I had turned from literature to commerce. I lived subordinate to others when, with my talents, I could have had important transactions under my control. But I have always preferred to wealth and comfort the understanding of things, good discipline and the mysteries of art.

This Jefferson might have said, although his interpretation of art would have inclined toward the useful rather than the ornamental arts.

The truth is that Jefferson, in spite of the time and intellectual energy he spent on architecture, was not an artist. His very honesty of mind, which (in addition to his weak voice) prevented him from being an orator, stopped him from paying too much attention to the actual way in which things are presented. The Ciceronian arts of persuasion, so carefully cultivated by the humanists, would have been distasteful to him. All art has in it an element of artifice which was foreign to the constitution of his mind. We may even question how much he allowed himself to be moved by works of art. Everyone knows his famous letter about the Maison Carrée at Nîmes – "Here I am, Madam, gazing whole hours at the Maison Carrée like a lover at his mistress. The stocking weavers and silk spinners around it consider me a hypochondriac Englishman." Strong words from Jefferson. There are other enthusiastic descriptions of architecture. On the other hand, when he was in Milan not only did he describe the cathedral as "a worthy object of philosophical contemplation, to be placed

among the rarest instances of the misuse of money," but he never noticed the architecture of Bramante or visited the masterpiece of the greatest of all universal men, Leonardo da Vinci's *Last Supper*. More surprising still, he does not seem to have tried to get on to Vicenza. That the devoted student of Palladio's writings should have made no attempt to see his original buildings is rather disappointing. But Jefferson's whole attention was concentrated on the cultivation of rice and raisins, and the amount of Italian rice that he could smuggle out in his pockets. Nor can we truly say that his interest in architecture was a later development, because he had begun work on Monticello ten years earlier. As Secretary of State he submitted a design for the President's residence based on the Villa Rotonda in Vicenza. Considering how notoriously difficult that famous building is to imitate, and still more to adapt, he would have been well advised to go and look at it. Perhaps it is just as well that to the eighteen recorded copies of the Villa Rotonda there was not added a nineteenth, and that we have Hoban's White House instead.

Finally, I see a considerable difference in what might be called the religious philosophy of Thomas Jefferson and that of the early Florentines. They were, it is true, united by a religion of work. The ideas of a *vita contemplativa* would have been equally contemptible to both of them. But this religion of work was held with different ends in mind. Jefferson, although in his lifetime he was attacked as an atheist, was in fact a religiously minded man with an entirely Christian approach. His composite Gospel, in four languages, from which miracles and revelations have been excluded, could have been compiled only by one for whom the moral teachings of Christ had supreme authority; and, as you know, Jefferson frequently spoke of himself as "a real Christian."

The humanists, on the other hand, had no Christian beliefs at all. Priests and theologians have always been fair game for satirists, but there is a difference in tone between the religious indignation of Erasmus' satires and the mere contempt of Valla. So what beliefs kept the early humanists on the path of duty? What induced Alberti to work so hard and recommend so earnestly a moral life? The answer is Platonism: or rather that form of stoic philosophy which derived its ideals from Plato, and was transmitted by Cicero. It was the Platonic conception of harmony that inspired Alberti's most interesting thoughts about architecture, and aroused that outburst of emotion at the spectacle of nature which Jacob Burckhardt interpreted in a romantic vein, and which I will therefore quote in a more literal translation:

> In summer the yellowing cornfields and fruit-laden trees brought tears to his eyes. "Look," he would exclaim, "how we are surrounded by witnesses accusing us of idleness. There is nothing in nature but brings, in the course of a year, some great gain to mankind. And what can I show well made according to the strength that is in me?"

Alberti worked because he felt that in doing so he was at one with the forces of nature. He believed in the Platonic concept of the universe as one great harmony. Thomas Jefferson, as you know, had a particular dislike of Plato; in fact the only man I have ever known who disliked Plato more was one of the great Americans of our own time, Judge Learned Hand. Jefferson would certainly not have shed tears at the sight of yellowing cornfields, but would have taken infinite pains to find out how to get a second crop. He

Alberti's bronze self-portrait.

believed, and it is revealed in all his writings, that the solution of moral problems was implicit in the successful life of action. Perhaps, after all, this is not so far from the beliefs of civic humanism up to about 1450. But the shadow of Plato was never far away, and in the second half of the century Platonism, in the writings of Pico della Mirandola and Marsilio Ficino, took control of Italian thought for over a century. Even the aging Alberti dutifully sat at the feet of the brilliant young teachers. My parallel between Thomas Jefferson and the founders of the humanist Renaissance is over. Of course it was always incomplete, because Jefferson was President of the United States, and the humanists were (relatively) small-town men. He had to deal with a huge, formless country, chaotic, divided, unsure of its aims and its future; a country that was dangerously poor (whereas Florence was dangerously rich) and perpetually seeking the foreign aid which it has since so generously dispensed. Half the continent was still French or Spanish. There were vast problems to be settled, to all of which he applied his remarkable intelligence and a diplomacy that is unexpected in so stubborn a character. There is really no comparison with the problems of Chancellors Salutati and Bruni. But we may remember that the wilful inscription on his tombstone – "and not one word more" – does not mention either the Presidency or the Louisiana Purchase. The three achievements for which Jefferson wished to be remembered – the Declaration of Independence, religious liberty in Virginia and the University of Virginia – are all aspirations that go back to the first age of humanism.

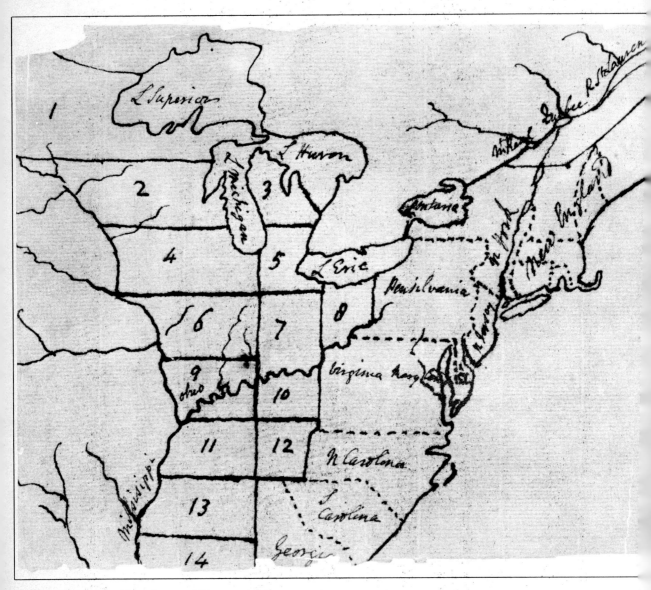

The Jefferson–Hartley Map of 1783–4. This map
shows Jefferson's proposed division of the West into
new states.

SAVAGE ENOUGH TO PREFER THE WOODS: THE COSMOPOLITE AND THE WEST

William Goetzmann

The ideas that governed the rise of the American West owed as much to the cosmopolitan imagination of revolutionary leaders as they did to the local ingenuity of practical settlers and frontier promoters. Most prominent of all the American revolutionary leaders who concerned themselves with the West was one of the new country's greatest cosmopolites – Thomas Jefferson. Even while dazzled by the sights of Paris, the conversation of far-ranging philosophers, the salons, the courtesans and women of brilliance and charm, Jefferson wrote in 1786, "I am savage enough to prefer the woods, the wilds and independence of Monticello, to all the brilliant pleasures of this gay capital."[1] Fond as he was of music and architecture, wines and wit, Jefferson still saw himself as a noble savage, who, in line with the Rousseauesque philosophy of the day, derived more value, if not pleasure, from the state of nature than from civilization. High on a mountaintop in the wilds of Virginia he had built his classical retreat – Monticello – facing west over vast tracts of land which he as a boy had helped to survey. Borrowing not from the baroque architectural fashions of Christopher Wren and other contemporary Europeans, Jefferson had gone back to Palladio and the Roman Vitruvius for the design of his substantial country villa. He had built a Roman country farmhouse in the pastoral or Virgilian mode which exemplified the agrarian simplicity of republican country life at the same time as it suggested patrician substance, abundance, and the future progress possible for man in nature's wilderness. Thus, Jefferson's vision of the West was a complex vision generated out of a feeling for the romantic richness of the classical past – timeless and free for all nations to draw upon – and the abundant, republican possibilities of unspoiled nature, itself equally timeless and in America open to adventurous men of all nations. The West, to Jefferson, *was* America, mankind's last best chance of regaining that lost world of simplicity, virtue and hope that had truly existed somewhere in the distant past. Such a world had been idealized by the Roman poets long before it had been hypothesized by Locke and Rousseau and other philosophers overburdened by the weight of contemporary civilization. To reach back in unspoiled America to Virgilian simplicity was to do more than recapture a myth of forgotten time. It was to bring mankind back into close contact with the great chain of nature's being and in tune with nature's fundamental laws, hence to restore morality to the world. Thus, to Jefferson, America, by virtue of being "an empire for liberty," was also an empire for morality. Both empires were made possible for the mass of Americans by the existence of an endless, unspoiled wilderness

stretching to the West, beyond Monticello, beyond the distant contours of the Blue Ridge Mountains, beyond the Ohio and the Mississippi and the "Stoney Mountains" to the far Pacific. The task of Americans who moved west was to make the wilderness safe for democracy and republican virtue and to avoid as much as possible the complexities of over-civilization. The American West was mankind's great second chance.

In documenting the American colonists' right to self-determination in pursuit of their second chance for happiness, Jefferson devised a doctrine combining the seeds of the "germ theory" of history, Frederick Jackson Turner's frontier hypothesis, and the recent concept of "the territorial imperative."[2] During his days as a neophyte lawyer in Williamsburg, Jefferson kept a *Commonplace Book* in which he recorded his extensive readings in history and his reflections upon these readings which amounted to a new view of the history and situation of colonial America. In effect he saw raw, frontier colonial America as a culture transported back in time to the equivalent of the later stages of Saxon culture that emerged from the German forests to conquer and settle prehistoric Britain. His was a process of thought similar to that of Frederick Jackson Turner who saw each stage of the American frontier, each "great leap forward" of settlement, as a reversion to the primordial, in a new and pristine beginning in a state of uncorrupted nature out of which grew, of necessity, democracy and republicanism. Jefferson's argument ran as follows:

> ... our ancestors, before their emigration to America, were the free inhabitants of the British Dominions in Europe, and possessed a right which nature has given to all men of leaving the country in which chance, not choice, had placed them, and of seeking out new habitations, and there establishing new societies under such laws and regulations as, to them, shall seem most likely to promote public happiness.

> ... their Saxon ancestors had, under this universal law, in like manner left their native wilds and woods in the North of Europe, possessed themselves of the Island of Britain, then less charged with inhabitants, and established there a system of laws which has been so long the glory and protection of that country.[3]

So, too, had Britons come to America and "no circumstance has occurred to distinguish materially, the British from the Saxon migration. America was conquered, and her settlements made firmly established, at the expense of individuals, and not of the British public."[4]

Thus, those Britons who had come to America had reverted to the classic "state of nature" – certainly the case in early, suffering Jamestown – and hence had become the sole masters of their individual and collective fates in the wilderness. They owed nothing to king or parliament, neither of whom had any real right to grant anything in the New World, nor any real right over the state of nature except such as a corrupt and benighted people had reluctantly granted them in England in the years following the Norman Conquest. Rather, in the New World state of nature, the territorial imperative had once again come into play:

> From the nature and purpose of civil institutions, all the lands within the limits, which any particular party has circumscribed around itself, are assumed by that society, and sub-

ject to their allotment; this may be done by themselves assembled collectively, or by their legislature, to whom they may have delegated sovereign authority; and if they are allotted in neither of these ways, each individual of the society, may appropriate to himself such lands as he finds vacant, and occupancy will give him title.[5]

In the forest, as in Saxon times, individual conquest, occupation and delegated authority yielded sovereignty. Such, to the young Jefferson, was the case with America which was, viewed from the wilds of Virginia, the living reincarnation of early Britain or the Saxon woodlands. From this analogy he derived the right of self-determination in a state of nature and eventually the right of revolution when a "foreign" king would attempt to impose his will upon a people far removed from his true domain. It was an eccentric but logical doctrine with which, as the impatient young Jefferson put it, "I have never been able to get anyone to agree ... but Mr Wythe" (his Virginia lawyer friend and drinking companion).[6] Eventually, however, it formed the broad revolutionary basis upon which rested the Declaration of Independence. Such a concept would not have been possible without two very powerful contributary influences: (1) the idea that world history, i.e. Saxon history in this case, offered an analogous experience upon which Americans could draw; and (2) the image of America as the West – a relatively vacant wilderness frontier where individuals had title to the land, as had the Saxons, by right of occupation.

The "germ theory" came into play as Jefferson saw the Saxon democratic governmental process transported to early Britain and then America. The "frontier hypothesis" was foreshadowed in Jefferson's rolling back of time on the American frontier and his view that republican and democratic institutions originated in a wilderness experience. And the "territorial imperative" concept became relevant when one speculated by what right an individual or a group had sovereignty over any part of nature. For Jefferson, the right of democratic revolution was inextricably bound up with the historical existence of a frontier or vacant wilderness, and even people in heavily populated and urban countries could harken back to this basis of individual rights in the cause of revolution as Locke, Rousseau and others in Europe continually reminded the intellectuals and political leaders. America, a living, tangible state of nature, merely served as a symbol for the rights and opportunities of all mankind, as Jefferson made so abundantly clear in the Declaration of Independence.

Long after the Revolution, Jefferson held to this idea of "squatter sovereignty" as each successive frontier emerged across the North American continent. Though he pledged his allegiance to the original union of thirteen American states, Jefferson was by no means committed to "manifest destiny," or the unwavering belief that every political arrangement in North America would inevitably fall under the purview of the United States. Rather, knowing something of geography and the difficulties of maintaining trans-Appalachian commerce, not to mention transcontinental commerce, Jefferson was inclined to believe that the future would spawn a series of "sister-republics" all across the western hemisphere, on both continents.[7] They would be governed by the same fundamental republican principles, and hence would be in such harmony with one another that, when the time was ripe, a great continental merger would take place producing the ultimate republic. Like similar atomic particles they would inevitably gravitate to one another.

None the less he believed very strongly, in a practical sense, in the immediate efficacy of the United States experiment; consequently, his most important revolutionary war measure as Governor of Virginia was to send General George Rogers Clark and a sizeable army of regulars west beyond to Ohio to capture the northwest and neutralize the British stronghold at Detroit which dominated the Great Lakes.[8] The frontier West as a future stage for an ever-expanding series of republican experiments was always on his mind and no American states-man so effectively concerned himself with it. If the Saxon forests stretched on to infinity over a boundless horizon, Jefferson wished Americans to be perpetually crossing over that frontier line into new and vacant territory. His bold stroke in sending George Rogers Clark to the West insured that that vast stage of opportunity would be available to republican Americans at the end of the Revolution.

Following independence, one of the most pressing problems confronting America *was* the role of the West, that continual "noise" at the back of the thirteen original colonies. Some of the larger colonies, like Virginia, claimed boundaries that extended west to the Pacific Ocean. The smaller "locked in" colonies such as Delaware, Rhode Island, and Maryland had no western lands and they felt at a disadvantage because, though they had all helped to win the Revolution, the costs of war fell most heavily upon them. Colonies or states with land to the west could sell the lands to new settlers and thus easily defray the expenses of the war. The smaller states did not have this option. Thus as the founding fathers struggled to unite the former colonies in a confederated government, the disposal of the West remained a formidable obstacle. Maryland, for example, absolutely refused to ratify the Articles of Confederation until her neighbor, Virginia, ceded its western land claims. Once again, however, Jefferson took the lead in establishing a plan for the West, and consequently for the new nation. As Governor, he persuaded his fellow Virginians to cede all western land claims, except for Kentucky and a military veterans grant, similar to those received by the other states, north of the Ohio between the Scioto and Little Miami rivers. Given this concession, Maryland and the other "have not" states ratified the Articles of Confederation and the first real American government was born. The consequences of Jefferson's actions in this instance were immense. He prevented, at the outset, the Balkanization of America, and in so doing insured, as much as was possible at the time, that the United States would be a large, potentially powerful continental nation that could not easily be divided and con-quered in the near future. In a sense he eliminated, as far as he could, the possibility of European nations playing off the former colonies against one another in a balance of power strategy. The undeveloped West had made this possible. Furthermore, the control over the distribution of western lands, which the Articles of Confederation government came to possess, represented the new government's most significant power. The West served as the cement of Union at a critical time as Jefferson fully realized it could.

Having acquired the vast western lands, however, the new American government had the further problem of their political organization and relevance to the new nation. Numerous groups of would-be settlers and land speculators were eager to move into and exploit the new lands in complete disregard of the Indian inhabitants. In a series of battles and Indian treaties, the red man was quickly disposed of and the land opened to settlers. Almost at the

outset America had acquired a colonial empire of its own and quickly faced the very problem of tension between colonists (westerners) and mother country (original thirteen colonies) that had torn the British Empire apart.

On the same day, 1 March 1784, that Virginia ceded her western lands, Congress appointed a committee composed of Thomas Jefferson, Elbridge Gerry, David Howell, Hugh Williamson and John Reed to determine the proper governmental organization of the new territories. This committee, led by Jefferson, whose ideas dominated their report of 22 March 1784, solved the problem of empire which Britain had been unable even to come to grips with. In its broadest terms the report of 1784 proposed a basis whereby people moving into the new western lands could organize themselves into territories for purposes of local government and then into states which were eligible for acceptance into the Confederation on an equal basis with the original thirteen states. They would have real instead of virtual representation as had been the case of the American colonies in the British Parliament.

The specific provisions of the report reveal clearly Jefferson's practical vision of the West and its future. First the land should be purchased from the Indians, not simply appropriated. Secondly in any territory so purchased the free males "of full age" had the right to call an assembly "for the purpose of establishing a temporary government." The temporary government would remain in force until the territory should have acquired twenty thousand free inhabitants when, upon receiving permission from Congress, they could establish a permanent government based on a permanent constitution. This permanent status was contingent upon the territory's remaining a part of the Confederacy of the United States and subject to Congress, assuming a share of the federal debt, forming a republican government with no hereditary titles, and, after 1800, abolishing slavery.

Whenever any territory should achieve a population of free inhabitants equal to that of the least populated of the original thirteen states, it could petition for admission to the Confederacy on a basis equal to the original thirteen states. When its petition was ratified by nine states and two-thirds of Congress, it could take its place as an equal partner in the Confederacy. But even while it remained in territorial status awaiting the pleasure of Congress, the candidate state had the right to have a delegate in Congress who could debate but not vote.[9]

Thus the people who moved into new wilderness lands could proceed by democratic and republican stages to parity in the Confederation with the founding states. This was a modified extension of Jefferson's Saxon migration view of man and free government in a state of nature. In his plan the people could organize at will their own territorial units and control their own immediate destinies while at the same time being free to affiliate, should they choose, with the larger political entity. So much did Jefferson view this process as Roman and republican in nature that he proposed elegant Latinized names for the new states such as Michigania, Sylvania, Cherronesus, Metropotamia, Polisipia, and Assenisipia (the latter proposed for present-day Illinois). He envisaged many states and territories scattered across the new West, all in various stages of progress and prosperity, and all of them republican and free and without slaves.

Jefferson's report of 1784 was ultimately rejected in part and modified. The anti-slavery clause was dropped, for example. But it eventually became the basis for the Northwest

Jefferson's odometer which he attached to his carriage
to measure the distance it traveled.

Ordinance of 1787 that finally laid down the conditions for political organization in the West in such a creative way as to indeed solve the problem of empire. Along with the Constitution proposed in the same year, it was perhaps America's most farsighted and creative piece of legislation. In some ways the Ordinance of 1787 was more conservative than Jefferson's plan in that it limited the number of new states, but it was also more liberal in that it terminated slavery immediately and it incorporated Jefferson's own measures as Governor of Virginia on behalf of freedom of religion, and the abolition of entail and primogeniture, thus prohibiting the concentration of land forever in the hands of a few key families. As one writer characterized it, the Northwest Ordinance of 1787 was more than a device for organizing new territories and states, it was also a bill of rights.[10] Though Jefferson was in France when it was adopted, it bore the unmistakable imprint of his vision and imagination – and his values.

Jefferson's cosmopolitanism and his intense curiosity about all of mankind and all of nature, which to him seemed to exist in a kind of inter-related simultaneous present, was also brought to focus on the West. Well aware of the frontier country's political and economic significance, Jefferson was also interested in its scientific dimensions. A follower of the great cosmopolitan German geographer, Alexander von Humboldt, who had explored the Amazon and the Orinoco, climbed Chimborazo, the highest mountain in the western hemisphere, and opened up Mexico to science for the first time, Jefferson lived in a world of boundless scientific curiosity that at times transcended national boundaries, even national allegiances, and caused him to speculate constantly in continental terms. In his mind science and its potential usefulness to mankind ran far ahead of national ambition, and it seems quite clear that Jefferson enjoyed his long term as President of the American Philosophical Society for the Promotion of Useful Knowledge as much as he enjoyed his two terms as President of the United States. Excavating Indian mounds and exhuming mastodon bones were only the most romantic evidences of his interest in science which ran from the mundane invention of plows and complicated clocks to the extensive collection and classification of plants and experiments in scientific gardening comparable to those of the Bartrams and Casper Wistar who stood at the center of the Philadelphia naturalist circle. Scientists of world renown such as Benjamin Franklin, Joseph Priestley, David Rittenhouse and Benjamin Rush were among his most honored friends, not only because they were companions in revolution, but because they were helping to expand mankind's knowledge of the great chain of nature's being at the rapid rate so characteristic of the eighteenth-century age of discovery. Like Jefferson, they all eagerly sought out nature's wonders and marvels, sometimes a bit too credulously, as when Jefferson believed the story of a Kentucky Indian chief to the effect that the mammoth still browsed among the forests of the Ohio country.[11]

Regarding the West beyond the Appalachians, Jefferson monitored every possible scrap of information to be gleaned from British or French explorers and fur traders. As he put it in a letter to Peter Du Ponceau, the corresponding Secretary of the American Philosophical Society, he possessed in his library at Monticello "every thing respecting America which I had been able to collect by unremitting researches, during my residence in Europe, particularly, and generally thro' my life."[12] He possessed the maps of the brothers

Arrowsmith, Britain's finest cartographers, those of Vancouver, De Lisle, d'Anville, Thornton, Ellicott, Mitchell, Moll, and Harmann among others,[13] and he eagerly followed the exploits of Peter Pond, Jonathan Carver, Samuel Hearne, and the great Alexander McKenzie, those intrepid explorers of Canada's wilderness who marched to the Arctic Circle and spanned the continent from east to west for the first time. McKenzie's first transcontinental trek in 1793 especially fired Jefferson's imagination, if not his competitive national instincts, and contributed directly to the launching of the Lewis and Clark expedition.[14]

But especially since his Paris days among the Humboldtean savants, Jefferson had been interested in learning more about the far side of North America – the northwest coast especially, which had been so tantalizingly revealed by Captains Cook and Vancouver. In 1785 he commissioned John Ledyard, a former officer under Cook, to undertake a fantastic global mission, across Europe, across Russia, and across the Pacific to learn the facts about the remote northwest coast of America. It seemingly never occurred to the cosmopolitan Jefferson that other countries might object to his explorers crossing their territory. But such was the case with Ledyard. The Empress Catherine of Russia turned him back from her lands after he had reached Siberia. Jefferson's mission was aborted and Ledyard himself died while trying to ascend the Nile for the sport of it.[15]

Jefferson likewise ran into difficulty in his own country when, in 1793, he sponsored the botanist and veteran French middle-east explorer, André Michaux, on an attempted trans-continental expedition across the United States via the Ohio River. The obnoxious Citizen Genet implicated not only Michaux in a plot to re-establish French grandeur in America, but also Jefferson's friend the American revolutionary hero, George Rogers Clark. Amidst the furor caused among both Republican and Federalist politicians over the Genet affair, Jefferson himself must have been somewhat surprised and not a little disappointed to find that Michaux, his French companion in pursuit of science, was indeed a spy bent on detaching the trans-Appalachian country from the United States. Science in Jefferson's view knew no boundaries, but often scientists were acutely aware of them.

Judging from his intense interest in the Canadian explorers and his somewhat reckless sponsorship of the Ledyard and Michaux expeditions, it is clear that Jefferson's great passion was for an American transcontinental exploring expedition in the interests of science, commerce, and strategic geopolitics. Therefore in February of 1801, after he had become President, Jefferson selected Meriwether Lewis as his personal secretary, not to attend to White House matters, but because of his "knolege [sic] of the Western country."[16] Even then Jefferson was planning his American transcontinental expedition and had selected Lewis as its potential leader. By December of 1802 he had casually inquired of the Spanish Ambassador if Spain would object to "a small caravan" which would "go and explore the course of the Missouri River in which they would nominally have the objective of investigating everything which might contribute to the progress of commerce; but that in reality it would have no other view than the advancement of geography." The Spanish Ambassador, no fool, wrote his Foreign Minister that

The President has been all his life a man of letters, very speculative and a lover of glory, and it would be possible he might attempt to perpetuate the fame of his administration . . .

by discovering or attempting at least to discover the way by which the Americans may some day extend their population and their interests up to the coasts of the South Sea.[17]

Clearly Jefferson had something like this in mind. He was truly interested in scientific information, but such information was "useful knowledge." He told the Spanish his purpose was literary while at the same time, in order to remain a strict constructionist and gain its assent to a modest appropriation, Jefferson told Congress his purpose was commercial. Actually he had all of these motives in mind, but his purpose was continental if not global. Lewis' expedition was to be the opening wedge of America's bid for a continental empire from sea to sea. If Lewis found the Northwest Passage that European explorers had sought for generations, then that strategic artery of commerce would be America's by right of discovery and actually by right of settlement if Lewis wintered on the northwest coast, as he eventually did at Fort Clatsop near the mouth of the Columbia. Though a dubious Congress granted $5,000 for the expedition and Spain granted its cautious assent, nobody could be quite certain of Jefferson's purpose. In short order, the Spanish Ambassador was sending dispatches to his garrison commanders at New Orleans and Santa Fé which ordered them to stop Lewis' expedition at all costs – a futile gesture that clearly illustrated the dire necessity for geographical knowledge of the Far West.[18]

Meanwhile Jefferson turned immediately to the training of his explorer who was to be "programmed" with detailed instructions as perhaps no other explorer in history before the days of the astronauts.[19] Lewis studied all the maps available and was provided with even the most recent Missouri River charts of Antoine Soulard, James Mackay, and John Evans who had traversed considerable stretches of the river, the latter having reached the Mandan Villages in present-day North Dakota. Lewis also learned the art of map-making and of mastering the use of the sextant and the theodolite which would enable him to calculate scientifically points of longitude and latitude. By this time, too, William Clark of the United States Army had been selected as second in command of the expedition and was learning these important techniques as well. Both men acquired a surprising expertise in scientific map-making, and though their longitudinal calculations were ultimately a thousand miles off, their great master map derived from the expedition was the most complete and accurate of its time.[20]

Significantly, in their scientific training Lewis and Clark were taught to examine the widest conceivable range of phenomena and to remain as flexible as possible as to the kinds of opportunities for commerce and settlement that might present themselves. Unlike Spanish explorers who searched for gold and fabled cities, or Canadian explorers – employees of the Hudson's Bay or Northwest Companies – who searched for furs or Indians with furs, Lewis and Clark in effect were to monitor the whole "great chain of being" in terms of human possibilities. This was characteristic of Jefferson's limitless mind. It was also characteristic of an emergent and flexible America.

Among the things they were ordered to do was to explore the Missouri and Columbia rivers to locate "the most direct and practicable water communication across this continent for purposes of commerce." They were also to make maps, fix astronomical positions at every opportunity, particularly at the mouths of rivers; they were to make friends with and

study very carefully the Indians they would meet, much in the manner of latter-day anthropologists; they were to study the climate, weather and soil of the country especially with an eye to the needs of an agricultural country; they were to collect information on animals, fossils, vegetables and minerals, especially metals, limestone, coal, salts, mineral waters and saltpeter. Jefferson even demanded accurate descriptive notes in multiple copies of any volcanoes active or inactive which they might encounter along the way.[21] The best thoughts, not only of Jefferson but of the entire Philadelphia naturalist circle, most notably Robert Patterson, Casper Wistar, Benjamin Rush and Andrew Ellicott, the great surveyor, had gone into Lewis' training as he spent a period of apprenticeship in that city. If Lewis and Clark succeeded in their mission exactly according to Jefferson's instructions, the results of their expedition would rival if not obscure Humboldt's best efforts. It was as scientifically trained agents of a "civilized and flexible nation" that Lewis and Clark set out on their great adventure.

As it turned out, the purchase of Louisiana made all the prior intrigue unnecessary. When they set out from Camp Du Bois just above St Louis in 1804, Lewis and Clark were traversing American territory. The detailed story of their expedition needs no retelling here. Their heroic voyage up the Missouri to its headwaters at the Three Forks, their overland crossover through the rugged Idaho wilderness, with the guidance of the Indian girl Sacagawea, to Lewis' Fork and then the Columbia, and their triumphant emergence on the Pacific shores has become an American epic. That they were aware of the magnitude of their accomplishment is signified by Clark's dramatic gesture when, ignoring a pelting winter rain, he carved on a tall yellow pine overlooking the Pacific: "William Clark December 3rd 1805. By Land from the U. States in 1804 and 1805."[22]

The significance of the Lewis and Clark expedition overshadowed even their epic wilderness achievement. Besides the incredible amount of scientific data they brought back, including Indian artifacts, animal skins and scientific specimens enough to fill Peale's entire museum in Philadelphia, they had gained a sense of the immensity of the continent and of the riches it contained. In looking for a Northwest Passage – which they did not find – Lewis and Clark had discovered the vast interior of North America and dramatized its potential for the new American republic. While European nations struggled half-heartedly and clumsily for control of North America, Lewis and Clark made it possible, indeed virtually inevitable, that citizens of the United States should take possession of it. They more than fulfilled the Spanish Ambassador's fears, and Jefferson's continental dream.

Understandably enough, the idea of the West so gripped Jefferson that he did not rest content with the achievements of Lewis and Clark's expedition. He also sent William Dunbar and John Hunter west in 1804 to explore the Red River and other southern tributaries of the Mississippi so as to chart the limits of his Louisiana Purchase. Their report he also submitted proudly to Congress.[23] And for a time he allowed General James Wilkinson, military governor of Louisiana, to send out expeditions under Zebulon Pike to the sources of the Mississippi and to the headwaters of the Arkansas which took Pike all the way to Spanish Santa Fé in an effort to explore and map the unknown West.[24] The years of Jefferson's Presidency were years of intense government and private fur trader exploring activity. The latter was encouraged by the government, and William Clark, soon established in St Louis

as the new Governor of Louisiana, continually collected every bit of information he could from trappers, traders, Indians and official explorers for incorporation into his master map of the West.

Even after his presidential years, Jefferson continued to urge exploring expeditions that contributed to American expansionism. In 1811 John Jacob Astor, the New York fur magnate, fired by stories he had heard in Montreal of the potential of the Columbia River country, devised a grand scheme to send out two expeditions to the mouth of the Columbia – one up the Missouri and overland, the other by sea aboard the *Tonquin*, one of his trading vessels. These expeditions were to meet and establish a permanent American outpost in the Northwest. It was a complex, globe-spanning, grandiose plan, and Jefferson encouraged it at every stage. In fact it is doubtful if Astor would have undertaken the venture at all without Jefferson's encouragement. But he did so and the result was another epic overland march led by Wilson Price Hunt, an intrepid three hundred pound heavyweight, who established Fort Astoria at the mouth of the Columbia – the first permanent American settlement in the region. Another of the Astorians, Robert Stuart, on his return from the Pacific, discovered the South Pass of the Rocky Mountains which would become the Cumberland Gap of the far West through which ran the Oregon and California Trails – the main emigrant routes to the west coast. The major casualty of Astor's venture was the *Tonquin*, which was overrun by hostile Indians off Puget's Sound and was blown up by the sole surviving crewman who sacrificed himself and several hundred aborigines for the cause.[25]

It appears then that through his long life Jefferson never forgot the West, even in retirement at Monticello. If he was not encouraging expeditions, he was continually inspiring protégés such as John B. Floyd of Virginia and Thomas Hart Benton of Missouri who in turn inspired still further western ventures. Benton, rising in Congress, pointed West and grandly, if somewhat misleadingly, declared "There lies the East. There lies India!" and sent his son-in-law John C. Frémont exploring to glory up and down and across the whole trans-Mississippi West until he became "the Pathfinder" to most Americans and a world-renowned scientific explorer praised even by the great Humboldt. Thus the Jeffersonian spirit and zest for scientific exploration of the American West lived on and grew through much of the nineteenth century.

Just as Jefferson's whole view of the American West derived from his cosmopolitan outlook – his sense of the frontier process as a function of world history including the Saxon-British experience, the value and life style of republican Rome, and the Humboldtean scientific vision of nature, so, too, did cosmopolitanism govern his views of the West's aboriginal citizens – the Indians. Nearly all his life Jefferson was fascinated with the red man. He vividly remembered the occasions when delegations of gorgeously plumed Virginia chieftains visited Governor Dunmore at Williamsburg, and in his famous letter to the Chevalier de Chastellux in 1785, he described with unbridled admiration the oration of the dying Mingo chief Logan, comparing him to Demosthenes and Cicero. "They [Indian orators] astonish you with strokes of the most sublime oratory," he wrote, "such as prove their reason and sentiment strong, their imagination glowing and elevated."[26] To Jefferson, the red chieftains were towering and exotic, indeed irresistibly moving figures who brought

forth his romantic sentiments in much the same way as the great Natural Bridge of Virginia or the beautiful craggy gorges of the Shenandoah.[27] They had many of the qualities of early Roman or Saxon warriors. He admired the simplicity of their way of life in the wilderness at the same time that he deplored the fact that the onrushing tide of civilization seemed to make their nomadic, hunter's way of life anachronistic. For Jefferson, as for European romantic thinkers like Rousseau and Chateaubriand, the savage was indeed noble, because of his simple way of life that was fast vanishing from the earth. His romantic affection for the Indian grew out of a nostalgia for the imagined purity of ancient times. The Indian, like the frontier, was a symbol of mankind's second chance; and as the Indian was rapidly vanishing, so, too, was the unspoiled frontier – the source of America's innate superiority over corrupt contemporary Europe.

This whole complex of romantic emotions was rudely challenged by the great French scientist Buffon when he declared that everything in America was physically smaller, from the animals and plants to the stature of the aboriginal inhabitants and even their "organs of reproduction." To refute this charge in 1785 Jefferson wrote his classic treatise in the Humboldtean tradition, *Notes on the State of Virginia*. In systematic fashion, following the German geographer's technique, Jefferson began with the physical dimensions, geology and landforms of Virginia and worked methodically tracing out the chain of being in his particular region. When he came to the Indian, Jefferson implied that the statements of Buffon had no more validity than "the fables of Aesop." But Buffon's strictures forced him to think through in more analytical fashion his whole position on the Indian. Clearly questions of stature, strength, size of sexual organ, amount of body hair, female fertility, and ardour in lovemaking, some of the questions raised by Buffon, were trivial and Jefferson in *Notes on Virginia* easily disposed of them. One wonders if he did not afford the sophisticated Frenchman some amusement in his earnest efforts to do so. Essentially humorless passages such as "I am able to say, in contradiction to this representation [Buffon's], that he [the Indian] is neither more defective in ardor, nor more impotent with his female, than the white reduced to the same diet and exercise...."[28] must have produced giggles if not guffaws in Paris salons. Surely Benjamin Franklin better caught the spirit of the Frenchman's inquiry when at dinner in Paris he replied by simply asking all Frenchmen and all Americans to rise, instantly revealing the fact that the Americans physically towered over the diminutive Frenchmen.

None the less Buffon's Socratic inquiry forced Jefferson to think about the Indian's place in human history and in so doing to relate him to his own broad statements about the equality of all the species of mankind. If all men were created equal, then why was the Indian fast vanishing before the white man? To begin with, and because the red man was after all "nature's nobleman," Jefferson flatly asserted in a letter to Chastellux, "I believe the Indian, then, to be, in body and mind, equal to the white man...."[29] The Indian was simply a variety of the human species descended from a common set of first parents. Like all the varieties of mankind he had, from the creation, been in the process of dispersion over the earth.[30] And though Linnaeus generally related the varieties of the human species to their characteristic continental habitat – Americanus, Europeaus, Asiaticus, Afer, etc. – Jefferson saw all varieties of mankind as being "originally equals in the order of creation." They came from common parents and were cosmopolitan as they spread over the earth. Jefferson did not

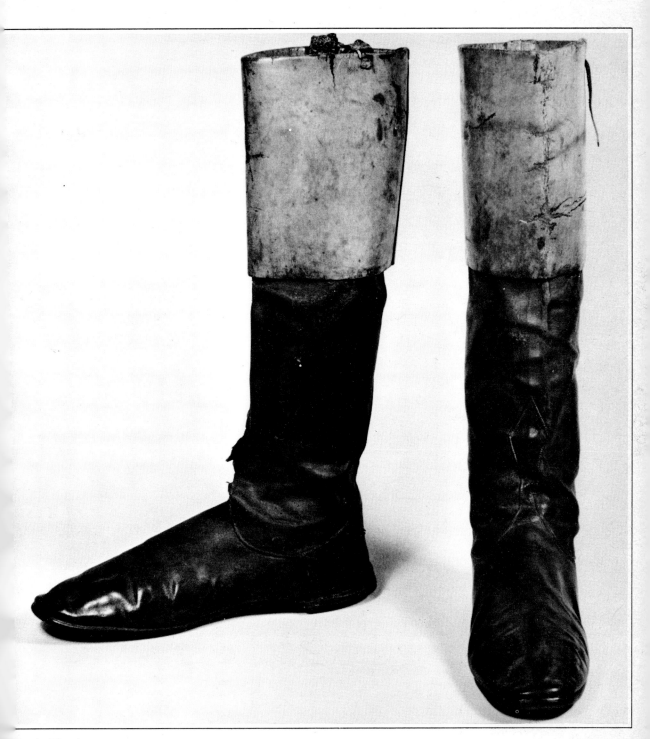

rson's riding boots.

believe, as did his friend, Benjamin Smith Barton, that there had been a separate creation of each of the races in each of the separate continents, and that like the animals peculiar to the continents, the specific varieties of man could only exist in specific continental or climatic environments. Rather Jefferson saw human nature distinguished from the animals by the fact of man's supreme adaptability to all climates and all places. Mankind, like the Roman, the Saxon and the Briton, was by nature a pioneer. He was cosmopolitan. He could adapt to new places and things. The Indian, too, was a pioneer. Like the Briton, a millennium later, the red man had migrated to America, possibly from parts of Europe, but almost certainly over the land bridge from Asia, as the researches of Captain Cook suggested.[31] To prove the latter, however, was a difficult matter. Primitive archeology and mound excavation of the sort that Jefferson had attempted so systematically at a site near Charlottesville yielded nothing beyond wild speculation by other students of the moundbuilders, like Josiah Priest,[32] that the Indians were variously descendants of the Phoenicians, Romans, Greeks, or Hebrews. In Jefferson's time the Ten Lost Tribes hypothesis was the most popular. Instead, Jefferson concluded that the proof of diffusion lay in the comparative study of languages and historical linguistics – in tracing the relationship of words used to refer to common things by different people and then looking for similarities. He was much encouraged by apparent congruencies between words used by Asiatic tribes and American Indians, and for over thirty years Jefferson assiduously collected Indian vocabularies. Unfortunately his collection was lost when a trunk containing them disappeared during the move back to Monticello from Washington following his Presidency.

Nevertheless, to Jefferson, the Indian, like the other heroic stocks he so admired, and like the "new man, the American," was a pioneer and hence an adaptable cosmopolitan. His current inferior status was the result of his environment – his isolation and his hard life in the forests where survival depended upon the hunt and hence constant difficult migrations under severe climatic conditions. The Indian's cultural progress had been temporarily arrested, due to environment and lack of numbers, at a barbarous stage in his development similar to that of the heroic Saxons.

> Before we condemn the Indians of this continent as wanting genius [Jefferson wrote], we must consider that letters have not yet been introduced among them. Were we to compare them in their present state with the Europeans north of the Alps when the Roman armies and arts first crossed those mountains, the comparison would be unequal because, at that time, those parts of Europe were swarming with numbers; because numbers produce emulation, and multiply the chances of improvement and one improvement begets another.[33]

Thus, ran Jefferson's argument, the red man was potentially equal to the white man, but his status was temporarily inferior due to environment and the opportunities for learning and emulation that come with large populations. But in this hypothesis, Jefferson implicitly adopted a scale of civilization, similar to that made explicit nearly one hundred years later by Lewis Henry Morgan in *Ancient Society*, where all mankind was assumed to be the same and evaluated on a scale that rose from "savagery" to "barbarism" to "civilization" depending upon such technological advances as the alphabet, pottery-making, and industrializa-

tion.[34] Thus in making the case for the Indian and his pre-industrial disadvantagement, Jefferson, though he clearly did not mean to do so, implicitly placed the American on a lower stage of civilization vis-à-vis Europe. Jefferson would not have recognized this, of course, because he saw cities and industrialism as artificial over-civilization. The Virgilian and pastoral mode of life was the golden mean – now possible of attainment in America and largely in the West where there was room enough for all.

The yeoman and the self-sufficient farmer were the ideal: the "chosen people of God." And on every occasion when he addressed the Indian, Jefferson held out the promise of this "American dream" to him. For example, in Washington on 7 January 1802, he told the "Miamis," "Powtewatamis," and "Weeauks:"

> We shall, with great pleasure, see your people become disposed to cultivate the earth, to raise herds of useful animals, and to spin and weave, for their food and clothing. These resources are certain; they will never disappoint you: while those of hunting may fail, and expose your women and children to the miseries of hunger and cold. We will with pleasure furnish you with implements for the most necessary arts, and with persons who may instruct you how to make use of them.[35]

This message he repeated countless other times to hundreds of other tribal chieftans. His policy, unlike so many frontiersmen, was not to make the Indian vanish, but rather to hold out to him an equal opportunity to rise on the scale of civilization and to share in the pastoral American dream that he regarded as the highest and best stage of mankind. Jefferson's was a policy of assimilation rather than cultural pluralism, but assimilation on an equal basis, and with profound respect, into what he regarded as the best of all ways of life. In a sense, if the Indian failed, or if the new American failed the Indian, and the West did not become a bucolic place of peace and prosperity insulated from the artificialities of corrupt European cities and life styles, then the whole American dream had failed and with it mankind had lost its second chance. Perhaps one can say from the vantage of hindsight that Jefferson had traded "cultural pluralism" – possibly a fiction of latter-day anthropologists – for a universal and cosmopolitan dream of man's future. But then Jefferson had seen "cultural pluralism" at work among the competitive nations of Europe where endless rivalries, religious strife and even linguistic frontiers had produced nothing but contention and war. Even as he preached his yeoman and republican gospel of cultural universalism to the red man in 1802, Jefferson was forced to look outward to the jungle of world diplomacy and competing nations in order to save the West itself as a future stage of opportunity for white men and red men alike.

The West was America's land of opportunity, but it was also its most vulnerable point. As settlers crossed over the Appalachians into Kentucky, Tennessee and the Ohio and Illinois country, their lines of communication and commerce with the seaboard states stretched precariously thin. Angered at the outset over the absentee ownership by easterners of large tracts of land in the West, westerners also felt that Congress was negligent in not building roads or canals over which they could ship their produce to eastern markets. As early as 15 March 1784, Jefferson recognized the precarious nature of the east–west relationship and

in a letter to Washington he proposed improving the upper Potomac and opening the Kanaway River so as to tap the trade of the West and bring it through Alexandria rather than New York via the Great Lakes and the Hudson River or the Mississippi and Spanish New Orleans. "Nature then, has declared in favor of the Potomac," he wrote, "and through that channel offers to pour into our lap the whole commerce of the Western world."[36] But Washington demurred,[37] and the West turned more and more to the Mississippi as its main artery of commerce.

The Mississippi, however, was controlled by Spain who patrolled it with a picturesque fleet of galleys and galleons.[38] New Orleans, the key port, was opened or closed to American commerce at the whim or caprice of the Spanish Intendant. Meanwhile Spanish undercover agents had employed General James Wilkinson, the American military governor of the western territories, as an agent who promised to help detach Kentucky from the United States and deliver it into Spanish hands.[39] In agreeing to act as such an agent, Wilkinson could argue that he was only serving the western people who desperately needed the right of transportation down the Mississippi and that survival could not stand on national allegiance in this case. Thus Spain played a tantalizing game, sometimes opening the Mississippi and New Orleans to show its promise to the westerner and at other times closing down that vital artery to demonstrate the consequences and the costs of allegiance to the United States.

Tensions were lessened somewhat by Pinckney's treaty of San Lorenzo in 1795 which guaranteed Americans the right to navigate the Mississippi and the right of deposit at New Orleans. Still commercial activities at New Orleans were restrictive and tedious and always contingent upon new instructions from Spain, making any annual business forecasting impossible. Control of the Mississippi and its mouth at New Orleans was essential to the security, indeed the political integrity of the United States.

This became all the more obvious in view of General Collot's overt reconnaissance of the Ohio and the Mississippi in 1796 signifying renewed French interest in Louisiana.[40] Everywhere rumors abounded that France intended to reclaim Louisiana from Spain and to use it as a basis for (1) reconstituting its lost empire in North America; (2) re-invading Santo Domingo and re-establishing a Caribbean empire; and (3) restricting the advance of Americans to the West. The Federalists who in any case regarded France with animosity were in a continual state of alarm and called more and more often for a closer alliance with Britain to protect the country from French "Jacobin" encirclement.

In the very year that Jefferson became President, Spain had secretly retroceded Louisiana to France by the treaty of San Ildefonso, signed on 1 October 1800. Though he had heard rumors of the treaty six months after it was signed, it was not until 1802 that Jefferson knew for certain that the retrocession had actually occurred. And when he learned of the news, Jefferson, as did most Americans, believed that the retrocession also included East and West Florida which would have made Napoleon Bonaparte master of two sides of the United States and would have completely closed off access to the Caribbean. Actually, Spain did not cede the Floridas to France, but none the less Bonaparte had formidable plans for New Orleans and the rest of Louisiana. He wished to make it the pivotal point in an attempt to re-capture the French islands in the West Indies. For the time being, New Orleans would

become an impregnable military bastion, raw materials and supplies would be drawn from Louisiana, and troops staged there for the invasion and re-capture of Santo Domingo. In 1801 Napoleon sent his brother-in-law, General Le Clerc and 50,000 picked troops to reconquer Santo Domingo and he reinforced New Orleans and Mississippi outposts.

Jefferson, well aware of the acute tensions in Europe, refused for a time to become alarmed. He believed that war between England, France and Spain was imminent, and in that event New Orleans and the Floridas would fall easily to the United States. Moreover he was reluctant to embrace Britain in an alliance because that would be tantamount to re-establishing British hegemony in North America. But domestic politics placed him in a precarious position. Panic-stricken Federalists and angry westerners in a political alliance clamored for action. Meanwhile Napoleon's aggressive plans for Louisiana and Santo Domingo became apparent. Jefferson's hand appeared to be forced. With great astuteness he picked James Monroe, a western landowner and a popular figure with western politicians, to be his special emissary to France with orders to try to purchase New Orleans and the Floridas for six million dollars. This bought him time on the domestic American political scene.

Meanwhile as early as April of 1802 he had sent a dispatch via his old friend Du Pont de Nemours to Robert Livingston, the American Minister in France, ordering him to apprise France of the gravity of the move she had made. In the letter, which he left open to Du Pont, Jefferson declared:

> There is on the globe one single spot, the possessor of which is our natural and habitual enemy. It is New Orleans through which the produce of three-eights of our territory must pass to market, and from its fertility it will ere long yield more than half of our whole produce and contain more than half our inhabitants. France placing herself in that door assumes to us the attitude of defiance.... The day that France takes possession of New Orleans fixes the sentence which is to restrain her forever within her low water mark. It seals the union of two nations who in conjunction can maintain exclusive possession of the ocean. From that moment we must marry ourselves to the British fleet and nation.[41]

He went on in the letter virtually to threaten war against France and to assure Napoleon that in the event of a war in Europe, the United States not only would side with Britain, but would seize New Orleans and the Floridas by force.[42] If France were to cede New Orleans to the United States, though Jefferson did not mention this in his letter, he was prepared to guarantee France free navigation of the Mississippi and the use of the port facilities at New Orleans.

Du Pont, however, was horrified at Jefferson's dispatch. He informed the President that threats of force would only harden Napoleon's resolve to keep his North American possessions. Instead he suggested that the United States offer to purchase the port and the Floridas.[43] It is quite possible that he worked directly to persuade the French government of the advisibility of such a sale. At any rate his advice persuaded Jefferson to secure an appropriation from Congress for this purpose and to send James Monroe on his important mission.

Meanwhile, in Santo Domingo, General Le Clerc and 50,000 French troops were dying of

tropical fever and the fierce resistance put up by the black Santo Domingan patriots. Moreover, the ships intended to carry an armada of reinforcements were frozen solid in Dutch ports in an unusually severe winter. The conquest of Santo Domingo, not to mention the strengthening of New Orleans, was rapidly becoming an impossibility. At the same time the Peace of Amiens between France and Britain was crumbling, and the European war that Jefferson had patiently expected was imminent. Time was running out on France. So, suddenly, the French Foreign Minister, Talleyrand, proposed to Livingston that America purchase from France, not the Floridas which she did not own, but New Orleans and all of Louisiana. On his own initiative Livingston agreed, and by the time Monroe reached France all that remained to be done was to haggle over price and work out the details. The treaty was signed on 30 April 1803, and all of Louisiana, including control of the entire Mississippi, was purchased for fifteen million dollars. "We have lived long," wrote Livingston, "but this is the noblest work of our whole lives."[44]

Within two weeks after the signing, France and England went to war. But this did not prevent the English banking house of Baring from loaning the United States ten million dollars to give to Napoleon in partial purchase of Louisiana.[45]

Having acquired the Mississippi and a territory twice as large as the original United States, Jefferson did not quite know what to do. Congress had voted him $6,000,000 to make the purchase of New Orleans, but he had authorized the loan and the larger purchase on his own. A strict constructionist of the Constitution, he believed ultimately that the purchase would require a constitutional amendment. He wrote his friend John Breckinridge on 12 August 1803:

> The Constitution has made no provision for our holding foreign territory, still less for incorporating foreign nations into our Union. The Executive in seizing the fugitive occurrence which so much advances the good of their country, have done an act beyond the Constitution. The Legislature in casting behind them metaphysical subtleties, and risking themselves like faithful servants, must ratify and pay for it, and throw themselves on their country for doing for them unauthorized what we know they would have done for themselves had they been in a situation to do it. It is the case of a guardian, investing the money of his ward in purchasing an important adjacent territory; and saying to him when of age, I did this for your good ... I thought it my duty to risk myself for you. But we shall not be disavowed by the nation, and their act of indemnity will confirm and not weaken the Constitution by more strongly marking out its lines.[46]

He might have added that "their act of indemity" also immeasurably strengthened the country and made it truly the continental nation that Jefferson had always, in some fashion, hoped it would be. He had indeed extended "the empire for liberty."

The purchase of Louisiana and the launching of Lewis and Clark's expedition were the most famous of Jefferson's contributions to the American West. The one act acquired an immense western domain, while the other revealed not only its dimensions but its value and potential riches. Both deeds dramatized the interior of North America not only to Americans but to the world. And even as Lewis and Clark made their way home down the Missouri river, they

"A canoe striking a tree," frontispiece of a journal of
the Lewis and Clark expedition.

encountered bands of traders heading upstream into the mountains bent on establishing outposts in the new American wilderness.[47] They were the vanguard of thousands of settlers who by the mid-nineteenth century would give the United States an empire that stretched to the Pacific.

But, as this account has shown, the purchase of Louisiana and the Lewis and Clark expedition were only the most obvious of Jefferson's interests in and contributions to the American West. A lover and scientific student of nature which he saw best exemplified in the West; a devotee, analyst and humane policy-maker for the American Indian; a revolutionary war strategist of the western campaigns; mastermind and designer of the Northwest Ordinance which made the West a functioning political part of the United States; economic planner of western development; guiding spirit of more than one scientific exploring expedition to the frontier; and finally a continental-minded diplomatist, Jefferson's whole career seems dominated by a never-ending concern for the West. In countless ways – whether in large vision or practical detail – Jefferson was the earliest and most important architect of American continental expansion. For him the West *was* the nation or at least the nation's future. If the Massachusetts puritan had built a "city upon a hill" as an example of God-fearing right living to the world, Jefferson chose to display a whole continent, populated with virtuous republican yeomen as his example for judgement by "the candid opinions of mankind." The frontier was America's utopian future, and in the vastness of the wilderness lay the source of America's virtue and its impregnable strength. Simple size, sublime, empty, unspoiled immensity, afforded the abundance and the space that gave democracy room to work and offered a boundless future for generations yet to come.

But even as he served as the architect and designer of the West as the nation, Jefferson did not do so as a western man. Rather he did so as a cosmopolitan who saw nature and world history and world civilization all of a piece. The experiences and models of republican Rome

were as real to him as the Virginia legislature or the Continental Congress. And the image of man, the migratory adaptable species descended from common parents and created equal, informed his judgements, his evaluations and his interpretation of the frontier experience. It was this vision of the timeless, universal quality of the American democratic experiment in the wilderness, so sharply focused by the actions and words of Thomas Jefferson, that formed the meaningful basis of what continues to be the fundamental agrarian myth of America. Thomas Jefferson, the romantic cosmopolitan, was the first to dramatize America's own "tale of the tribe" in its pursuit of life, liberty and happiness.

1. Letter to the Baron de Geismer, 6 April 1785, quoted in Gilbert Chinard, *Thomas Jefferson, the Apostle of Americanism* (Ann Arbor Paperback edition), Ann Arbor, Michigan, 1962, p. 163.
2. For a discussion of Jefferson's Anglo-Saxon theory see Chinard, pp. 48–51. The application of "the germ theory," the Turner frontier hypothesis, and the theory of "the territorial imperative" to Jefferson's thoughts are the present author's interpretation.
3. Quoted in Chinard, pp. 48–9.
4. Quoted in ibid., p. 51.
5. Quoted in ibid., p. 50.
6. Quoted in ibid., p. 51.
7. See Jefferson to John Breckinridge, 12 August 1803.
8. See Jefferson to General George Rogers Clark, 25 December 1780.
9. See Report on Temporary Government for Western Country, 1 March 1784, and Report on Western Territory, 22 March 1784.
10. This observation was made by Thomas D. Clark in *Frontier America*, New York, Charles Scribner's Sons, 1959, p. 145.
11. Quoted in Daniel Boorstin, *The Lost World of Thomas Jefferson*, Boston, Beacon Press, 1948, p. 37. The original quote is from *Notes on Virginia*.
12. *Documents Relating to the Purchase and Exploration of Louisiana*, reprinted from the original manuscripts in the American Philosophical Society, Boston and New York, Houghton Mifflin & Co., 1904, p. 9.
13. See ibid., fn. p. 27, and William H. Goetzmann, *Exploration and Empire*, New York, Alfred A. Knopf Inc., 1966, p. 6, fn. 8.
14. See, for example, Louis André Pichon to the Minister of Foreign Affairs, 4 March 1803, Edward Thornton to Lord Hawkesbury, 9 March 1803, pp. 22 and 26 respectively in Donald Jackson, ed., *Letters of the Lewis and Clark Expedition*, Urbana, Illinois, University of Illinois Press, 1962.
15. See William H. Goetzmann, *When the Eagle Screamed*, New York, London, Sydney, John Wiley and Sons, 1966, p. 4.
16. See Jefferson to Lewis, 23 February 1801, in Jackson, *Letters*, p. 2.
17. See Carlos Martinez de Youjo to Pedro Cervallos, 2 December 1802, in Jackson, *Letters*, pp. 4–5.
18. See Marqués de Casa Calvo to Pedro Cervallos, 30 March 1804, in Jackson, *Letters*,

pp. 173–4.

19. For Jefferson's instructions to Lewis, see Jackson, *Letters*, pp. 61–6.

20. Clark's "master map" is now in the Yale Western Americana Collection, Beinecke Library, Yale University. For an early version of a Lewis and Clark map see Jackson, illus. V, following p. 106.

21. Jefferson's Instructions, see note 19 above.

22. Quoted in William H. Goetzmann, *Exploration and Empire*, p. 7.

23. For the Dunbar and Hunter Report see note 12 above.

24. Goetzmann, *Exploration and Empire*, pp. 43–50.

25. Ibid., p. 32. Also see Washington Irving, *Astoria, or Anecdotes of an Enterprise Beyond the Rocky Mountains*, 2 vols., Philadelphia, Carey, Lea, and Blanchard, 1836, vol. 1, pp. 119–20.

26. Quoted in Winthrop Jordan, *White Over Black*, Baltimore, Maryland, Penguin Books, 1969, pp. 477–8.

27. For example see Jefferson, *Notes on Virginia* in Adrienne Koch and William Peden, eds., *The Life and Selected Writings of Thomas Jefferson*, New York, Modern Library Edition, 1944, p. 193.

28. See ibid., p. 210.

29. Boorstin, *Lost World*, p. 94.

30. My discussion of Jefferson's view of the Indian in the following pages owes much to Boorstin, *Lost World*, pp. 59–108.

31. Jefferson, *Notes*, p. 255.

32. Josiah Priest was the author of a curious book entitled *American Antiquities and Discoveries in the West* ..., (Albany, N.Y., 1833) which saw America as being peopled by most of the nations of the ancient world, including the Ten Lost Tribes of Israel.

33. Jefferson, *Notes*, pp. 212–13.

34. See Lewis Henry Morgan, *Ancient Society*, Cleveland, Ohio, World Publishing Co., 1877.

35. Jefferson to Miamis, etc., 7 January 1802, in Koch and Peden, eds., p. 333.

36. Jefferson to Washington, 15 March 1784.

37. Washington to Jefferson, 29 March 1784.

38. For a vivid description of these see Abraham P. Nasatir, *Spanish War Vessels on the Mississippi, 1792–96*, New Haven and London, Yale University Press, 1968.

39. Goetzmann, *Exploration and Empire*, pp. 43–4.

40. Goetzmann, *When the Eagle Screamed*, p. 7.

41. Jefferson to Robert Livingston, 18 April 1802.

42. Ibid.

43. See Jefferson's acknowledgement of Du Pont de Nemours' letter which suggests the Frenchman's reaction, 1 February 1803. Also see Alexander De Condé, *A History of American Foreign Policy*, Charles Scribner's Sons, 1963, p. 77.

44. Quoted in De Condé, *American Foreign Policy*, p. 81.

45. Ibid., pp. 81–2.

46. Jefferson to John Breckinridge, 12 August 1803.

47. Goetzmann, *Exploration and Empire*, pp. 13–35.

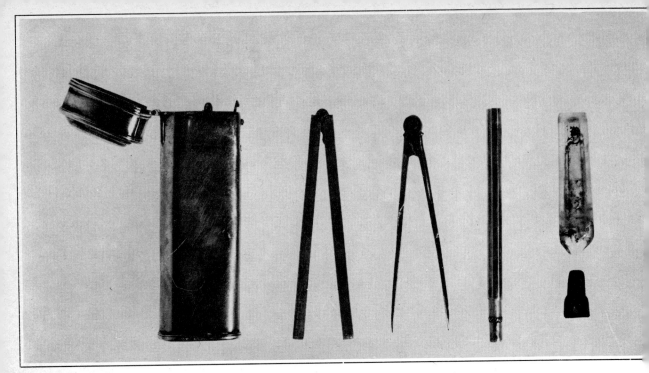

A set of silver drafting instruments owned and used by Jefferson.

The polygraph, a copying machine, which enabled Jefferson to make a copy of every letter he wrote. What he wrote with one pen was duplicated by the other.

JEFFERSON, MAN OF SCIENCE

"Science is my passion, politics my duty," commented Thomas Jefferson. Jefferson was an inventor and compulsive gadgeteer. Among the inventions associated with his name were his revolving chair, a walking stick which could be turned into a folding chair, musical stands and a writing box which could serve as a reading stand as well as a writing surface. He had a genuine love of timepieces of all types; during his last year as Secretary of State he contracted for the construction and installation of the great clock at Monticello. He surveyed his own lands and purchased a number of the finest surveying instruments available. To his final days his preoccupation with science never diminished nor his confidence in the future of a nation in which science had its place.

SILVIO BEDINI

...ra obscura which was used to make silhouettes. Jefferson owned several of these.

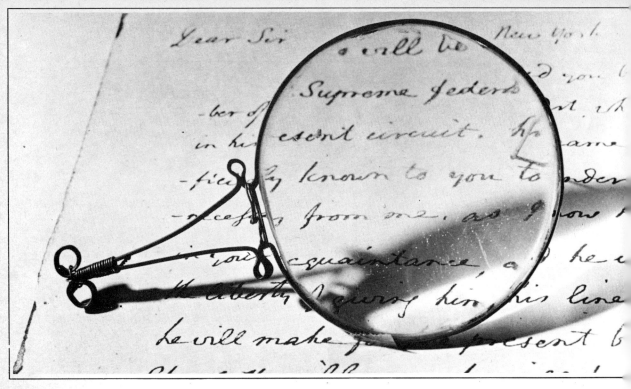

Jefferson's pocket magnifying glass.

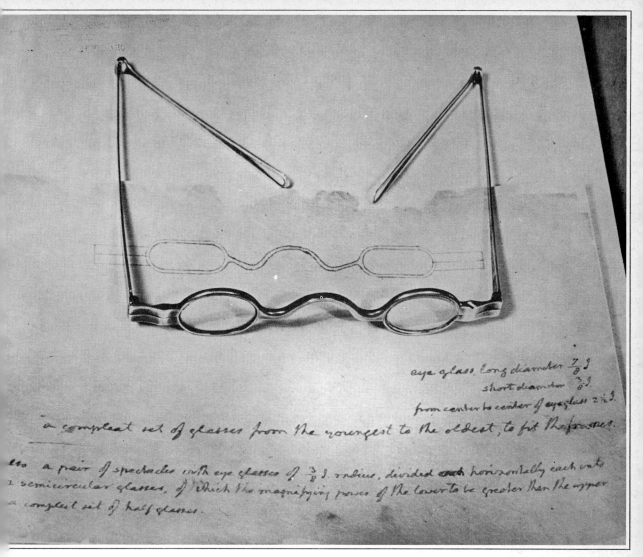

eye glass, long diameter $\frac{7}{8}$ I.
short diameter $\frac{3}{8}$ I.
from center to center of eye glass 2 $\frac{1}{8}$ I.

a compleat set of glasses from the youngest to the oldest, to fit the frames.

ls̄o a pair of spectacles with eye glasses of $\frac{3}{8}$ I. radius, divided each horizontally each into
2 semicircular glasses, of which the magnifying power of the lower to be greater than the upper
a compleat set of half glasses.

...rson's spectacles and a letter specifying
... design.

A surveying instrument owned by Jefferson.

Dear Sir   Monticello Aug. 27. 16.

As you were so kind as to give me your invention of the handsome peculiarly American capitel, I must give you mine of the new dial to which that capitel has led. I had placed the capitel on a pedestal of the size proper to it's diameter, and had reconciled their confluence into one another by interposing plinths successively diminishing. it looked bald for want of something to crown it. I therefore surmounted it with a globe and it's neck, as is usual on gate posts. I was not yet satisfied; because it presented no idea of utility. it occurred then that his globe might be made to perform the functions of a dial. I ascertained on it two soles, delineated it's equator and tropics, described meridians at every 15.° from tropic to tropic, and shorter portions of meridian intermediately for the half hours quarter hours, and every 5. minutes. I then mounted it on it's neck, with it's axis parallel to that of the earth by a hole bored in the Nadir of our latitude, affixed a meridian of sheet iron, moveable on it's poles, and with it's plane in that of a great circle, of course presenting it's upper edge to the meridian of the heavens corresponding with that on the globe to which it's lower edge pointed. I then meridianised the globe truly, and presenting the outer edge of it's moveable meridian to the sun, the shade of it's thin plane, as a thread, designates on the hour lines of the globe, the meridian of the heavens on which he then is.

My globe is of locust, 10½ I. diameter, equal to the collar of the capitel, & enables me to judge within one or two minutes of the solar time. this device may be usefully applied to the ornamental balls on gate-posts; or mounted on a balluster, or the frustrum of a column, for the purpose of an ordinary dial. it is easily made by a common turner with materials which every one possesses, and requires no calculation of hour-lines, being adapted to every latitude by only fixing it on the point corresponding with the Nadir of the place. — perhaps indeed this may be no novelty. it is one however to me, and I offer it to you as an architectural embellishment which you may sometimes perhaps find occasion to use in your profession, and as a testimony of my readiness to embrace every occasion of renewing to you the assurances of my constant esteem & respect.

B. H. Latrobe esq.   37037   Th. Jefferson

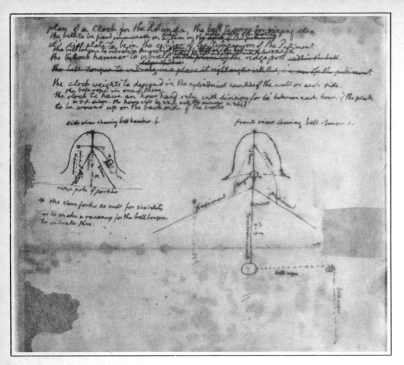

Jefferson's sketch of the clock bell for the Rotunda of
the University of Virginia.

A weather vane which was installed above the east
portico of Monticello.

The wind rose and vane on the ceiling inside the east
portico of Monticello.

A view of the reception hall at Monticello showing
the clock designed by Jefferson. In this hall Jefferson
displayed paintings, fossil bones, and busts of
Hamilton, Turgot and himself. The antlers hanging
over the door were brought back by Lewis and Clark
from their western expedition.

Jefferson's description of the Great Clock at Monticello. The clock, designed by Jefferson, was run by cannon ball weights. The top weight marked the day of the week by its position on the wall.

the great clock.
the works are 15.I. deep, from the plate to the farthest point in the
a circle of 12.I. radius round the center of
the hour circle, will barely cover the remotest
point of the works.

The center of vibration of the pendulum is 7.I. a-
-bove the ~~point~~ back end of the axis of the hour hand.

the arc of vibration is (at the ~~uttermost~~ most) 18.I.

the same arc, at 7.I. below the center, will be 3.I.

then a toothed wheel of 2.I. on the back end of the axis of the hour
hand, taking in an equal wheel whose axis will be
I course 2½.I. horizontally from that of hour hand, will
be clear of the vibration of the pendulum, and may
turn an hour hand on the reverse face of the wall
on a wooden hour plate of 12.I. radius. there need
be no ~~second~~ minutes hand, as the hour figures will be 6.I.
apart. but the interspace should be divided into
arters and 5. minute marks. the fore & back hour.
~~plates will not be concentric.~~
the ~~center~~ axis of the second hand 4⅙ I. from that of the
hour hand (i.e. their centers)
the radius of the second circle (i.e. length of hand) 1¾.I.

41588

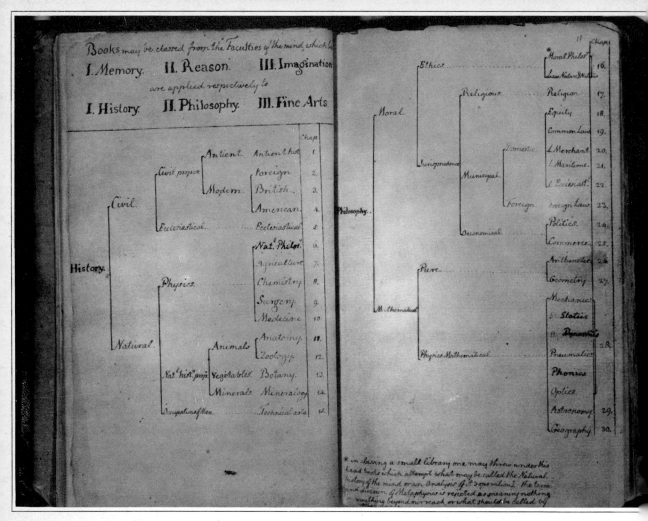

Jefferson's catalogue of his library.

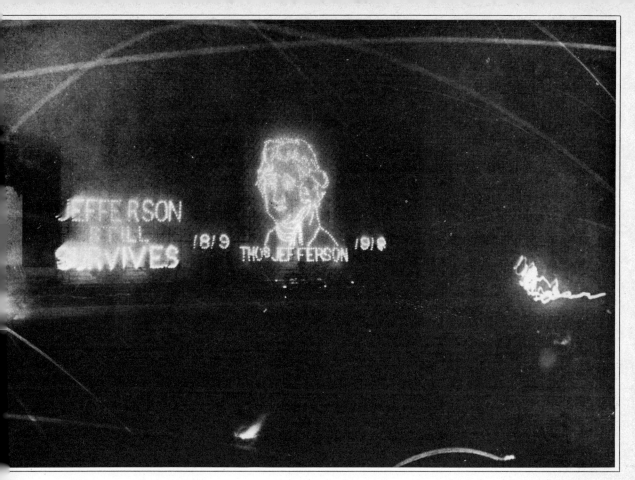

...ennial celebration of the chartering of the
...ersity of Virginia.

The Aurora, a leading Republican newspaper, favored
Jefferson in the election campaign of 1800. Jefferson
was elected in spite of the slurs cast on him by the
Federalist press.

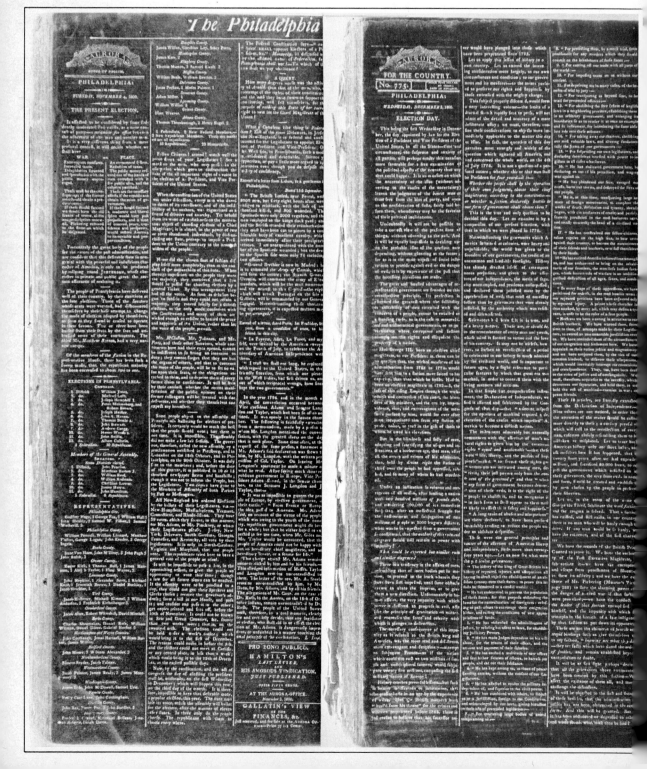

JEFFERSON AND THE PRESS

James R. Wiggins

Thomas Jefferson better understood the inseparable connection between a free press and a free society than any of his predecessors, contemporaries or successors in American public life. That understanding seems to have come initially from his own inquiry into the fundamental principles of liberal institutions, but it was broadened by a lifetime of experience with the press of his own country and with that of England and Europe.

The colonial press of Jefferson's first experience was a fledgling press but its importance to the agitation of the American Revolution can hardly be exaggerated. John Holt of *The New York Journal* told Sam Adams, "It was by means of News papers that we receiv'd & spread the Notice of the tyrannical Designs formed against America, and kindled a Spirit that has been sufficient to repel them." The typical newspaper of the day usually was a poorly printed, four-page sheet some ten by fifteen inches in size. The type was small and often poorly arranged. There were only twenty-one newspapers in all the colonies when the Stamp Act crisis developed in 1765.

Philadelphia was the very center of newspaper activity in the colonies when Thomas Jefferson arrived there in the summer of 1775 to succeed Peyton Randolph on the Virginia delegation to the Continental Congress. So astute an observer as Jefferson could not have failed to note, during the sessions of the Continental Congress which he attended, the powerful influence of the Philadelphia press. It was an advocate press that he saw, both in the city, and in the rest of the colonies whose papers circulated in Philadelphia and which were widely reprinted there. Many of the newspapers freely opened their columns to conflicting views, but they were as one in the patriot cause.

When Jefferson was sent to France as the American Minister, he saw another sort of press. The newspaper which most strongly influenced him, of all the newspapers he saw in England and in France, was *The Leyden Gazette*, a dignified political journal on which European diplomats much relied and which Jefferson continued to read on his return to the United States. He was so much impressed with it that he frequently succeeded in getting excerpts from it reprinted in American newspapers. In a letter to John Jay he described it as "the best in Europe." He respected its sober, factual and impartial reporting of events in Europe.

Jefferson's feelings about British newspapers were hostile, and subsequent inquiry has supported his suspicion that the British papers of the time were often creatures of the

current ministry. The British government, in the years before the French Revolution, was spending some five thousand pounds a year on press subsidies and the press was usually in the pay of the ministry or of the opposition. The seventeen London newspapers of 1775 had a daily sale of 41,615 copies. They were widely mistrusted for the publication of half-truths and rumor. One critic thought that not an article in twenty could be believed.[1] Jefferson's hostility, nevertheless, was excessive. Nearly all the influential press had been sympathetic with the American cause during the Revolution.

When George Washington was inaugurated President on 30 April 1789, his new government had virtually unanimous press support. Within a few months, however, divisions began to appear inside the government, in the country, and in the press. By mid-1791, Jefferson was convinced that the *United States Gazette*, published by John Fenno, was a Tory organ, and he began to wish for another newspaper. He hired Phillip Freneau as a translator in the State Department and encouraged him to set up the *National Gazette*, which started on 21 October 1791. Jefferson always denied he wrote for it, but he acknowledged getting Freneau to carry European news from *The Leyden Gazette* and he and other "Whigs" helped to get subscriptions for it. Until 1793, it was the foremost opposition journal. The *United States Gazette* criticized the new paper and questioned the propriety of its sponsorship by the Secretary of State, in view of its attacks on the Washington administration.

Freneau denied that his paper was advised or influenced by Jefferson. Jefferson wrote to Washington to explain his connection with the paper. His letter, of 9 September 1792, is a most extraordinary communication in which he laid out the basis of his disagreements with Hamilton. He bluntly accused Hamilton of subverting the legislature, planning the abuse of the general welfare clause, interfering with foreign affairs, wishing the amendment of the Constitution to provide a House of Lords and a king, desiring to extinguish the power of the states and of libeling the Secretary of State in Fenno's newspaper by declaring Jefferson opposed to the Constitution during the ratification struggle.

Jefferson said he had encouraged Freneau to set up a newspaper because he thought it might be useful for getting printed "material" parts of *The Leyden Gazette*, in order to put before the President and the country "a juster view of the Affairs of Europe than could be obtained from any public source." Otherwise, he said, "I can protest, in the presence of heaven, that I never did by myself, or any other, or indirectly, say a syllable, nor attempt any kind of influence."

Then Jefferson put down a much-quoted paragraph:

> No government ought to be without censors; and where the press is free, no one ever will. If virtuous, it need not fear the fair operation of attack and defense. Nature has given to man no other means of sifting out the truth, either in religion, law, or politics. I think it as honorable to the government neither to know, nor notice, its sycophants or censors, as it would be undignified and criminal to pamper the former and persecute the latter.[2]

Freneau and his newspaper continued a source of friction in the Administration. Jefferson recounted in his diary a conference with Washington on 23 May 1793. He said the President

adverted to a piece in Freneau's paper of yesterday; he said he despised all their attacks on him personally, but that there never had been an act of the Government, not meaning in the executive line only, but in any line, which that paper had not abused. He was evidently sore and warm, and I took his intention to be that I should interpose in some way with Freneau, perhaps withdraw his appointment of translating clerk to my office. But I will not do it. His paper has saved our Constitution, which was galloping fast into monarchy, and has been checked by no one means so powerfully as by that paper. It is well and universally known, that it has been that paper which has checked the career of the monocrats; and the President, not sensible of the designs of the party, has not with his usual good sense and sang froid, looked on the efforts and effects of this free press, and seen that, though some bad things have passed through it to the public, yet the good have preponderated immensely.

By the end of 1793 Jefferson was out of the Washington administration and Freneau had lost his clerkship and the *National Gazette* had been suspended. Thereafter, the leading Republican journal was the *Philadelphia General Advertiser*, later known as *The Aurora*. Benjamin Bache was its editor until 1798 when he was succeeded by William Duane.

The Aurora gained great credit for its summaries of the congressional debates and its reports of the transactions of the government. Jefferson had frequent communication with Bache and supported the paper in many ways.

Other Republican papers included *The Boston Independent Chronicle, The Boston Gazette, The New York Argus, The Baltimore American,* and *The Richmond Examiner*. The Republican press was outnumbered two to one by the Federalists' newspapers. Although it was out-numbered, the Republican press is believed to have been decisive in the Republican victory of 1800.[3]

Jefferson did not contribute to the Republican newspapers himself, but he urged others to do so. A letter to James Madison, written from Philadelphia on 5 February 1790, acknowledged the good effect of a piece published in the Bache paper. He wrote:

> The public sentiment being now on the gain, and many heavy circumstances about to fall into the republican scale, we are sensible that this summer is the season for systematic energies and sacrifices. The engine is the press. Every man must lay his purse and his pen under contribution. As to the former, it is possible I may be obliged to assume something for you. As to the latter, let me pray and beseech you to set apart a certain portion of every post day to write what may be proper for the public. Send it to me while here, and when I go away I will let you know to whom you may send, so that your name shall be sacredly secret.[4]

Jefferson frequently solicited aid for *The Aurora*. He praised it generously on leaving the presidency. He thought Duane had rendered "incalculable services to republicanism through all its struggles with the federalists." Even when Duane changed his affiliations, Jefferson still conceded his earlier merit and spoke of the paper's "unquestionable effect in the revolution produced in the public mind."[5]

The fury of the newspaper battle in the election campaign of 1800 is indicated by the

notice which appeared in *The Gazette of The United States* on 27 September 1800. It stated:

THE GRAND QUESTION STATED.
At the present solemn moment the only
question to be asked by every American
is "Shall I continue in allegiance to
GOD – AND A RELIGIOUS PRESIDENT
or impiously declare for
JEFFERSON AND NO GOD?"

Other Federalist newspapers were also violent and severe. While Jefferson was Vice President, the *Evening Post* printed a story that he would soon resign. Another newspaper reported that he was "mortally ill" and had been given up by attendant physicians. The *Columbian Centinel* printed a series of insulting open letters denouncing Jefferson.[6]

Others accused Jefferson of being an infidel because he denied that shells found on mountain tops were proof of the great flood and favored Greek and Roman history instead of Bible reading for children. One pamphlet said that if he were elected "the character of the United States will sink in the estimation of foreign people ... religion will be destroyed ... immorality will flourish ... the very bonds of society will be loosed."[7]. But Jefferson won the election.

Jefferson's most satisfactory relationship with an individual editor no doubt was that with Samuel Harrison Smith. In the spring of 1800, Jefferson encouraged Smith to set up a new paper in Washington as the journal of the new administration. Smith agreed, and on 31 October 1800 the first issue of the *Intelligencer* appeared. It was a four column, four-page, three-times-a-week publication. Of his policy as editor, Smith wrote:

> While the Editor classes with our dearest rights the Liberty of the Press, he is decidedly inimical to its licentousness. As on the one hand, the conduct of public men and the tendency of public measures will be freely examined, so, on the other, private character will remain inviolable, nor shall indelicate ideas or expressions be admitted, however disguised by satire or enlivened by wit.[8]

The tone of the paper is shown in an article in the issue of 3 April 1801. Smith disavowed intention to be on the side of partisan factions or to carry on "the sharpness and subtlety of personal altercations on public questions." In his newspaper, he said, the news columns would be "consecrated to spreading information useful and important to the people." He said that the *Intelligencer*, "possessing as it does the peculiar advantage of publishing from the seat of the government, will from time to time, make such statements and explanations as may appear necessary, and with which it is hoped, honesty and real patriotism will be satisfied."

The *Intelligencer* was looked upon generally as the organ of the Jefferson administration. Jefferson no doubt stuck to his own rule of never writing for the newspapers, but he was a source of information for Smith and he urged others to write for him. The congressional debates printed by the *Intelligencer* made it indispensable to other newspapers. Its coverage of

government was excellent. A typical issue in 1804 carried eight columns of debate in the Senate, five columns of proceedings in the House, a report of a committee on the impeachment of Judge Chase, acts and resolutions of Congress, messages of governors, election returns and other governmental matters. In all, it presented a survey of government probably more complete than is found in newspapers today. Of course it had little general news outside of government. And it had no comics, sports, or women's pages.

Personal relations between editor and President were cordial throughout the Jefferson administration.

Thomas Ritchie, editor of the *Richmond Enquirer*, was another editor with whom Jefferson was long on friendly terms. The high standards of Ritchie are indicated in a piece printed in the issue of 6 August 1805:

> We may consider our newspapers as the purifying chronicles of the times. Sometimes conductors may take upon themselves the dignified office of commentators; but their principal character is that of an historian. They may reason; they may argumentatively expatiate upon the incidents which successively solicit their attention; but their first duty is to furnish such facts as may add to the amusement or such materials as may excite or assist the investigating spirit of their readers.

The *National Intelligencer* and the *Richmond Enquirer* were several cuts above the press that Jefferson knew generally in his lifetime. The strictures against the press which marked his later years confirm the judgement of many critics.

Pamphlets were quite as potent a political force in Jefferson's time as newspapers, and Jefferson had relations, some unfortunate, with the most famous (and infamous) pamphleteers of his day.

James Callendar was one of the victims of the sedition law. Jefferson befriended him as he did other victims of the persecution of the press in the Adams Administration. His charity was misconstrued by many persons whom Callendar libeled, as support for and endorsement of the pamphleteer's views and opinions. Callendar himself misconstrued one bit of support as a bribe to suppress a libel on Jefferson. He became so disgruntled over Jefferson's failure to get him a job as postmaster at Richmond that he circulated the most outrageous attacks on Jefferson, including the allegation that Jefferson had intimate relations with a female slave and seduced the wife of a friend. His attacks on Washington and Adams in the pamphlet *The Prospect Before Us* were blamed on Jefferson by his Federalist critics.

Thomas Paine, the great pamphleteer of the Revolution, who wrote *The Crisis* and *Common Sense*, was also a source of embarrassment to Jefferson. Jefferson wrote what he thought was a private comment on *The Rights of Man*, and a Philadelphia printer put it in a preface of the American edition of that work. In 1800, when Paine's life was in danger in France, Jefferson arranged to give him passage to the United States on an American warship which had taken an American diplomat to Europe. Paine did not avail himself of the offer. When he did come to the United States two years later, he was under attack for his assault on religion and for an abusive letter he had written to George Washington, just after the first President's retirement. He visited the city of Washington and saw Jefferson several times, but apparently felt Jefferson had not paid him sufficient attention. He then released

Jefferson's friendly invitation to use a United States ship for his passage. Federalists promptly assailed Jefferson for his friendship toward an atheist and a traducer of Washington.

William Cobbett, an émigré Englishman, who was the pamphleteer "Peter Porcupine" from 1794 to 1795, made Jefferson the object of many scurrilous attacks. Cobbett came to the United States with a letter of introduction to Jefferson. He solicited a job in the government and Jefferson wrote him that none was available. After an interval during which he espoused French and Republican sentiments, Cobbett turned into a violent pamphleteer on the Federalist and British side. He described Jefferson as

> a man who is a deist by profession, a philosopher by trade, and a Frenchman in politics and morality: a man who has written a passport for Tom Paine's Rights of Man, and would, if necessary, write another for his infamous letter to General Washington: a man, in short, who is at the head of the prostituted party by which he has been brought forward and is supported. If this man is elected President, the country is sold to the French and as plantations are generally sold with the livestock on them, I shall remove my carcass; for I am resolved never to become their property. I do not wish my family vault to be in the guts of cannibals.[9]

Jefferson's experience with newspapers and newspapermen and pamphleteers no doubt caused him to elaborate his theories on the freedom of the press, but even the most unhappy ordeals seem to have very little changed his estimate on the place of a free press in a free society. While many people have been struck by the apparent inconsistency between some of his professed beliefs in the principle of press freedom and his emphatic criticisms of newspapers in his later years, it is clear that he found no conflict between his high estimate on the value of a free press and his low opinion of some newspapers.

His theory ranges from the liberal view he expressed in commenting on press criticisms of John Jay to the conservative opinion he voiced in urging some state prosecutions for libel. On 28 January 1786 he wrote to James Currie deploring an attack on Jay. And he concluded: "It is however an evil for which there is no remedy. Our liberty depends on the freedom of the press, and that cannot be limited without being lost."[10] On 25 January 1786 he had similarly written to Jay: "However it is a part of the price we pay for our liberty, which cannot be guarded but by the freedom of the press, nor that be limited without danger of losing it."[11]

At the other boundary of Jefferson's estimate of the proper limit on press freedom is his famous letter to Thomas McKean, in 1803. He wrote: "... I have therefore, long thought that a few prosecutions of the most prominent offenders would have a wholesome effect on restoring the integrity of the presses. Not a general prosecution, for that would look like persecution; but a selected one."[12]

The rest of his expressions, almost without number, on the theory of a free press, lie somewhere within these boundaries.

Jefferson's first draft of the Virginia Constitution of 1776 contains one of his earliest formulations on press freedom. It stated: "Printing presses shall be free, except where by commission of private injury they shall give cause of private action."[13] Jefferson's several

drafts of a press clause for the Virginia Constitution of 1783 did not greatly differ, running thus: "Printing presses shall be subject to no other restraint than liableness to legal prosecution for false facts printed and published."[14]

It is important to remember these proposals were for a state constitution.

Jefferson's reaction to the American Constitution was voiced in a letter he wrote James Madison on 20 December 1786, in which he first listed what he liked in the document and then what he disliked. He objected to

> First, the omission of a bill of rights providing clearly and without the aid of sophisms for freedom of religion, freedom of the press, protection against standing armies, restrictions against monopolies, the eternal and unremitting force of habeas corpus laws, and trials by jury in all matters triable by the laws of the land and not by the law of Nations.[15]

He wrote Madison again, on 28 August 1789, saying that there ought to be provision that "the people shall not be deprived or abridged of their right to speak to write or otherwise to publish anything but false facts affecting injuriously the life, liberty, property, or reputation of others or affecting the peace of the confederacy with foreign nations."[16]

There is again that interesting reference to "false facts," but also the restriction on publication "affecting the peace of the confederacy with foreign nations," a limitation not subsequently brought up in his letters and not remembered by Madison in framing the First Amendment.

Jefferson's letter of 16 January 1787 to Edward Carrington probably is the most quoted of all his comments on the press. He wrote:

> The people are the only censors of their governors: and even their errors will tend to keep these to the true principles of their institution. To punish these errors too severely would be to suppress the only safeguard of the public liberty. The way to prevent these irregular interpositions of the people is to give them full information of their affairs thro' the channel of the public papers, and to contrive that those papers should penetrate the whole mass of the people. The basis of our governments being the opinion of the people, the very first object should be to keep that right; and were it left to me to decide whether we should have a government without newspapers, or newspapers without a government, I should not hesitate a moment to prefer the latter.[17]

But it was in Jefferson's Second Inaugural Address, delivered on 4 March 1805, that he viewed with the most tranquility and maturity the issues involved in press freedom. No compendium of Jefferson on the press could exclude its eloquent testimony.

> During this course of administration, and in order to disturb it, the artillery of the press has been levelled against us, charged with whatsoever its licentiousness could devise or dare. These abuses of an institution so important to freedom and science, are deeply to be regretted, inasmuch as they tend to lessen its usefulness, and to sap its safety; they might, indeed, have been corrected by the wholesome punishments reserved and provided by the laws of the several States against falsehood and defamation; but public duties more

The Aurora on 27 December 1800 reported on progress of the Presidential campaign.

urgent press on the time of public servants, and the offenders have therefore been left to find their punishment in the public indignation.

Nor was it uninteresting to the world, that an experiment should be fairly and fully made, whether freedom of discussion, unaided by power, is not sufficient for the propagation and protection of truth – whether a government, conducting itself in the true spirit of its constitution, with zeal and purity, and doing no act which it would be unwilling the whole world should witness, can be written down by falsehood and defamation. The experiment has been tried; you have witnessed the scene; our fellow citizens have looked on, cool and collected; they saw the latent source from which these outrages proceeded; they gathered around their public functionaries, and when the constitution called them to the decision by suffrage, they pronounced their verdict, honorable to those who had served them, and consolatory to the friend of man, who believes he may be intrusted with his own affairs.

No inference is here intended, that the laws provided by the State against false and defamatory publications, should not be enforced; he who has time, renders a service to public morals and public tranquility, in reforming the abuses by the salutary coercions of the law; but the experiment is noted, to prove that, since truth and reason have maintained their ground against false opinions in league with false facts, the press, confined to truth, needs no other legal restraint; the public judgment will correct false reasonings and opinions, on a full hearing of all parties; and no other definite line can be drawn between the inestimable liberty of the press and its demoralizing licentiousness. If there be still improprieties which this rule would not restrain, its supplement must be sought in the censorship of public opinion.[18]

This is beyond doubt, Jefferson's most reflective, mature, balanced, and deliberate expression on press freedom, given with the advantage that a long public career added to his initial theories developed as a philosopher and student of free institutions.

A little more than two years later, on 11 June 1807, Jefferson wrote one of his most intemperate criticisms of newspapers in a letter to a young man asking how a newspaper should be conducted. His comment to John Norvell was, by his own description, a "hasty communication" and it lacked poise, restraint and balance. The press, long before the restrained statement in the second Inaugural Address, had exhibited much more malignancy about him than it since had, so the intemperance of the Norvell letter is somewhat inexplicable, except as the off-hand release of pent-up resentment, accumulated in a lifetime of public service and generally contained beneath a calm and unruffled exterior. Jefferson wrote his young correspondent:

It is a melancholy truth, that a suppression of the press could not more completely deprive the nation of its benefits, than is done by its abandoned prostitution to falsehood. Nothing can now be believed which is seen in a newspaper. Truth itself becomes suspicious by being put into that polluted vehicle. The real extent of this state of misinformation is known only to those who are in situations to confront facts within their knowledge with the lies of the day. I really look with commiseration over the great body of my fellow citizens, who, reading newspapers, live and die in the belief that they

have known something of what has been passing in the world in their time; whereas the accounts they have read in newspapers are just as true a history of any other period of the world as of the present, except that the real names of the day are affixed to their fables.... I will add, that the man who never looks into a newspaper is better informed than he who reads them; inasmuch as he who knows nothing is nearer to truth than he whose mind is filled with falsehoods and errors. He who reads nothing will still learn the great facts, and the details are all false.[19]

There were similar comments in the years of his retirement. He wrote to Walter Jones, in December 1814: "I deplore, with you, the putrid state into which our newspapers have passed, and the malignity, the vulgarity, and the mendacious spirit of those who write for them;..."[20]

To James Monroe, he wrote, on 1 January 1815: "A truth now and then projecting into the ocean of newspaper lies, serves like a headland to correct our course."[21]

These effusions of discontent with newspapers, it is to be noted, did not swerve him from first principles or induce him, even in his private impatience, to advocate abandoning freedom of the press.

That freedom involved, in the eighteenth century as it does now, more than a lack of government restriction on publication, important as that is. It involved, in all its essentials, the right to get information, the right to print it without prior restraint, the right to print without fear of punishment for innocent publication, and the right to distribute printed material.

The Jefferson record on access to information and the right of the people to get it and the duty of the government to disseminate it is abundant. It is generally as affirmative as Jefferson's views on prior restraint and on penalties for publication. This is not remarkable, of course, for it would be quite ridiculous to assure the press that it could print what it wished to print without government restraint if the government, at the same time, prevented the press from obtaining anything to print. The dissemination of information was one of the most important responsibilities of government, in Jefferson's view.

A letter to Andrew Ellicott, written on 18 December 1800, while the election was still pending in the House of Representatives, aptly expresses Jefferson's general philosophy on the government's duty to give out information. He wrote: "My own opinion is that government should by all means in their power deal out the materials of information to the public in order that it may be reflected back on themselves in the various forms into which public ingenuity may throw it."[22]

His instinctive mistrust of secrecy in government was previously voiced in a letter to John Adams while the Constitutional Convention was sitting. He wrote: "I am sorry they began their deliberations by so abominable a precedent as that of tying up the tongues of their members. Nothing can justify this example, but the innocence of their intentions, and ignorance of the value of public discussion."[23]

If he was convinced that the government ought to give out information, he was even more convinced that the information given out by government should be honest and accurate. Recounting in a letter to Matthew Carr, on 19 June 1813, an episode of the revolutionary

war, in which there was a motion in Congress to suppress or garble the news, Jefferson wrote: "The whole truth was given in all its details, and there never was another attempt in that body to disguise it." He was convinced, he said, that a "fair and honest narrative of the bad, is a voucher for the truth of the good."[24] In line with a policy of fullest information, Jefferson's Administration introduced a strict regime of publicity as to the salaries of officials and employees. In his first annual message to Congress, Jefferson said:

> We may well doubt whether our organization is not too complicated, too expensive; whether offices and officers have not been multiplied unnecessarily and sometimes injuriously to the service they were meant to promote. I will cause to be laid before you an essay toward a statement of those who, under public employment of various kinds, draw money from the Treasury or from our citizens.[25]

Congress was given a roster of federal officials and agents on 17 February 1802. Later, department heads were required to report the names of clerks, year by year.

In retirement, Jefferson advocated an overseas information program, to be conducted by American embassies abroad. In stressing the importance of this, he said that "the advantage of public opinion is like that of the weather-gauge in a naval action." He continued, in a letter to James Monroe,

> I hope that to preserve this weather-gauge of public opinion and to counteract the slanders and falsehoods disseminated by the English papers, the government will make it a standing instruction to their ministers at foreign courts, to keep Europe truly informed of occurrences here, by publishing in their papers the naked truth always, whether favorable or unfavorable. For they will believe the good if we candidly tell them the bad also.[26]

Jefferson's views on the disclosure of diplomatic matters fluctuated somewhat with his own situation and with his views as to the importance of confidentiality to the national interest.

When he was Minister to France he was much embarrassed by breach of the confidentiality of some of his letters to John Jay, American Secretary of State. He also was angered by publication of a letter "as from me" to the Count de Vergennes. He said the published account was "surreptitious and falsified, and both the true and untrue parts very improper for the public eye" and wrote C.W.F. Dumas, in Holland, on 25 December 1786 to "endeavor to prevent its publication" in *The Leyden Gazette*.[27] Writing to Jay on 9 January 1787 he said he feared disclosure would prevent Vergennes from future confidential exchanges; would "inspire the same diffidence into all other ministers with whom I might have to transact business" and "damp that freedom of communication which the resolution of Congress of May 3, 1784 [enforcing confidentiality for diplomatic matters] was intended to re-establish."[28]

In 1793, President Washington was considering the wisdom of laying before Congress the content of Pinckney's negotiations with the British on violations of the frontier and interference with American trade. The reply which Jefferson wrote on the issue sets forth an

interesting distinction between situations in which diplomatic confidentiality should be maintained and those in which it should be abandoned.

He felt that secrecy would not be maintained by Congress even if it were enjoined; that secrecy would withhold information only from Americans, since the British obviously knew all about the negotiations; and that only in cases where the public good would be injured and because it would be injured should secrecy be maintained. If the negotiations were at an end, he thought they should be disclosed because they would be of more interest now than later.

In 1790 another issue of publication of diplomatic material arose. William Temple Franklin left for England with the intention of publishing the papers of Benjamin Franklin. Jefferson wrote him on 27 November 1790, voicing this admonition: "I am sure your delicacy needs no hint from me against the publication of such letters or papers of Dr Franklin as Minister Plenipotentiary of the US as might not yet be proper to put into the possession of every body."[29]

In 1795, when the Jay Treaty came before the Senate, Jefferson had retired as Secretary of State. The treaty reached this country in November of 1794. Washington kept it secret. It was sent to the Senate under a rule of secrecy. Even when it was approved, the Senate enjoined members not to divulge the exact text. At this point Bache's *Aurora* got an abstract of the treaty from Senator Stevens T. Mason of Virginia and printed it. Jefferson, in a letter to Randolph, 6 September 1795, praised this disclosure as a "bold act of duty in one of our senators."[30]

Another instance of Jeffersonian support for disclosure of diplomatic information happened in January 1799 when Jefferson was Vice President. Elbridge Gerry of Massachusetts was one of three commissioners sent to discuss peace with France. The others were Charles Pinckney and John Marshall. Marshall and Pinckney came home to report that they had refused to pay tribute to French officials, in the famous XYZ affair. Congress asked for the files and Adams furnished them. The country was at a war fever over French insults. The Republicans were discomfited and embarrassed. Jefferson mistrusted the official report of the commissioners to France. He appealed to Gerry, who had remained behind when his colleagues came home, for a full account of the proceedings.

Clearly, Jefferson thought, at the very height of the XYZ excitement, that unless contradictory disclosures by Gerry were made, the country would be driven into a needless war with France. Jefferson was mistaken, to the degree that war did not ensue. But Jefferson was not mistaken as to the attitude of the French government. He suspected the French to be more receptive to negotiations than the reports of Marshall and Pinckney indicated. He was right. He came close, however, to urging a diplomatic representative to betray his chief and compromise diplomatic security, a position that he would have criticized under ordinary circumstances.

The Aaron Burr case precipitated two incidents concerning executive privilege. One case involved Congress; the other the Supreme Court. On 16 January 1807, the House asked Jefferson to furnish it information on the so-called Burr Rebellion. It limited its request to preclude the production of such papers "as he [the President] may deem the public welfare to require not to be disclosed." Jefferson wrote the House on 22 January 1807, that the mass

of the material in his hands had not been given under oath and this apparently satisfied the House, which did not press the issue to a test of executive privilege. The Chief Justice, John Marshall, on 13 June 1807, issued a *subpoena duces tecum*, requesting government papers relating to the Burr case. Jefferson offered the papers involved, chiefly a letter of General Wilkinson, and explained reservations on his personal attendance as inconsistent with a separation of powers. He wrote to government counsel at Richmond an extensive comment on the executive right to withhold. He said:

> With respect to papers, there is certainly a public and a private side to our offices. To the former belong grants of land, patents for inventions, certain commissions, proclamations, and other papers patent in their nature. To the other belong mere executive proceedings. All nations have found it necessary, that for the advantageous conduct of their affairs, some of these proceedings, at least, should remain known to their executive functionary only. He, of course, from the nature of the case, must be the sole judge of which of them the public interests will permit publication. Hence, under our Constitution, in requests of papers, from the legislative to the executive branch, an exception is carefully expressed, as to those which he may deem the public welfare may require not to be disclosed; as you will see in the inclosed resolution of the House of Representatives, which produced the message of January 22d, respecting this case. The respect mutually due between constituted authorities in their official intercourse, as well as sincere dispositions to do for everyone what is just, will always ensure from the Executive, in exercising the duty of discrimination confided to him, the same candor and integrity to which the nation has in like manner trusted in the disposal of its judiciary authorities.[31]

The papers actually relevant to the Burr trial were produced in the trial at Richmond and neither Court nor Executive pushed the test of executive privilege to a summit test. In the more than a century and a half since, no one has more clearly defined the boundaries of executive privilege. The Jefferson position in the Burr memo stating that the Executive must be the sole judge of what may be safely divulged would never satisfy Congress, the courts or the public. But it may be best viewed as a political question. Probably neither Congress, nor the Court, can compel a President to divulge matter which he thinks covered by executive privilege; but the President's critics sometimes can make him wish he had disclosed. This ambiguity, in the end, may be better unresolved; but Jefferson devised a statement of the due bounds which has not been much improved upon since.

Late in life, Jefferson developed, in correspondence with John Adams, some interesting theories on the privacy of personal correspondence. Shortly after Jefferson and Adams resumed writing to each other, after a long lapse, Jefferson on 10 August 1815 wrote to Adams: "I presume that our correspondence has been observed at the postoffices, and thus has attracted notice. Would you believe, that a printer has had the effrontery to propose to me the letting him publish it? These people think they have a right to everything, however secret or sacred."[32] On 1 June 1822, he wrote Adams again on this subject: "I should wish never to put pen to paper: and the more because of the treacherous practice some people have of publishing one's letters without leave. Lord Mansfield declared it a breach of trust, and punishable at law. I think it should be a penitentiary felony...."[33]

Thomas Jefferson's views on access to information about government can be quite fully reconstructed from his remarks here quoted. He clearly believed generally in disclosure of government information when that could be done without clear injury to the public interest. At the same time, he thought a right of privacy existed with respect to private communications of individuals. Secrecy in the foreign correspondence of government seemed to him essential to the conduct of foreign affairs during their pendency, and, as his Franklin letter shows, for a decent interval thereafter; but his comment on Pinckney's negotiations shows and the remarks on the Jay treaty disclosure confirm, that he favored publication of documents essential to public understanding of policy, on completion of negotiations. He adhered to the belief that there is a public and a private side to government papers, but he was diffident and cautious about pushing the doctrine of executive privilege. He yielded to Congress when he thought disclosure would not compromise individuals or impair the conduct of foreign policy. He yielded to the courts, if the judicial demand was relevant and specific. No President in history has gone farther in acknowledging limits on governmental secrecy.

Prior restraint issues did not arise in Jefferson's lifetime. Even the authors of the Sedition Act in the Adams administration supported the Blackstone theory construing freedom of the press to mean complete freedom from prior restraint. Jefferson did not believe that freedom of the press consisted solely of immunity to prior restraint. Many of his opponents did.

The Federalist authors of the Sedition Act believed it appropriate to punish for publication prejudicial to the State or to private persons. This was what the row over the Sedition Act was all about. This debate put Thomas Jefferson first in the ranks of those in American history who have defended the press against federal reprisal for publication. It is almost inexplicable that a President as upright and honorable as John Adams, and that Federalist congressmen as intelligent as Robert Goodloe Harper of South Carolina, John Allen of Connecticut, and Harrison Gray Otis of Massachusetts, could have been led so far astray by party spirit as to have put forward or countenanced the Sedition Act. President Adams, in later years, defended his own position by saying that he had not asked Congress for the law, but he helped to inflame the party spirit that led to its passage and he applied it against Republican editors. At no subsequent period in American history has the virulence of party spirit produced the factional animosity that divided Republicans and Federalists in the Adams administration.

Jefferson, while Vice President, early noted with alarm the intemperance of the Adams attacks on France and on Republican friends of France and he anticipated administration efforts to silence the critics in the opposition press.

His expectations were fulfilled when on 6 June he wrote Madison,

the Federalists have brought into the lower house a sedition bill, which among other enormities, undertakes to make printing certain matters criminal, tho' one of the amendments to the Constitution has so expressly taken religion, printing press etc. out of their coercion. Indeed this bill and the alien bill are so palpably in the teeth of the Constitution as to show they mean to pay no respect to it.[34]

In the House debate on the bill, Otis argued that the First Amendment only reaffirmed Blackstone on press freedom, which, he said, was "nothing more than the liberty of writing, publishing, and speaking one's thoughts, under the condition of being answerable to the injured party, whether it be the Government or an individual, for false, malicious and seditious expressions, whether spoken or written; and the liberty of the press is merely an exemption from all previous restraints."[35]

All Federalists supported the bill, with the exception of John Marshall, who announced that had he been in Congress, he would have opposed it. The Act as passed provided punishment by a fine not exceeding two thousand dollars and by imprisonment not exceeding two years for writing or printing defamation of the government or its officials. It permitted truth as a defense, but this proved to little purpose for defendants when biased Federalist judges decided what the truth was.

The Federalists brought actions for sedition against seventeen newspapers. Proceedings were begun against four of the five leading Republican newspapers – the Philadelphia *Aurora, The Boston Independent Chronicle, The New York Argus* and the *Richmond Enquirer.* Four newspapers in addition to these were prosecuted by Secretary of State Pickering in the summer of 1799. Two of them ceased publication. No Federalist newspapers were indicted. The enemies of the administration, not only in the press, but in Congress, were targets of the government and Vermont Congressman Matthew Lyon was the first object of attention.

Jefferson and Madison set to work at once to obstruct the enforcement of the law, to defend editors and congressman, and to arouse the country to this threat to freedom of speech and the press. One of the instruments of this campaign was the Virginia and Kentucky Resolutions which declared the law a "nullity." Jefferson also contributed liberally to defense funds for prosecuted editors.

When he was elected in 1800, Jefferson allowed outstanding prosecutions to lapse and freed editors still under prosecution. The law itself was for a fixed period which had expired.

While Jefferson's views on federal libel laws are clear, his attitude toward state libel laws differs. He often attacked the Federal prosecutions of editors by saying this was the domain of the states. He quarreled with state laws only when they did not permit truth as a defense.

The case of Henry Croswell, editor of the *Wasp*, in Hudson, New York, is often cited as an example of Republican inconsistency on the theory of libel. Jefferson has never been linked to the case in any way, but the case involved a libel on him. The *Wasp*, on 9 September 1802, printed a paragraph saying Jefferson had paid Callendar to call Washington a traitor, robber and perjurer and Adams an incendiary.

The Republican administration of George Clinton prosecuted the *Wasp* in about the same spirit that the Federalists had prosecuted the Republican press. Croswell was convicted. Alexander Hamilton was brought into the case and appealed the decision to the State Supreme Court. He made his historic argument for truth as a defense against libel. He lost the case, but the New York legislature adopted in 1805 a law making truth a defense. This was really in conformity with Jefferson's own doctrine. The *Wasp* was put out of business, as many of its Republican colleagues had been in the Adams administration.

Jefferson frequently expressed his impatience with the insecurity of the mails – a form of obstruction to distribution needed to make press freedom effective – but there seem to have

been no celebrated cases of post office refusal to accept newspapers for distribution in the eighteenth century, at least none to compare with the frequent controversies over mailability in later decades.

Measured by his theories on the right to get information, the right to print without prior restraint, the right to publish without unjust reprisal by the federal government and the right to distribution, Jefferson emerges with very high marks indeed. His views on access to information were more enlightened than those of his contemporaries and more liberal than those of his successors, even to this day. He shares with James Madison the credit for the First Amendment ban on congressional action restricting the freedom of the press. In the fight that he and Madison made on the Sedition Act, Jefferson fixed the immunity for publication alleged to be seditious more firmly in the American tradition than it was established by the First Amendment. His views on the right of the individual to protect the privacy of his own letters against the inquiry of the press or the government have not acquired legal or judicial sanction but they deserve respectful consideration in a day when privacy is more precarious than it was in Jefferson's day. His opinions on the security of diplomatic correspondence and the proceedings of government exhibit a commonsense estimate of the papers entitled to protection against disclosure and those that the people may justly demand access to in order to be informed of the acts of government.

Thomas Jefferson believed in freedom of the press more unreservedly than any President of the United States before or since and more completely than any public man in American history, with the possible exception of Associate Justice Hugo Black. He came to this belief before he had any extensive practical experience with American newspapers. No doubt it was strengthened by the role the patriot press played in preparing the country for the American Revolution and fortified by the effectiveness of the Republican newspapers in the election of 1800.

His belief in the theory of a free press did not blind him to the abuses of a licentious press or prevent frequent expressions of anger, disgust and contempt at the irresponsibility and mendacity of individual newspapers and newspapermen, but their faults did not have any visible effect on his fundamental beliefs. When he had a choice, he preferred sober, serious and respectable newspapers such as the objective and balanced European paper, *The Leyden Gazette*, the *National Intelligencer* and the *Richmond Enquirer*, but he had his favorites among the advocate press such as *The Aurora* and Freneau's *National Gazette*. No doubt the clash of hostile opinion reconciled him to some of the excesses of the press of his day; and the increasing absence of that competition would alarm him now.

In the conflict arising from the perhaps intentional ambiguities of the Constitution on the powers of government, Jefferson habitually came down on the side of disclosure as a matter of policy, but the national interest figured importantly in his views on diplomatic secrecy and the confidentiality of some of the papers of government.

In nearly two hundred years, American history has not produced a more invariable, more eloquent or more effective advocate of freedom of the press.

1. Arthur Aspinall, *Politics and the Press 1780–1850*, Home & Van Thal Ltd, 1949.
2. *Writings of Thomas Jefferson*, edited by Andrew A. Lipscomb, Thomas Jefferson Memorial Association, 1904, vol. 8, pp. 403, 404, 406.
3. Donald Stewart, *The Opposition Press of the Federalist Period*, State University of New York Press, 1969, p. 629.
4. Lipscomb, vol. 10, p. 96.
5. Stewart, p. 634.
6. James E. Pollard, *The Presidents and the Press*, Macmillan, 1947, p. 83.
7. John Bach McMaster, *History of the People of the United States*, Appleton & Co., 1914, vol. 2, p. 502.
8. Frank van der Linden, *The Turning Point*, Luce, 1962, p. 210.
9. Pierce W. Gaines, *William Cobbett and the United States*, American Antiquarian Society, 1972, p. 69.
10. *The Papers of Thomas Jefferson*, edited by Julian Boyd, Princeton University Press, 1954, vol. 9, p. 239.
11. Ibid., p. 215.
12. *Jefferson's Papers*, edited by Paul Leicester Ford, vol. VIII, p. 218.
13. Boyd, op. cit., vol. 1, pp. 344 and 363.
14. Ibid., vol. 6, p. 304.
15. Ibid., vol. 12, p. 440.
16. Ibid., vol. 15, p. 367.
17. Ibid., vol. 11, p. 49.
18. Lipscomb, op. cit., vol 3, p. 380.
19. Ibid., vol. 11, p. 222.
20. Ibid., vol. 14, p. 46.
21. Ibid., vol. 14, p. 226.
22. Ibid., vol. 19, p. 121.
23. Henry S. Randall, *The Life of Thomas Jefferson*, Derby & Jackson, 1858, vol. 1, p. 487.
24. Lipscomb, op. cit., vol XIII, p. 264.
25. *Messages and Papers of the Presidents 1789–1894*, edited by James D. Richardson, Bureau of National Literature, 1913, vol. 1, p. 316.
26. Lipscomb, op. cit., vol. 14, pp. 226–7.
27. Boyd, op. cit., vol. 10, p. 630.
28. Ibid., vol. 11, p. 30.
29. Ibid., vol. 18, p. 87.
30. Ford, op. cit., vol. 7, p. 28.
31. Randall, op. cit., vol. 3, p. 211.
32. Lipscomb, vol. 4, p. 344.
33. Ibid., vol. 15, p. 372.
34. Ford, op. cit., vol. 7, p. 266.
35. James Morton Smith, *Freedom's Fetters*, Cornell University Press, 1956, p. 136.

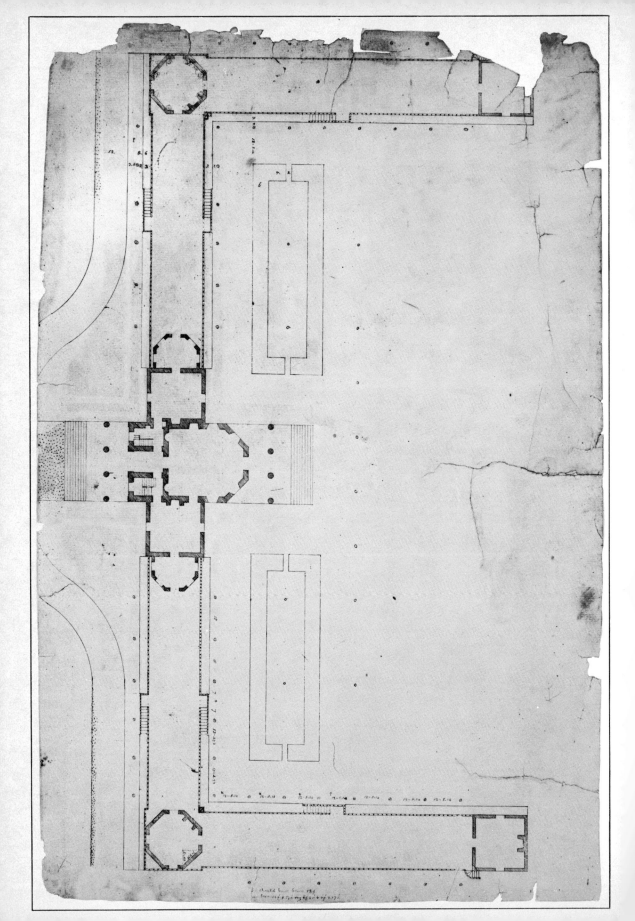

THOMAS JEFFERSON, ARCHITECT

Walter Muir Whitehill

The Chevalier (later Marquis) de Chastellux, having visited Thomas Jefferson on 13 April 1782, thus described Monticello:

> This house, of which Mr Jefferson was the architect, and often the builder, is constructed in an Italian style, and is quite tasteful, although not however without some faults; it consists of a large square pavilion, into which one enters through two porticoes ornamented with columns. The ground floor consists chiefly of a large and lofty *salon*, or drawing room, which is to be decorated entirely in the antique style; above the *salon* is a library of the same form; two small wings, with only a ground floor and attic, are joined to this pavilion, and are intended to communicate with the kitchen, offices, etc., which will form on either side a kind of basement topped by a terrace. My object in giving these details is not to describe the house, but to prove that it resembles none of the others seen in this country; so that it may be said that Mr Jefferson is the first American who has consulted the Fine Arts to know how he should shelter himself from the weather.

Chastellux, a professional soldier by inheritance and inclination, had entered the French army at the age of thirteen as a second lieutenant in the Auvergne Regiment. Twenty-four years later, when he visited Monticello, he was a *maréchal de camp*, serving as one of the major generals under Rochambeau in the French expeditionary force. Nevertheless he was thoroughly at home in the world of the *Encyclopédistes* and *philosophes* and knew his way around the best Paris *salons*. He had traveled in Italy. His two-volume philosophical treatise, *De la Félicité Publique*, published in 1772, won him the admiration and friendship of Voltaire. Three years later, when Chastellux became one of the forty Immortals of the French Academy, his *Discours de Réception* dealt with the subject of taste and its formation, from antiquity to the enlightened year of 1775. Clearly such a man's observation about consulting the fine arts was founded in experience and thought.

Thomas Jefferson, on whose thirty-ninth birthday Chastellux came to Monticello, knew the world of the *philosophes* and the fine arts only through books. Jefferson obtained, while still an undergraduate of William and Mary, his first book on architecture from an old cabinetmaker, who lived near the gate of the college. Architecture in colonial Virginia was the province either of craftsmen who had grown up in one of the building trades or of gentleman amateurs, like Richard Taliaferro of Williamsburg, whose flair for design was

Monticello: the first floor and dependencies, as shown on the final plan.

stimulated by the study of imported books. As Taliaferro, active from 1725 to 1755, was George Wythe's father-in-law, it is highly probable that the young Jefferson knew him.

There was little in Williamsburg, or anywhere in Virginia, that contributed to the development of Thomas Jefferson as an architect. In his *Notes on the State of Virginia*, written in 1781–2, he had little good to say of the architectural taste of his neighbors. He described the College and Hospital at Williamsburg as "rude, mis-shapen piles, which, but that they have roofs, would be taken for brick-kilns" and continued:

> The genius of architecture seems to have shed its maledictions over this land. Buildings are often erected, by individuals, of considerable expence. To give these symmetry and taste would not increase their cost. It would only change the arrangement of the materials, the form and combination of the members. This would often cost less than the burthen of barbarous ornaments with which these buildings are sometimes charged. But the first principles of the art are unknown, and there exists scarcely a model among us sufficiently chaste to give an idea of them.

Thomas Jefferson was twenty-three before he ever went outside Virginia. A three months' journey to Annapolis, Philadelphia, and New York, beginning in May 1766, provided his first glimpse of the outside world.

Soon after Thomas Jefferson's return from his provincial grand tour, he began planning for a new house for himself on a mountain top above Shadwell. The site was a conspicuous one, with striking views in many directions. Chastellux on approaching the region noted:

> We had no difficulty in recognizing on one of the summits the house of Mr Jefferson, for it may be said that "it shines alone in this secluded spot." He himself built it and chose the site, for although he already owned fairly extensive lands in the neighborhood, there was nothing, in such an unsettled country, to prevent him from fixing his residence wherever he wanted to. But Nature so contrived it, that a Sage and a man of taste should find on his own estate the spot where he might best study and enjoy Her. He called this house *Monticello* (in Italian, Little Mountain), a very modest name indeed, for it is situated on a very high mountain, but a name which bespeaks the owner's attachment to the language of Italy and above all the Fine Arts, of which Italy was the cradle and is still the resort.

Note again the influence of books as the secret of self-cultivation, for Jefferson was absorbed in the study of Italian in 1764, two years before he first went outside Virginia. He learned the language so well that Dr Philip Mazzei, who at Jefferson's instigation brought Tuscan vignerons to Albemarle County in 1773 to introduce the culture of the grape and olive, observed: "Jefferson knew the Italian language very well, but he had never heard it spoken. Nevertheless, speaking with my men he understood them and they understood him. I was impressed by their demonstrations of joy at the circumstance."

In 1767 Jefferson was planting on his new mountain top, for in the *Garden Book* in which he entered memoranda concerning the process of the seasons, he wrote on 3 August 1767: "inoculated common cherry buds into stocks of large kind at Monticello;" this is the first mention of the name in his writings. Although he was absent from home on law cases and

The final version of the west front of Monticello drawn by Robert Mills who studied architecture under Jefferson.

visits to Williamsburg and elsewhere during a good deal of 1768, he arranged for John Moore to level an area two hundred and fifty foot square on the top of the mountain as a site for his future house. In 1769 the excavation and construction of the new house began. Initially there seemed no great need for haste, for Jefferson's law practice was increasing, and his election to the House of Burgesses in 1769 required extended stays in Williamsburg. But on 1 February 1770 Shadwell, the house in which he had been born and which he had inherited, burned, entailing the loss of most of his possessions, including his books. Being thus rendered homeless, Jefferson felt it necessary to accelerate construction. On 26 November 1770 he moved up the hill to a pavilion, called an "outchamber" that had been completed, from which he wrote to James Ogilvie on 20 February 1771: "I have here but one room, which, like the cobler's, serves me for parlour, for kitchen and hall. I may add, for bed chamber and study too. My friends sometimes take a temperate dinner with me and then retire to look for beds elsewhere. I have hopes however of getting more elbow room this summer."

In the course of sheltering himself from the weather, Thomas Jefferson became an architect while still in his twenties. There is scant evidence concerning his earliest architectural thoughts, for the Shadwell fire consumed, as he wrote to John Page, "every paper I had in the world, and almost every book." Fortunately the *Garden Book* was not in the house on the fateful day. For the fifty-six years of Jefferson's life after the fire, the architectural evidence is rich, thanks to the methodical care with which he preserved his papers and the diligence of his editors and biographers.

The great collection of his architectural drawings, now in the Massachusetts Historical Society, was acquired from cousins in Virginia in 1911 by his great-great-grandson, Thomas Jefferson Coolidge, Jr (1863–1912). His widow arranged for their study by Fiske Kimball. The resulting folio, *Thomas Jefferson Architect*, which contained magnificent reproductions of the drawings with a perceptive essay and notes by Fiske Kimball, was privately printed in 1916 for Mrs Coolidge, who distributed it to friends and libraries as a memorial to her husband. As this sumptuous publication soon went out of print, the Massachusetts Historical Society in 1960 issued in its Picture Book Series *Thomas Jefferson's Architectural Drawings*, a modestly priced reproduction of selected drawings, introduced by a succinct but comprehensive essay, "Thomas Jefferson's Architectural Development," by Frederick Doveton Nichols, now Cary Langhorne Professor of Architecture at the University of Virginia. To subsequent editions of this Picture Book, published jointly by the Society, the Thomas Jefferson Memorial Foundation, and the University Press of Virginia, Professor Nichols added a check list of all known Jefferson architectural drawings, including those scattered through other institutions. In 1968 the Da Capo Press reproduced for general sale Fiske Kimball's *Thomas Jefferson Architect* of 1916, with a new introduction by Professor Nichols and reproductions freshly made by the Meriden Gravure Company from the Massachusetts Historical Society originals. Thus Jefferson drawings are available today both in sumptuous and in readily accessible and inexpensive forms.

Fiske Kimball and his wife, having been intimately concerned with the restoration of Monticello after its purchase by the Thomas Jefferson Memorial Foundation in 1923, continued their Jeffersonian studies for the remainder of their lives. The three volumes of

"All my wishes end, where I hope my days will end, at Monticello."

Marie Kimball's unfinished biography, *Jefferson The Road to Glory 1743–1776, Jefferson War and Peace 1776–1784,* and *Jefferson The Scene of Europe 1784–1789*, are especially helpful for details of her subject's tastes in the arts. Dumas Malone's multi-volume *Jefferson and His Time*, still in progress, is also enlightening in regard to architectural matters, while Julian P. Boyd's great edition *The Papers of Thomas Jefferson*, of which eighteen volumes (through March 1791) have appeared, provides the definitive text of Jefferson's writings. The *Garden Book* and the *Farm Book*, edited by the late Edwin Morris Betts, have been published by the American Philosophical Society. E. Millicent Sowerby's five volume *Catalogue of the Library of Thomas Jefferson*, published by the Library of Congress, is a thorough study of his books, including those on architecture and other arts. Altogether there is a wealth of resources to supplement the visual evidence of surviving buildings designed by Thomas Jefferson.

This is fortunate so far as Monticello is concerned, for the house changed from decade to decade as he planned, built, demolished, remodeled, added, and improved. For half a century workmen were about and something was under way. Late in life Jefferson is said to have remarked to a visitor that "architecture is my delight, and putting up and pulling down one of my favorite amusements." Not even his family could always keep abreast of changes, for in 1797 his daughter Maria, who had just married John Wayles Eppes, not only tumbled through a floor of Monticello into the cellar, without injury, but a little later suffered a sprain by falling out of a doorway! In spite of the richness of documentation it is not always possible to be certain what was being built at Monticello at a particular moment. During 1771, when Jefferson's home on the mountain consisted of his one-room outchamber, he was often away on legal business. He was, moreover, courting Martha Wayles, widow of Bathurst Skelton, whom he married on New Year's Day 1772.

Although the prospect of a wife would seem to have furnished reason for getting on with the construction of a house, it is not clear exactly what was accomplished at Monticello during 1771. In his *Account Book* for that year are notes on landscape fantasies that were never achieved, among them the elaboration of a spring in a manner that would have charmed an Italian humanist. This involved terraces, a cascade falling into a cistern under a temple whose roof might be "Chinese, Grecian, or in the taste of the Lantern of Demosthenes at Athens," with sleeping nymphs in sculpture with Latin inscriptions, distant vistas, and possibly even an Aeolian harp concealed under the temple – all very appropriate notions for a literary young man who was in love. Actually he brought his bride up the mountain late in January when there was three feet of snow on the ground – "the deepest snow we have ever seen." Family tradition has it that the last eight miles were of necessity traversed on horseback; that servants were in bed and fires out when the bride and groom arrived and that only the one-room outchamber was ready for occupancy.

The design of Monticello owed its initial inspiration to the work of Andrea Palladio and his English disciples. Jefferson early owned and used Palladio's *Four Books of Architecture* in Leoni's edition, James Gibb's *Rules for Drawing the Several Parts of Architecture* and *Book of Architecture*, and Robert Morris's *Select Architecture*. As originally built, the house was scarcely half the size of today's Monticello, and very different in exterior style. It consisted on the first floor of a central rectangular drawing room, flanked by the dining room to the

north and a bedroom (without alcove) to the south, both of which were square. Occupying only a part of the site of the present spacious hall was a small entrance from a two-story portico, Tuscan below and Ionic above, flanked by a pair of small enclosed stairways. These led to a second-floor library in the tall central pavilion and, presumably, bedrooms in the lower wings. A western portico, as today, led to the garden from the drawing room but without the dome which now rises above it.

Kitchens, stables, and other dependencies were first projected in form of two flanking wings, connected with the main house by arcades. As these would have restricted the view from the house, Jefferson put them out of sight in a characteristically ingenious way. His solution amounted to taking a Palladian entrance courtyard, turning it wrong side out (so that buildings were entered from the outside), dropping its level, and putting it on the back of the house. Thus he achieved a plan for terraces above his garden, below which the dependencies were neatly hidden, with exterior entrances at a lower level, leading in L-shapes to outchamber pavilions. Early in this campaign a large bow was added to the drawing room, resulting in its present form, and smaller separate bow rooms were added to the dining room and the bedroom. In spite of absences in Philadelphia at the Continental Congress and in Williamsburg at the Virginia House of Delegates, Jefferson had his house fairly complete by 1779, although the terraces and the northwest outchamber were still to be built, and there is doubt whether the second-story Ionic eastern portico (shown in the architectural drawing) had been completed. It was this two-story, essentially English Palladian house that in 1782 excited the admiration of the Marquis de Chastellux.

Mrs Jefferson died in the autumn of 1782. For the next eleven years her sorrowing widower had little inducement or opportunity to develop his property, for he was constantly away from home as a member of the Continental Congress, as Minister Plenipotentiary to France, and as Washington's Secretary of State. The years 1784–9 that he spent in Europe gave him, among many things, his first direct experience of European architecture. They also enlarged and changed his taste. Roman antiquities and their interpretation by architects under Louis XVI captivated him. He gazed at the old Maison Carrée at Nîmes "like a lover at his mistress" and at the new Hôtel de Salm in Paris with equal ardor. In the spring of 1786 he visited London and a number of great English country seats. A year later he traveled through Burgundy to Provence, on to northern Italy, returning to Paris by way of Toulouse, Bordeaux, and the west of France. When diplomatic business took him to Amsterdam in 1788 he seized the opportunity to come back by way of the Rhine through Cologne to Strasbourg. He left Paris in the autumn of 1789, anticipating that after a period of home leave he would be returning to France and determined to remodel Monticello to conform with his new enthusiasms. But on landing at Norfolk he found that having been nominated by President Washington as Secretary of State, and confirmed by the Senate, he was already a high official of the new federal government of the United States. Although he never again went to Europe, the recollections of Roman and contemporary French buildings dominated his architecture for the rest of his life. For all but four of the next twenty years he held a succession of the highest public offices. During that private respite in Washington's second administration between his service as Secretary of State and as Vice-President he applied his newly acquired European architectural experience to the rebuilding of Monti-

The east front of Monticello as Jefferson rebuilt it
after his return from France in 1789.

k sketch of Jefferson's first plan for Monticello.

cello. The Duc de la Rochefoucauld-Liancourt, who happened by in 1796, thus summarized what was going on in Mr Jefferson's mind:

> The house stands on the summit of a mountain, and the tastes and arts of Europe have been consulted in the formation of the plan. Mr Jefferson had commenced the construction before the American Revolution; since that epoch his life has constantly been engaged in public affairs, and he has not been able to complete the execution of the whole extent of the project which it seems he had at first conceived. That part of the building which is finished has suffered from the suspension of the work, and Mr Jefferson, who two years since assumed the habits and leisure of private life, is now employed in repairing the damage occasioned by this interruption, and still more by his absence; he continues his plan and even improves on it, by giving to his buildings more elevation and extent. He intends that they shall consist of only one story, crowned with balustrades; and a dome is to be constructed in the center of the structure. The apartments will be large and convenient; the decoration, both outside and inside, simple, yet regular and elegant. Monticello, according to the first plan, was infinitely superior to all other houses in America, in point of taste and convenience; but at that time Mr Jefferson had studied taste and fine arts in books only. His travels in Europe have supplied him with models; he has appropriated them to his design; and his new plan, the execution of which is already much advanced, will be accomplished before the end of next year, and then his house will certainly deserve to be ranked with the most pleasant mansions in France and England.

The duke, like everyone, was optimistic about the time required, for the next year, when things were still in a state where daughter Maria could fall through into the cellar, Jefferson returned again to public life. Four years as Vice-President and eight years as President of the United States did nothing to speed the completion of Monticello.

The new plans involved the destruction of the second-floor library, which must have been a wrench, and doubling the width of the house. The Tuscan eastern portico was moved out well beyond its original position, and the upper Ionic order of the original plan (if ever actually built) was suppressed, for, as Jefferson put it, "All the new and good houses are of a single story." The present high-studded hall was built between the drawing room and the new location of the Tuscan portico. To the eastward of the original dining room and bedroom were built transverse corridors, with tiny compact staircases, with two further rooms in front of each. On the north and south facades open loggias, which he called piazzas, were added between the old and new bows. Although the ceilings of the four rooms in the new eastern section were low enough to permit an *entresol* above them, in the French manner, the windows of both floors were treated continuously on the exterior to carry out the much desired single-story illusion. By this means he sought to bring his old-fashioned English Palladian house, inspired by books before he had ever crossed the Atlantic, up to current Parisian standards. This is evident from these remarks:

> The method of building houses 2, 3, or 4 stories high, first adopted in cities, where ground is scarce, and thence without reason copied in the country, where ground abounds, has for these 20 or 30 years been abandoned in Europe in all good houses newly built. In

Paris particularly all the new and good houses are of a single story. That is of the height of 16 or 18 feet generally, and the whole of it given to rooms for entertainment: but in the parts where there are bedrooms they have two tiers of them from 8 to 10 feet high each, with a small private staircase. By these means great staircases are avoided, which are expensive and occupy a space which would make a good room in every story.

The Hôtel de Salm, with which Jefferson had been "violently smitten" while it was under construction in Paris, had not only this one-story effect but was ornamented by a low dome. Consequently this second feature of Parisian elegance entered into his redesign of Monticello. In the center of the west facade, he added, beginning work in 1800, a dome "precisely on the same principles as those of the meat market in Paris." This dome rose above the Doric portico that led from the drawing room to the garden. Below it was the "sky room," a noble apartment with no reasonable access and no obvious use. Although Jefferson was an eminently practical man who could make things work admirably when he chose, he was blessedly free from the theory which has hamstrung later architects that form *must* follow function. If he wanted a dome, he had a dome whether it covered anything useful or not. He enjoyed designing and building it. And no one can deny that it lends great distinction to the west facade as seen from the curving garden paths.

The new bedrooms added during this reconstruction had the bed alcoves that Jefferson had seen in France. One was also built into his original bedroom, with an opening knocked through into the south bow room beyond, thus creating a situation by which he could leap into his bed from either of two rooms. This arrangement, designed for ventilation, is sometimes erroneously hailed as a device by which husband and wife could each have their own room and still sleep in the same bed. Unfortunately it was achieved at a time when Jefferson no longer had a wife to share his bed. He could go directly from his bed to the books in his library, or vice versa. Control of both ventilation and light was augmented by the skylights in the center of the ceilings of the tall bedroom and dining room which serve a function similar to the *teatinas* that are so common in Peruvian houses. An even greater convenience were the interior privies that he installed, opening from his bedroom and from halls on each floor. Shafts in the thickness of the walls led down to an air tunnel in which were removable receptacles in small carts. In 1804 Jefferson installed the folding glass doors between drawing room and hall that operate in such mysterious unison by means of a concealed chain sprocket. By 1809 the house in its present form was substantially completed, although it was 1824 – only two years before Jefferson's death – when the terrace railings were finally installed.

Visitors to Monticello today cannot help subscribing to the appraisals of the Marquis de Chastellux and the Duc de la Rochefoucauld-Liancourt, although there are curious quirks to the interior of the house. The two staircases are vertiginously narrow and inconvenient, but they were cheaper to build and took up less space than the monumental ones that consumed so disproportionate a part of the cubic content of many Virginia houses. Possibly Jefferson overreacted to such conspicuous waste of space, but he was deliberately trying to achieve a one-story French house in which *entresol* and attic rooms were private. A few other interior awkwardnesses reflect half a century of changing taste and adaptive construction, yet the

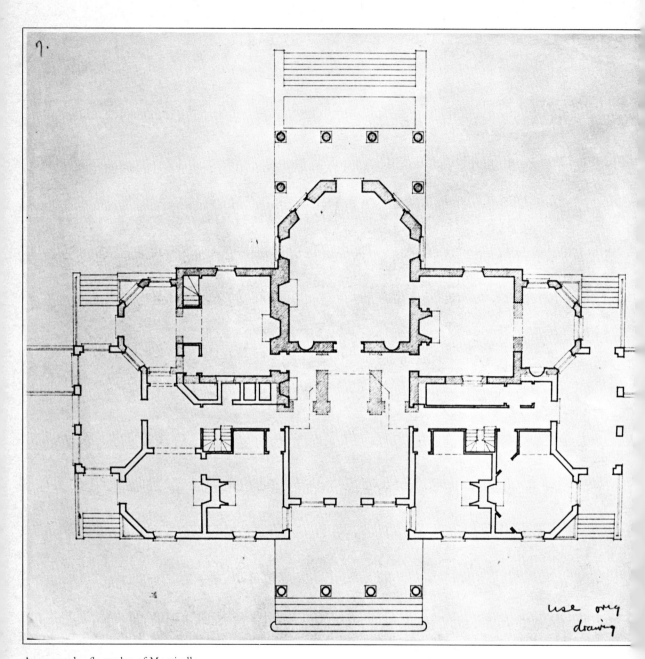

A present day floor plan of Monticello.

exterior of Monticello in its final form is remarkably felicitous from any point of view. The house stands superbly on its mountain top, with views in every direction, which are never impeded by the workaday aspects of daily life. Because of the utilitarian nature of the dependencies, the forecourts of many great European houses are sometimes more impressive in an architect's rendering than in actuality. Often barnyard fowl stray into the court of a French château and have to be restrained from trespassing in salons and libraries. By concentrating all the dependencies out of sight *behind* Monticello under the terraces, and having them entered from the outside at a lower level, Jefferson achieved unimpeded approach from the east and felicitous access to the gardens on the west. But the dependencies were adequately connected by exterior arcades under the L-shaped terraces, and invisible from house and garden, and also connected with each other by an all-weather passageway through the basement of the main house. Thus kitchens, cellars for wine, beer, and cider, a smoke house, dairy, laundry, and quarters for horses and carriages were conveniently accessible dry-shod in any season, with maximum invisibility, while the terraces above them provided an elegant transition between house and garden. This is indeed consulting the fine arts and still being uncommonly practical about it.

Jefferson's country retreat at Poplar Forest in Bedford County, some ninety miles from Monticello, which he began to build in 1806, is octagonal in plan, with symmetrical rooms disposed with geometric ingenuity. The 5,101 acres that he owned in that region – only a slightly smaller property than he had Albemarle County – had come to him through his wife's marriage settlement. Although distance made it difficult for him to exercise any close supervision of this Bedford County property, he eventually determined to build a house there to which he might retire when the flood of visitors at Monticello became oppressive. The plan, which was inspired by a plate in William Kent's 1737 *Designs of Inigo Jones*, he had first prepared as a possible house for his younger daughter, Maria Eppes, to be built on the land at Pantops, north of Monticello. As her death in 1804 put an end to that project, he used the plan at Poplar Forest instead.

This gloriously symmetrical little pyramidally-roofed house, which is thought to be the first one of octagonal plan to be built in the United States, has a tall square dining room in the center, lighted from above. The remaining space is neatly divided into four long, eight-sided areas, which, with four chimneys on the diagonal walls, exactly fill the exterior octagon. From the entrance portico a corridor leading into the central dining room divides one of the four outer rooms into two six-sided rooms, each with its own fireplace. On the opposite side of the house is a long parlor, with a fireplace at each end, which gives onto the second story of a rear portico. The two bedrooms, on opposite sides of the dining room, each have in the center a bed alcove, with passages on either side, thus recreating the double-approached bed of Jefferson's own rooms at Monticello. Although each bedroom had a small projecting dressing room or closet, Poplar Forest lacked the indoor conveniences of Monticello. By 1809 Jefferson was able to stay in the house, although it was not fully completed and decorated until a few years before his death.

The grounds were designed to enhance the form of the house. On the north was a forecourt of clipped yew. On the south, in order to provide an excuse for a two-story portico, Jefferson excavated a depressed lawn, which he bordered with terraces and planted with

lines of trees. The earth removed in this excavation was used to construct artificial mounds to the east and west of the house that conceal octagonal privies. Altogether Poplar Forest was a very handsome creation. It has survived as a private house, even though it has suffered from inept restoration following a fire of 1846, and the planting of the forecourt has grown out of proper bounds.

Throughout his life Jefferson constantly "consulted the Fine Arts" to know how he should shelter from the weather not only himself and his friends but the governments and public institutions that he served in so many capacities. At the request of Lord Dunmore he prepared in 1771 or 1772 a plan for an addition to the College of William and Mary. This called for a great rectangular arcaded quadrangle, strongly resembling a Palladian palace courtyard, to the west of the earlier building. Although construction was begun, it never proceeded beyond the foundations, for by 1777 work had been "discontinued on account of the present troubles."

For the improvement of the Palace at Williamsburg, begun in 1706 as a residence for royal governors, Jefferson made a number of plans between 1772 and the burning of the building in 1781. Elected Governor of Virginia on 1 June 1779, Thomas Jefferson occupied the Palace for a few months, but when the government moved to Richmond in the spring of 1780 he established himself there in a rented house. His improvements to the Palace were never carried out, but even after Williamsburg had ceased to be the capital he had not lost interest in possible improvement of the building for private use, for in *Notes on the State of Virginia* he wrote: "The Palace is not handsome without: but it is spacious and commodious within, is prettily situated, and with the grounds annexed to it, is capable of being made an elegant seat." The destruction of the Palace by fire in December 1781 put an end to such hopes.

Another unachieved building is an octagonal chapel, surrounded by a Tuscan peristyle, for which Jefferson drew a plan in 1770; on this he noted the Temple of Vesta at Tivoli, and Palladio, Book 4, plates 38–9, as his models. As such a building would have been beyond the resources of Albemarle County at the time, it is presumed that his chapel was designed for Williamsburg. He conceived in neo-classical terms a type of church hitherto unimagined in the colonies.

The removal of the capital of Virginia from Williamsburg to Richmond had originally been proposed in a bill drawn by Thomas Jefferson in 1776, which contained the then-original provision of separate buildings for the executive, legislative, and judicial branches of the new government. Although this bill was rejected, a similar one passed in 1779. When the move to Richmond was made in the spring of 1780, a committee of nine, headed by Governor Jefferson, was appointed to construct the public buildings. With characteristic energy, the Governor drew designs for enlarging the town on a gridiron plan, and made studies for several of the necessary buildings. The Capitol he envisioned in the then-unimagined form of a rectangular classical temple with porticos at both ends. The confusions of war delayed the completion of final plans; when Jefferson sailed for France in July 1784 nothing had been undertaken on construction in Richmond.

The following summer in Paris he received an urgent request from the Richmond committee "to consult an able architect on a plan fit for a Capitol, and to assist him with the information of which you are possessed." The letter indicated that Jefferson's unprece-

dented plan of separate buildings for the different branches of government had been abandoned; "fearing that the Assembly would not countenance us in giving sufficient magnificence to distinct buildings, we obtained leave to consolidate the whole under one roof." Haste was urged, for a bricklayer had already been hired. Having long admired in engravings the Maison Carrée at Nîmes, Jefferson turned to Charles Louis Clérisseau, an architect enamored of antiquity, whose *Antiquités de France, Monuments de Nismes* had been published in 1778. As he long afterwards recalled the circumstances:

> Thinking it a favorable opportunity of introducing into the state an example of architecture, in the classical style of antiquity, and the Maison quarrée of Nismes, an ancient Roman temple, being considered as the most perfect model existing of what may be called Cubic architecture, I applied to M. Clerisault, who had published drawings of the Antiquities of Nismes, to have me a model of the building made in stucco, only changing the order from Corinthian to Ionic, on account of the difficulty of the Corinthian capitals. I yielded, with reluctance, to the taste of Clerissault, in his preference of the modern capital of Scamozzi to the more noble capital of antiquity. This was executed by the artist whom Choiseul Gouffier had carried with him to Constantinople, and employed, while Ambassador there, in making those beautiful models of the remains of Grecian architecture, which are to be seen at Paris. To adapt the exterior to our use, I drew a plan for the interior, with the apartments necessary for legislative, executive and judiciary purposes; and accommodated in their size and distribution to the form and dimensions of the building. These were forwarded to the Directors, in 1786, and were carried into execution, with some variations, not for the better.

Jefferson's plans, completed with the collaboration of Clérisseau, were forwarded to Virginia in January 1786, although almost another year passed before the model went on its way. In these plans numerous liberties beyond the substitution of the Ionic for the Corinthian order had to be taken with the Maison Carrée. The six-column portico is only two rather than three columns deep. Pilasters were omitted from the lateral walls and necessary windows substituted. Although the interior was planned for contemporary use, the temple ancestry of the building was recalled by a monumental hall, designed for Houdon's standing statue of General Washington. As construction had already begun before the final plans arrived, certain modifications had to be made. Nevertheless the result was better than might have been expected in a public building project where the architect was on the other side of the Atlantic. When Jefferson first saw the building, still unfinished, in December 1789 on his return from France, he wrote:

> Our new Capitol when the corrections are made of which it is susceptible will be an edifice of first rate dignity. Whenever it shall be finished with the proper ornaments belonging to it (which will not be in this age) it will be worthy of being exhibited along side the most celebrated remains of antiquity. Its extreme convenience has acquired it universal approbation.

The Duc de la Rochefoucauld-Liancourt unequivocally called the Richmond Capitol, "beyond comparison the most beautiful, the most noble, and the greatest in all America." It

was, incidentally, the first effort anywhere to create a large public building in the form of a Roman temple. Not until the Madeleine was begun in Paris in 1807 under Napoleon was this idea used in Europe. As the critic Fiske Kimball observed:

It was to the statesmen and rulers, like Jefferson, Napoleon, Catherine II, and Ludwig, rather than to the professional architects, that the direct reproduction of classical models made its appeal – the Virginia Capitol and the Madeleine are similar products of their creation.... Jefferson's provincial insistence upon the support of classical authority thus anticipated by twenty years the attempt of Napoleon to gain the same sanction for his own empire. Not merely in America, but in the development of modern classic architecture as a whole, the design of the Virginia Capitol is a landmark of the first importance.

Jefferson helped shape the architecture of the capital of the nation as well as that of his own state. He constantly endeavored to impress the principles of classical order upon the seat of the new government. When Thomas Jefferson reported to President Washington and took over his duties as Secretary of State on 21 March 1790, the seat of government was New York City. But by July the Residence Act of 1790 had been passed which provided that after ten years in Philadelphia, the capital was to be established on the banks of the Potomac River at a site to be determined by the President. The Secretary of State was soon advising the President with a view to creating a capital on an ordered plan. In a memorandum of 29 August 1790 he urged that the permission to acquire "a territory not exceeding ten miles square" be interpreted to include enough land not only for public buildings but for a new city laid out in streets of 100 to 120 feet in width, "at right angles as in Philadelphia," with preference for "squares of at least 200 yards each way, which will be of about 8 acres each." He proposed lots of fifty-foot frontage, their depths to extend to the diagonals of the square; as to restrictions on building, he wrote:

I doubt much whether the obligation to build the houses at a given distance from the street, contributes to its beauty; it produces a disgusting monotony. All persons make this complaint against Philadelphia. The contrary practice varies the appearance, and is much more convenient to the inhabitants.

In Paris it is forbidden to build a house beyond a given height, and it is admitted to be a good restriction. It keeps down the price of ground, keeps the houses low and convenient, and the streets light and airy.

Although Jefferson drew sketches of a city plan in which he proposed the relationship of the President's House and the Capitol that was subsequently adopted, the plan for the federal city achieved by Major Pierre Charles L'Enfant superimposed upon Jefferson's rectangular grid a complicated system of diagonal avenues, with circles and squares at their intersections. Nevertheless Jefferson aided Major L'Enfant by the loan of plans of Frankfurt, Karlsruhe, Amsterdam, Strasbourg, Paris, Orléans, Bordeaux, Lyons, Montpellier, Marseilles, Turin, and Milan that he had procured during his travels. On 10 April 1791 he wrote L'Enfant:

Having communicated to the President, before he went away, such general ideas on the subject of the Town, as occurred to me, I make no doubt that, in explaining himself to you

on the subject, he has interwoven with his own ideas, such of mine as he approved: for fear of repeating therefore, what he did not approve, and having more confidence in the unbiassed state of his mind, than in my own, I avoid interfering with what he may have expressed to you. Whenever it is proposed to prepare plans for the Capitol, I should prefer the adoption of some one of the models of antiquity, which have had the approbation of thousands of years, and for the President's House I should prefer the celebrated fronts of modern buildings, which have already received the approvation of all good judges. Such are the Galerie du Louvre, the Gardes meubles, (Gabriel buildings facing the Place de la Concorde) and the two fronts of the Hotel de Salm.

On the same day he wrote President Washington with an ingenious suggestion for raising the architectural quality of the private buildings of the new capital.

While in Europe I selected about a dozen or two of the handsomest fronts of private buildings of which I have the plates. Perhaps it might decide the taste of the new town, were these to be engraved here, and distributed gratis among the inhabitants of Georgetown. The expense would be trifling.

Alas, this good idea was never tried.

When Major L'Enfant, who was to have designed the public buildings of the federal city (named "Washington" in the fall of 1791), was dismissed before he could begin, Jefferson suggested architectural competitions for the Capitol and the President's House. For the latter he personally tried his hand at two designs; one based on the Parisian models he had suggested to L'Enfant, and the other, which he submitted anonymously in the competition, an enlargement of Palladio's Villa Rotunda. The prize was awarded in July 1792 to James Hoban, an Irish architect living in Charleston, South Carolina, for the design of the Georgian country seat that all Americans know today as the White House. Although Jefferson did not prepare a finished design for the Capitol competition, he passed to Stephen Hallet, a French architect then settled in Philadelphia, a sketch for a domical structure with four projecting wings, based on the Pantheon in Paris. The prize was, however, awarded to an amateur, Dr William Thornton, for another domical design with wings. The cornerstone for the new Capitol was laid on 18 September 1793.

The ten years spent by the United States government in Philadelphia were not sufficient to make the new capital on the Potomac elegant or habitable. When President John Adams arrived in Washington in November 1800 the White House was still far from finished; Vice President Jefferson lodged as best he could in Conrad's boarding house at the corner of New Jersey Avenue and C. Street. This was within easy reach of the Capitol, of which only the north or Senate wing was completed. The Capitol and the White House were separated by a muddy, mile-long morass through which Pennsylvania Avenue extended as an inadequate causeway. When Thomas Jefferson was elected as President of the United States, he moved to the President's House, on 19 March 1801. A newspaper writer jocularly described the White House as "big enough for two emperors, one pope, and the grand lama in the bargain." Being in a position to influence official architecture, President Jefferson took bold steps to improve the capital.

One of his first acts was to dignify Pennsylvania Avenue by the planting of rows of trees

that, in the manner of a Parisian boulevard, separated roadways from footways. He offered the post of Surveyor of Public Buildings to the English-trained architect Benjamin Henry Latrobe, who pushed forward the construction of the south wing of the Capitol and made interior alterations in the already completed north wing. Although Jefferson and Latrobe discussed modifications in Dr Thornton's plan for the central domed structure, work was not undertaken on this crowning feature of the Capitol. When President Jefferson left office in 1809 the Capitol consisted simply of independent north and south wings, linked only by a temporary wooden passageway. The President's House, although completed on the exterior, was only partially plastered within, and no provision had been made for adequate dependencies or treatment of the grounds. Although President Jefferson preferred to expend on the Capitol any substantial sums available, something was accomplished in the house year by year. In 1804 he drew plans for connecting it by colonnades with the executive departments that flanked it. As the ground fell away to the south, he proposed to have cellars, stables, and other dependencies entered from the colonnades as at Monticello, with terraces for promenades above them. In 1807 Latrobe drew plans for future alterations, incorporating Jefferson's suggestions, which included a great semi-circular portico on the south facade.

When Jefferson reached an age where he considered the accomplishments by which he most wished to be remembered, he provided his grandson with an inscription for the obelisk above his grave that described him as "Author of the Declaration of American Independence of the Statute of Virginia for religious freedom, and Father of the University of Virginia." Just as the last of these for him outweighed his service as President of the United States, so the design of the University of Virginia represents the culmination of his career as an architect. While still President, Jefferson had in 1804–5 dreamed of building a university in the form of "an academical village rather than of one large building." In 1810 he expressed the idea in words that foreshadowed what he began to create at Charlottesville after his two-term presidency:

> A small and separate lodge for each professorship, with only a hall below for his class, and two chambers above for himself; joining these lodges by barracks for a certain portion of the students, opening into a covered way to give a dry communication between all the schools. The whole of these arranged around an open square of grass or trees.

Although the University of Virginia was only chartered by the General Assembly in 1819, Jefferson completed in 1817 a plan for the first professorial pavilions, with their accompanying dormitories. From private subscriptions, money was raised to buy land and to begin to make Jefferson's educational and architectural plans a reality. Construction began with the present Pavilion VII, West Lawn, whose cornerstone was laid on 6 October 1817. The following year the Assembly appropriated $15,000 to found a state university and appointed a commission, of which Jefferson was chairman, to select a site and bring the institution into being. The commission agreed that the new university should be established in Albemarle County. The Board of Visitors of the University of Virginia, created by the 1819 charter, promptly elected Jefferson Rector, thus enabling him to carry out his ideas for the choice of faculty, courses of study, the purchase of books, and the construction of the necessary

buildings. Thus in his seventies, ostensibly in retirement at Monticello, he embarked upon still another career.

Four days after the authorization of the first pavilion, on 9 May 1817, he wrote to Dr William Thornton describing his plan and saying:

> Now what we wish is that these pavilions, as they will show themselves above the dormitories, shall be models of taste and good architecture, and of variety of appearance, no two alike, so as to serve as specimens for the Architectural lecturer. Will you set your imagination to work and sketch some designs for us? No matter how loosely with the pen, without the trouble of referring to scale or rule; for we want nothing but the outline of the architecture, as the internal must be arranged according to local convenience. A few sketches such as need not take you a moment will greatly oblige us.

Dr Thornton replied promptly, sending two sketches, and making various suggestions. Jefferson then wrote in similar vein to B.H. Latrobe, who made significant contributions to the evolution of the plan. Jefferson's early site plan had provided for nine pavilions, placed at equal distances from each other around three sides of an open-ended square. Thornton and Latrobe had both been concerned about the weakness of the corners in this early plan. Latrobe not only proposed placing pavilions at the corners, but suggested enlarging the central pavilion at the end of the square into a monumental structure with a hexastyle portico and a Roman dome over a circular lecture hall.

Jefferson wholeheartedly embraced Latrobe's suggestion of a dome, which gave him the opportunity to experiment with one of his favorite classical forms. He had a predilection for cubes and spheres. In designing the Capitol at Richmond he was inspired by the Maison Carrée, which he regarded "as the most perfect model existing of what may be called Cubic architecture." The Pantheon in Rome, which he considered the nearest thing to perfection in spherical architecture, provided him with a point of departure for the Rotunda, which was to become the dominating central feature for the whole "academical village." In adapting it for use at the University of Virginia, he reduced it to half-scale and made important changes in its form. Although the interior of the Pantheon seemed to Jefferson one of the world's finest rooms, he considered its exterior "dumpy," for it was actually not so much a sphere as a relatively low segment of a cylinder, surmounted by a dome. In his design he increased the height to a point where the vertical dimension equalled the horizontal, thus achieving a perfect sphere, as will be seen in his drawings for section and elevation of the Rotunda. This gave him under his "Dome Room," which was to be the library, an additional lower floor, 16 feet high. On that level he created three magnificent oval rooms, two of them 48 by 28 feet and one 37 by 16 feet. These with a 57-foot hall in the shape of an hourglass neatly filled his circle. Rooms of similar shape, but with lower ceilings, were in the basement. Thus he provided needed space for administration, religious worship, and public examinations in the finest group of oval rooms constructed in the United States. The circular library on the second floor, ringed by a gallery supported by twin columns, preserved the proportions of the Pantheon in its relation to the dome. Arcades on either side of the Rotunda at the basement level were designed as gymnasia.

Although the construction of Pavilion VII, West Lawn, had already begun, Jefferson

radically altered his site plan, substituting for the open square a narrow rectangle, which was better suited to the contours of the ground. The Rotunda dominated the north side of the rectangle. On the east and west sides were five pavilions each. In this final version, pavilions and student rooms were no longer symetrically disposed. There was, rather, a pavilion at each end of the West and East Lawns, while the number of student rooms between pavilions increased as the plan moved from north to south in order to create an illusory perspective that made the rectangle seem longer. On the West Lawn there are four student rooms between Pavilions I and III; between III and V there are six; between V and VII seven, and between VII and IX ten; the same *trompe l'œil* naturally prevails on the East Lawn.

Just as the Rotunda reflects the Pantheon, so the ten pavilions "serve as specimens for the Architectural lecturer" in offering a variety of Roman or Palladian orders. On the West Lawn the pavilions represent: I Diocletian's Baths: Doric; III Palladio: Corinthian; V Palladio: Ionic with modillions; VII Palladio: Doric; IX Temple of Fortuna Virilis: Ionic. Those on the East Lawn offer this sequence: II Temple of Fortuna Virilis: Ionic; IV Albano: Doric; VI Theatre of Marcellus: Ionic; VIII Diocletian's Baths: Corinthian; X Theatre of Marcellus: Doric. Although Pavilion VII was inspired by Dr Thornton's suggestion, and V, III, VIII, IX and X owe something to Latrobe's, in all cases the final drawings and detailed execution were Jefferson's.

Behind each of the ten pavilions were gardens, enclosed by serpentine walls, while behind the gardens on each side groups of five buildings called the Ranges contained students' rooms, entered from exterior colonnades. The end and central buildings of both East and West Ranges were varied by "hotels" which served for dining. Only five years after the cornerstone of Pavilion VII was laid, Jefferson was proudly able thus to report on the progress of construction:

[We] have completed all the buildings proposed ... ten distinct houses or pavilions containing each a lecturing room with generally four other apartments and the accommodation of a professor and his family, and with a garden, and the requisite family offices; six hotels for dieting the students, with a single room in each for a refectory, and two rooms, a garden and offices for the tenant, and a hundred and nine dormitories, sufficient each for the accommodation of two students, arranged in four distinct rows between the pavilions and hotels, and united with them by covered ways; which buildings are all in readiness for occupation, except that there is still some plaistering to be done now in hand, which will be finished early in the present season, the garden grounds and garden walls to be completed, and some columns awaiting their capitals not yet received from Italy.

The Rotunda had still not been begun, for want of funds, but construction started in 1823. By 5 October 1824 it was roofed, and on the twelfth of that month a public dinner for General Lafayette was held in the Dome Room. Classes opened at the University on 7 March 1825, although many final details of the Rotunda were still incomplete when Jefferson died on 4 July 1826. This masterpiece of his architecture was gravely damaged by fire in 1895. In spite of unanimous agreement by the faculty that the interior should be restored to its original form, Stanford White, the architect charged with reconstruction, radically altered its form to accommodate a growing library. Happily in 1972 federal and private funds were obtained that will permit the restoration of the interior to Jefferson's design.

Nineteenth-century print of the University of Virginia:
"I contemplate the University of Virginia as the future bulwark of the human mind in this hemisphere."

The west front of Monticello.

The creation of the University of Virginia was, both architecturally and intellectually, the crowning accomplishment of Jefferson's life. When one considers that he designed the buildings, supervised country workmen in their construction, extracted funds from a reluctant Assembly, prevented legislators from tampering with designs, and in addition created a curriculum and rounded up a faculty, it is a fantastic accomplishment for only eight years; it is even more fantastic that he achieved it between his seventy-fifth and eighty-second years! Monticello is a distillation of the mature taste of an architect who, with time running against him, created the most elegant and harmonious "academical village" that the United States has ever seen, or is ever likely to see. Jefferson was clearly as competent an architect as he was a public servant. Fiske Kimball summed matters up well when he wrote:

The estimate of Jefferson as architect cannot now be doubted. Though not a professional, he was nevertheless an architect in the true modern sense, making the preliminary studies, working drawings, and full-size details, specifying the materials, and supervising the erection of a large number of buildings, usually without assistance from any one. Even where he collaborated with others or asked their advice, as on the Virginia Capitol and the University, the chief honors of the design remain with him. His architectural draughtsmanship, as early illustrated in the drawings for Monticello, was beyond comparison with the crude methods of other native designers of the same time, and remained unrivaled here until the advent of trained architects from abroad during the last decades of the eighteenth century. In constructive ingenuity he yielded to none, though lacking in sobering apprenticeship and prone to let artistic enthusiasm overrule practical judgment. Although like Bulfinch and Thornton, men widely honored today as architects, he had no formal instruction in the art, and gained his knowledge from travel and from books, he had advantages over them in both respects, and had, besides, a contact with foreign professionals which they had never enjoyed. In draughtsmanship Bulfinch never surpassed him; in extent of practice Thornton fell far behind. Both were equally with him amateurs in spirit, and he was equally with them a professional, in all but the acceptance of money for his services.

The University of Virginia: "Our university is the last of my mortal cares, and the last service I can render my country."

The Declaration of Independence, by John Trumbull,
painted about 1787.

THE DECLARATION OF INDEPENDENCE

Henry Steele Commager

On 26 May 1776, that indefatigable correspondent, John Adams, who represented Massachusetts at the second Continental Congress, wrote exultantly to his friend James Warren that "every post and every day rolls in upon us independence like a torrent." Well might he rejoice, for this was what he and his cousin Samuel and his new friend Thomas Jefferson had hoped and worked for almost since the Congress had convened in May of the previous year, this rallying of public opinion to the cause of independence. It helped, to be sure, that the fatuous George III had proclaimed the colonies in rebellion, and thus helped the Americans to take him at his word. But the turning point, certainly in public opinion, had come with the publication, in January 1776, of the sensational *Common Sense*, from the pen of Thomas Paine, the most gifted political propagandist in all history. And as if to vindicate Paine's aphorism that it was ridiculous for a continent to belong to an island, Washington proceeded to drive General Howe out of Boston, thus demonstrating that Americans need not stand on the defensive, but could vindicate themselves in military strategy quite as well as in political.

All that spring the political current flowed toward independence. In February the Congress had taken the ominous step of authorizing privateers; in March it ventured into diplomatic independence by sending the hapless Silas Deane to France to negotiate for aid; in April it declared economic independence by opening its ports to the trade of all nations – except Britain. No less impetuous was the radical change of sentiment in the states. As early as 26 March, South Carolina adopted a constitution which by implication repudiated the royal connection. Early the next month her sister state to the north instructed her delegates to the Congress to support independence, and in May Rhode Island followed suit. Now Massachusetts and Virginia, from the beginning the leaders in organizing resistance to Britain, took action that proved decisive. On 10 May the Provisional Congress of Massachusetts voted to sound out the towns on the question of independence, and the towns declared that they were ready. Virginia did not lag behind. On 15 May a convention met at the historic Raleigh Tavern in Williamsburg and voted unanimously to call upon Congress to declare for independence. On the very day of the Virginia resolution, the Congress took the fateful step of voting that "every kind of authority under the Crown should be totally suppressed," and recommended that the states set up independent governments.

Now the stage was set for the historic event. On 7 June, Richard Henry Lee of Virginia – "the Cicero of America" – introduced three resolutions calling for independence, foreign alliances, and confederation. The radicals wanted unanimity, and voted to postpone the final vote for three weeks, thus allowing time for debate, and for the hesitant and the faint-hearted to come over – or step out. Meantime Congress appointed a committee to prepare "a declaration of independence": Dr Franklin, John Adams, Roger Sherman, Robert Livingston, and, the youngest of all, Thomas Jefferson.

Jefferson had come up to the Continental Congress the previous year bringing with him "a reputation for literature, science and a happy talent of composition." His writings, said John Adams, who rarely had any good to say of others, "were remarkable for the peculiar felicity of expression." Back to Virginia in December 1775, Jefferson had not found it possible to return to the Congress until mid-May of the next spring, just in time to achieve immortality. In part because of that "peculiar felicity of expression," in part because he already had a reputation of working with dispatch, in part because it was thought that Virginia, as the oldest, the largest, and the most deeply committed of the states should take the lead, the committee unanimously turned to Jefferson to prepare a draft declaration. We know a good deal about the composition of that draft: that Jefferson wrote it standing up at his desk (still preserved) in the second-floor parlor of a young German bricklayer named Graff and that he completed it in two weeks. We have his word for it (which is not quite the same as knowing) that he "turned neither to book nor pamphlet" and that all the authority of the Declaration "rests on the harmonizing sentiments of the day, whether expressed in conversation, in letters, printed essays, or in the elementary books of public right, as Aristotle, Cicero, Locke, Sidney, etc." We know, too, that the body of the Declaration – that long and depressing catalog of the train of abuses and usurpations "designed to reduce the American people under absolute despotism" – was taken over from a parallel list of grievances which Jefferson had included in his draft constitution for Virginia only a few weeks earlier. And we can readily accept Jefferson's statement made fifty years later that the object of the Declaration was "an appeal to the tribunal of the world" – that "decent respect to the opinion of Mankind" invoked in the Declaration itself; certainly it was

> not to find out new principles, or new arguments, never before thought of; not merely to say things which had never been said before; but to place before mankind the common sense of the subject, in terms so plain and firm as to command their assent, and to justify ourselves in the independent stand we are compelled to take. Neither aiming at originality of principle or sentiment, nor yet copied from any particular and previous writing, it was intended to be an expression of the American mind, and to give to that expression the proper tone and spirit called for by the occasion.

In the end the Declaration was adopted pretty much as Jefferson had written it. There were, to be sure, a good many verbal changes – some twenty altogether (mostly improvements) – and Jefferson was persuaded to add three short paragraphs to his original text. The most grievous change, in his eyes, was the elimination of what John Adams called his "vehement philippic" against Negro slavery and the slave trade – one of the earliest expressions of Jefferson's lifelong detestation of the "peculiar institution." In some ways it

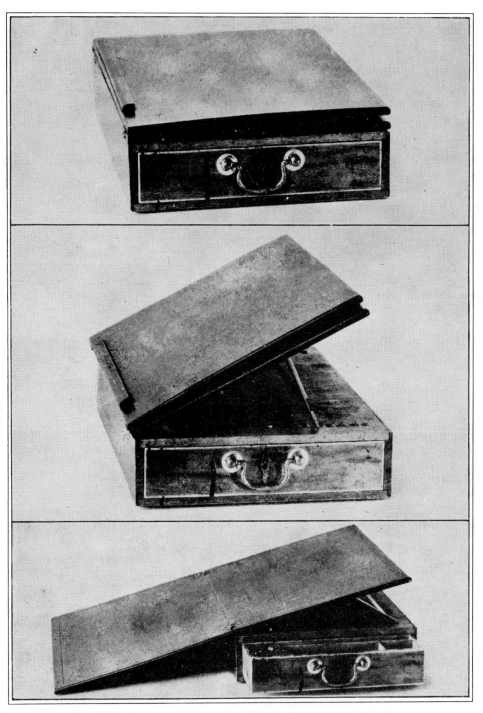

Jefferson's portable writing desk on which he wrote
the Declaration of Independence.

was well that that paragraph dropped out, for in a curious way it struck a false note: it was rhetorical without being passionate, and it was bad history. Alas, these were not the reasons why it was eliminated, it was rather the reluctance of southern delegates to endorse so extreme an attack upon slavery.

After almost three days of debate Congress adopted the Declaration of Independence, though New York still refrained from voting. Jefferson remembered later that on the 4th of July "the Declaration was signed by every member present except Mr Dickinson," and that legend has entered American history and art: witness the famous John Trumbull painting now hanging in the Library of Congress. Actually, however, it was not until 19 July that Congress provided that the Declaration be engrossed on parchment, and it was on 2 August that the document, "being engrossed and compared at the table" with Jefferson's original, was signed by all the members present.

Interestingly enough it is not Jefferson, but the more passionate and volatile John Adams, who has left us the most moving commentary on the events of this week when the declaration was proposed, debated and voted:

> You will think me transported with enthusiasm [he wrote to his wife Abigail], but I am not. I am well aware of the toil and blood, and treasure that it will cost us to maintain this declaration and support and defend these states. Yet through all the gloom I can see the rays of ravishing light and glory. I can see that the end is more than worth all the means, and that posterity will triumph in that day's transaction, even although we should rue it, which I trust in God we shall not.

When Jefferson wrote that the Declaration was "an expression of the American mind," what he referred to was almost certainly the Preamble. That Preamble was an expression of more than the American mind; it was an expression of the mind of the Enlightenment – of the Age of Reason. It was because Jefferson was so broadly cosmopolitan that he could sum up the thinking of the Enlightenment in the realm of political philosophy, and because he was so authentically American that he could transform that philosophy into American principles and realize it in American institutions.

Nothing is more fascinating than this Preamble, which summed up with matchless lucidity, logic, and eloquence the philosophy which presided over the argument for the Revolution, for the creation of a new political system, and for the vindication of the rights of man – and all in less than two hundred words! It is here that we find the expression of what is universal rather than parochial, what is permanent rather than transient, in the American Revolution. For where most of the body of the Declaration was retrospective, the Preamble was prospective: in the years to come it would be translated into the basic institutions of the American Republic, and not of the American alone.

Consider the opening words of the Declaration: "When, in the course of human events...." That places the Declaration, and the Revolution, at once in the appropriate setting, against the background not merely of American or of British but of universal history; that connects it with the experience of men everywhere, not at a moment of history, but in every era. This concept of the place of America in history is underlined by successive

phrases of that great opening sentence. Thus the new nation is to assume its place "among the powers of the earth;" it is not the laws of the British Empire, or even of history, but of "Nature and Nature's God" which entitle Americans to an equal station; and it is "a decent respect to the opinions of *mankind*" that requires this justification. No other political document of the eighteenth century proclaimed so broad a purpose; no political document of our own day associates the United States so boldly with universal history and the cosmic system.

Turn then to those principles which Jefferson, serenely confident of their ultimate vindication, called "self-evident truths." Let us list them in order:

> That all men are created equal;
> That they are endowed with "unalienable rights;"
> That these rights include life, liberty, and the pursuit of happiness;
> That it is to *secure* these rights that government is instituted among men;
> That governments so instituted derive their powers from the consent of the governed;
> That when a form of government becomes destructive of these ends, men may alter or abolish it; and
> That men have the right, then, to institute new governments designed to effect their safety and happiness.

Now neither Jefferson nor the American people invented these principles. They were drawn from classical literature (with which all educated men of that day were familiar); they were elaborated by the generation of Lilburne, Cromwell, Sidney, Milton, and above all John Locke in seventeenth-century England; they were an integral part of the assumptions of the Age of Reason; they were – or appeared to be – rooted in American colonial experience. Jefferson's "self-evident truths" were no more original than were the arguments of Tom Paine's *Common Sense*; the Declaration of Independence was itself simply the common sense of the matter. That is one reason why it was so readily and so generally accepted; that was why it was read with rapture in so many parts of the globe. For the Declaration inspired radicals such as Joseph Priestley, and Horne Tooke, and John Cartwright in England, and rebels like Grattan and Fitzgerald in Ireland; it inspired the enthusiasm of those *philosophes* who were the precursors of the French Revolution, such as Mirabeau, Condorcet, Brissot, and Lafayette; it gave comfort to liberals everywhere: Johan Moser and Christoph Ebeling in Germany, Vittorio Alfieri and Gianrinaldi Carli in Italy, the intrepid Francis van der Kemp in Holland, who found refuge in America, Henrick Steffens in Denmark, and Isaac Iselin in Basle. It fired the spirit of Francisco Miranda, and of many other leaders of the South American crusade for independence, and perhaps freedom. It entered into the mainstream of history, and worked like a ferment all through the nineteenth and twentieth centuries; in 1945 Ho Chi Minh proclaimed the independence of Vietnam with a declaration modelled on that which Thomas Jefferson had written 170 years earlier.

What Americans did was more important than invent new principles; in the telling phrase of John Adams "they *realized* the theories of the wisest writers." They actualized them, they legalized them, they institutionalized them. That was, and remains, the supreme achievement

John Adams, the second President of the United
States. Adams and Jefferson died on the same day,
4 July 1826. Adams' last words were, "Thomas
Jefferson still survives."

of the American Revolution; indeed, in the longer perspective, that *was* the American Revolution.

Thus – if we take up Jefferson's principles one by one – the idea of natural rights was as old as Greek philosophy, and one which had been invoked again and again over the centuries. But it was only then, for the first time, that it was formalized and written into constitutional guarantees, only then that the notion which had for so long lingered in the realm of the abstract was endowed with life and clothed in the majestic raiment of the law. Thus for over two thousand years philosophers had argued that government is limited; the revolutionary generation went further, and insisted that God himself was bound by his own laws of justice and mercy. All well enough as long as men gave only lip service to this revolutionary idea. For in fact no government ever had been really limited, not voluntarily anyway: the history of government (as Americans read it) had been an unbroken record of tyranny, and every monarch in Europe still exercised tyranny: even George III, particularly George III. When Jefferson wrote that it was "to preserve rights" that governments were instituted among men, he meant just what he said, and so did those who signed the Declaration: that the function of government was to preserve the inalienable rights of men, and that if government failed in this duty, it forfeited its claim to legitimacy. After all, even before he wrote the Declaration, Jefferson had drawn up a model constitution and bill of rights for Virginia (neither was adopted but some of his suggestions were incorporated into both) and both these documents were designed to limit the power of government with the utmost care. Soon constitution makers were busy in every state of the new nation doing what Jefferson and his associates had done so well in the oldest of American commonwealths.

So, too, with the principle that government is formed by compact, and that governments thus formed derive all their power from that compact and are limited by its terms. An old theory, this, one which had bemused philosophers for centuries and had received classic formulation by John Locke in the seventeenth and Jean Jacques Rousseau in the eighteenth centuries. Whether in some remote past men ever had come together to set up government, we do not know; what we do know is that this was the way government originated in America, and the way it continued to originate for two centuries: in the compact in the hold of the tiny *Mayflower*; in those *Fundamental Orders* which the freemen of three frontier towns along the Connecticut drew up in 1639; in the constitution formed by the pioneers of the short-lived Transylvania colony in 1775; by the settlers of early Oregon who in 1843 convened the so-called Wolf conventions, took affairs into their own hands, and drew up the first Organic Law west of the Rockies; by the followers of John Frémont, who in 1846 launched the Bear Flag revolt, and met together to set up a "Republican Government which shall ensure ... liberty and virtue."

Thus, too, with what now seems a kind of intuitive genius, Americans solved that most intractable problem: how men make government; they institutionalized the solution in the constitutional convention, a contrivance which has some claim to be the most important political institution of modern times, for it provided the basic mechanisms of democracy. And along with these, it provided a legal way for men to "alter or abolish" governments: to alter by amendments, or to abolish by wiping the slate clean and drawing up a wholly new constitution. Thus, for the first time in history men legalized revolution. As Alexander

Hamilton wrote, the Constitutional Convention "substituted the mild influence of the law for the violent and sanguinary agency of the sword." Jefferson put it more elaborately: "Happy for us that when we find our constitution defective and insufficient to secure the happiness of our people, we can assemble with all the coolness of philosophers and set it to rights, while every other nation on earth must have recourse to arms to amend or restore their constitutions."

The implementation of other principles in the Preamble was more difficult if only because they did not lend themselves so readily to institutionalization. What, after all, did Jefferson mean by such terms as "created equal," or "pursuit of happiness?" These are not only difficult questions, they are in a sense unfair questions. No language, as James Madison observed, "is so copious as to supply words and phrases for every complex idea or so correct as not to include many equivocally denoting different ideas."

There is little doubt that Jefferson used, and that his associates in the Congress endorsed, the term "created equal" in a quite literal sense, for that is the sense in which the Enlightenment embraced and applied the term. What Jefferson meant was that in the eyes of nature (and doubtless of God) every child was *born* equal. All subsequent inequalities, those of race, color, sex, class, wealth, even of talents, derived not from nature but from society, or government, or law. Nature, after all, did not decree the inequality of blacks to whites. Nature did not decree the subordination of the female to the male – there was some ground for thinking it might be the other way around. Nature did not impose class distinctions, or political distinctions, or religious distinctions; it was not even certain that nature imposed physical or intellectual distinctions. Give every child an equal chance, from birth, at health, education, and happiness, and who could foresee the result? This was not merely Jefferson's idea, but one widely held by the *philosophes* whose pervasive principle was that men were everywhere and at all times fundamentally the same. Yet neither the *philosophes* nor the enlightened despots of the Old World made any effort to translate this principle of equality into practice, as did the Americans, Jefferson among them. That they did not succeed is a reflection on their authority, not on their wisdom. After all we of the twentieth century have not succeeded either, yet we do have the authority. What we lack is the will.

"Pursuit of happiness" is a more elusive phrase, yet the idea that God and nature intended that men should be happy was a commonplace of eighteenth-century thought. In the Old World, however, happiness tended to be an elitist concept, something that the privileged few might possibly achieve by cultivating beauty and wisdom and leisure and the social graces: an expensive business, this, and not ordinarily available to the masses of the people. As America had no elite – not, certainly in the Old World sense of the term – happiness here was presumed to be available to all who were white, and it consisted, not in the enjoyment of art and literature, science and philosophy, and social position, but rather in material comfort, freedom, independence, and access to opportunity. Happiness meant milk for the children, and meat on the table, a well-built house and a well-filled barn, freedom from the tyranny of the state, the superstition of the church, the authority of the military, and the malaise of ignorance. Jefferson, who knew and indulged himself in the Old World forms of happiness, was entirely willing to abandon them – and indeed to banish them from his own country – in favor of the more simple, the more innocent, and the more just happiness which he

Thomas Jefferson II. ✗ 441

A portrait of Thomas Jefferson by Charles St. Mémin.

thought available in his own country. And to the attainment of these, and their preservation, he made not only philosophical contributions but practical contributions as important and as far-reaching as those made by any other man of his time.

A VIEW of the BOMBARDMENT of Fort McHenry, *near Baltimore, by the British fleet taken from the Observatory under the Command of Admirals Cochrane & Cockburn, on the morning of the 13 of Sep. 1814 which lasted 24 hours, & thrown from 1500 to 1800 shells in the Night attempted to land by forcing a passage up the ferry branch but were repulsed with great loss.*

The bombardment of Fort McHenry in 1814 during
the War of 1812. Jefferson favored the war: "The
sword once drawn, full justice must be done.
'Indemnification for the past and security for the
future,' should be painted on our banners."

JEFFERSON AS A
CIVIL LIBERTARIAN
Leonard Levy

There is a story about two Roman soothsayers whose job was to edify the populace with prophecies that were intended to sustain the ancient faith. While solemnly examining the entrails of an ox for signs and portents, they winked at each other. Historians who perpetuate an idealized image of Jefferson should be no less realistic about their own craft. William James once wrote that the notion of God's omnipotence must be relinquished if God is to be kept as a religious object, because the only God worthy of the name must be finite. Similarly the notion of Jefferson's perfection as a libertarian must be relinquished if he is to be kept as a model of values to which we aspire as a nation. The only worthy Jefferson must also be finite. Yet the Jefferson who has seized the American historical imagination is the Jefferson of nearly infinite wisdom on questions of personal freedom.

Although history can be quoted to support any cause, just as scripture can be quoted by the devil, no wrenching of the past can alter a transcending fact about Thomas Jefferson: he believed in the right and capacity of the ordinary man to live responsibly in freedom. Lincoln testified for the ages that the principles of Jefferson were "the definitions and axioms of free society." It is Jefferson, if not Lincoln himself, who is the central figure in the history of American democracy. He fervently believed that the will and welfare of the people were the only prop and purpose of government. Others pitted liberty and equality against each other as if a tension, even a contradiction, existed between them. To Jefferson liberty and equality were complementary qualities of the condition to which man had a moral right. He suffused the Declaration of Independence with an ethical philosophy – not merely a political or legal one – that permanently nourished the American spirit.

Jefferson's principles sprang from the deepest aspirations of the people. A communion of sentiment tied him to them, despite his tendency to shrink from too close a personal contact. He expressed himself in literary utterance that was a model of clarity and beauty – understandable, appealing, and almost unfailingly humane. With crisp eloquence he memorably voiced the noblest hopes for human fortune on earth. In so doing, he somehow illuminated the lives of his compatriots – their needs, their best values, their ambitions. His deepest sympathies belonged to the disadvantaged and downtrodden; his deepest trust was in the power of his fellow men to do justice and to fulfil themselves on their own terms, self-reliant and self-governing, as long as they had the opportunity to make informed, unfettered choices; his deepest faith was in the emancipating effect of education and freedom on the

human personality. His confidence in popular government, bounded only by respect for minority rights, was anchored in a belief that counting heads was a much better way to rule than breaking them. It secured sounder policies, more beneficial to the general welfare, than those determined by the privileged few.

Jefferson "still survives," to quote the famous deathbed words of John Adams, because a free people still cherishes the spirit of liberty and its foremost exponent among the founders of the Republic. Jefferson hated tyranny and war, poverty and privilege, bigotry and ignorance; he hated whatever crippled man's spirit or body. His influence was zealously devoted to securing the conditions of freedom that would make possible the "pursuit of happiness" by all. He championed free public education and attacked the aristocratic system of entail and primogeniture. He condemned slavery and recommended its gradual abolition. He saved untold thousands from bondage by championing the end of the foreign slave trade. He reformed the criminal code of his state, and he tightened the constitutional definition of treason to prevent the use of the criminal law as an instrument of political oppression. He advocated freedom of the press and resisted the noxious Alien and Sedition Acts. He insisted on subordination of the military to the civil authority. He converted Madison to the cause of adding the Bill of Rights to the new federal Constitution. He supported a broadening of the base of popular government by public-land grants that would enable every citizen to meet the property qualifications on the right to vote. Almost always Jefferson's impulses were generous and liberating. And on some matters, like religious liberty, he displayed a principled consistency.

When religious persecution still menaced Virginia, thanks to the legal establishment of the Church of England, Jefferson, in a magnificent collaboration with Madison, led a ten-year battle – the severest, said Jefferson, in which he had ever engaged – culminating in a victory for the free exercise of religion and separation of church and state. He believed, as had Roger Williams, that "compulsion stincks in God's notrils." Toleration, a mere concession from the state, was only less repugnant; at its best it implied no enforced tithes or civil disabilities. Jefferson believed that religion was a private duty which free men owed their Creator. The manner of discharging that duty was none of the state's business. It was, rather, an unquestionable and illimitable natural right to be exercised freely according to the dictates of conscience.

Although the Virginia Declaration of Rights of 1776 recognized the principle of religious liberty rather than toleration, Jefferson lost on the main issue of the relation of church to state. The legislature reserved for future decision the question of whether religion ought to be supported on a nonpreferential basis by a new establishment in which all denominations would proportionally share tax proceeds. When Patrick Henry, with the backing of Washington, Randolph, and Lee, introduced a measure to create a multiple establishment benefitting all churches, Jefferson countered with his Bill for Establishing Religious Freedom. It was a classic expression of the American creed on intellectual as well as religious liberty, although Jefferson never applied its "overt acts" test to the expression of political opinion. The test, which insured the widest possible latitude for the expression of religious opinion, was "that it is time enough for the rightful purposes of civil government for its officers to interfere when principles break out into overt acts against peace and good order."

The bill provided also that no man should be compelled to frequent or support any worship whatever, nor be restrained in any way on account of his religious opinions. The bill became law in 1785. Jefferson's pride of authorship was so great that he ranked the bill with the Declaration of Independence as contributions for which he most wanted to be remembered.

He faithfully adhered to the principles of his bill throughout his life. As President he departed from the precedents of Washington and Adams by refusing to recommend or designate any day for national prayer, fasting, or thanksgiving. For the President to recommend exercises of a religious character would, in his opinion, constitute an establishment of religion in violation of the First Amendment. Only a totally principled commitment to the privacy and voluntary nature of religious belief explained so exquisite a constitutional conscience.

Jefferson's consistency in applying the principle of the separation of church and state was also evident in the field of education. He was the complete secularist, opposed to the use of public funds for the teaching of religion in schools. His various proposals for establishing a system of public education in Virginia omitted religious instruction at a time when it was a prominent feature in the schools everywhere else. He was instrumental in the abolition of the school of divinity at the College of William and Mary, and when he founded the University of Virginia, neither the professorships nor the curriculum related to religion. Everywhere else in the colleges and universities of the country, ministers were commonly presidents and members of the boards, daily chapel attendance was compulsory, courses in religion were required, and professors of divinity had a prominent place on the faculties.

Jefferson cared very deeply about religious liberty. Diligent study and thought had given him a systematic theory, the most advanced of his age, and he put it into practice. His position was clearly defined, publicly stated, and vigorously defended. Although it exposed him to abusive criticism he carried on his fight for separation of church and state, and for the free exercise of religion, throughout his long public career without significant contradictions. In sum his thought on religious liberty was profoundly libertarian, and his actions suited his thought.

However, Jefferson's ideas on many other issues were not always libertarian; and when they were, his practice did not always match his professions. Between his words and deeds on religious liberty there was an almost perfect congruence, but it was not one that was characteristic of Jefferson as a civil libertarian. Historians and biographers have fixed a libertarian halo around his brow as if he were a plaster saint or a demigod in the pantheon of freedom. He has been depicted as a noble figure caught in a mythic stance: swearing eternal hostility to every form of tyranny over the mind of man. But Jefferson had his darker side: it should be recognized and understood.

His baffling complexity on all matters other than religious liberty has been the subject of critical analysis from his own time to the present. Historians have been fascinated with him as a figure of contradictions and ambiguities. The incandescent advocate of natural rights was a slaveholder; the strict constructionist of constitutional powers purchased Louisiana and adopted the Embargo; the philosopher wrote the *Manual of Parliamentary Practice*; the aristocrat championed democracy; and the democrat never introduced a proposal for universal manhood suffrage. A chiaroscuro of Jefferson would fill a huge canvas. But one

A map of Washington, D.C. engraved by Robert King
in 1818 showing the east front of the Capitol of the
United States as originally designed by William
Thornton and the south front of the President's
House as designed and executed by James Hoban.

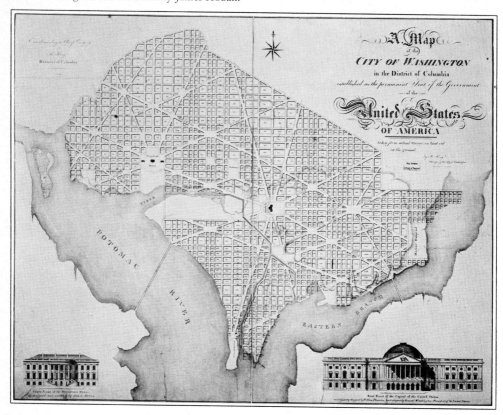

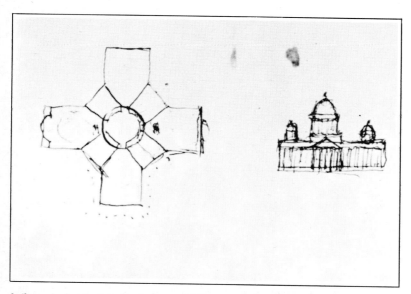

Jefferson's sketch of the Capitol, 1792. Jefferson set up
an architectural competition for the Capitol which
was won by William Thornton.

image has remained relatively pure and undisputed, if not indisputable: Jefferson as the apostle of liberty. Occasional inconsistencies between his actions and libertarian values have been regarded as momentary aberrations, the exceptions that proved the rule. Even unsympathetic historians have endorsed the traditional image that lays claim to our devotion and admiration, without ever suggesting more than the possibility that the democratic idol had a toe of clay. Sympathetic historians, including Commager, Malone, and Peterson, who are represented in the pages of this book, have written of Jefferson as wholly committed to the rights of man.

Freedom's apostle was not its apostate. Yet Jefferson's thoughts and actions on a variety of occasions and issues over an extended period followed a pattern that does not easily square with the conventional image. The familiar Jefferson is the one who, in his *Notes on the State of Virginia*, condemned temporary dictatorships even in time of war and impending invasion. The unfamiliar Jefferson, who requires our attention, is the one who wrote the following letter shortly after the acquittal of Burr and his fellow conspirators:

> I did wish to see these people get what they deserved; and under the maxim of the law itself, that *inter arma silent leges*, that in an encampment expecting daily attack from a powerful enemy, self-preservation is paramount to all law, I expected that instead of invoking the forms of the law to cover traitors, all good citizens would have concurred in securing them. Should we have ever gained our Revolution, if we had bound our hands by manacles of the law, not only in the beginning, but in any part of the revolutionary conflict? There are extreme cases where the laws become inadequate even to their own preservation, and where the universal resource is a dictator, or martial law.

The unfamiliar Jefferson at one time or another supported loyalty oaths; countenanced internment camps for political suspects; drafted a bill of attainder; urged prosecutions for seditious libel; trampled on the Fourth Amendment's protection against unreasonable searches and seizures; condoned military despotism; used the army to enforce laws in time of peace; censored reading; chose professors for their political opinions; and endorsed the doctrine that the means, however odious, were justified by the ends.

The conventional image of Jefferson has been partially fashioned from a national impulse to have a libertarian hero larger than life. When the American people honor Jefferson as freedom's foremost exponent, they reflect their own ideals and aspirations more, perhaps, than they reflect history. The darker side of both Jefferson and of the American experience is not venerated, but its existence is undeniable. American history yields more than one tradition. Abridgements of civil liberty are as old a story as the nation itself; Jefferson embodied and reflected both traditions.

From the standpoint of civil liberties Jefferson's conduct during the revolutionary war conformed with the maxim that the laws are silent in time of war. The benefits of another maxim, more congenial to the spirit of liberty, let justice be done though the heavens fall, were denied to citizens suspected of tory thoughts and sympathies. The imperatives of victory and political survival superseded the moral and legal values that normally claimed the respect of humane, libertarian leaders. Jefferson, like the others, believed that there could be no toleration for serious differences of opinion on the issue of independence, no

acceptable alternative to complete submission to the patriot cause. Everywhere there was unlimited liberty to praise it, none to criticize it. Jefferson, as a member of Congress, a leader of the Virginia legislature, and a wartime governor, declared himself to be an enemy to traitorous views. He and John Adams drafted the first American Articles of War, punishing "traitorous or disrespectful words" against the United States. In 1806 President Jefferson signed into law the bill that altered this provision by punishing any "contemptuous or disrespectful words" against the President or Congress. This clause, adopted in time of peace and under a Constitution protecting freedom of speech – and passed after the Sedition Act of 1798 which it resembled – showed a Jeffersonian insensitivity to the First Amendment.

During the Revolution, Virginia's civilian counterpart of the military code against traitorous opinions consisted of a vicious loyalty oath and an act against crimes injurious to independence but less than treason. Jefferson supported both and had a hand in writing the loose prohibition against any "word" or attempt to "persuade" in behalf of British authority. This act passed the abyss between defensible war measures such as the punishment of incitement to seditious conduct, and the repression of opinion such as punishment of a toast to the king's health. The same statute, which was broadened when Jefferson was Governor, was used as a dragnet against persons suspected of treason or disaffection but against whom proof was lacking.

The loyalty oath, which in Jefferson's phrase was aimed at "traitors in thought, but not in deed," stripped non-jurors of their civil rights. They could not vote, sue, or sell property; Jefferson himself wrote the amendment subjecting them to triple taxation. He also helped write the act retroactively legalizing the internment of political suspects in time of danger, and when Governor he supported a similar bill authorizing him to jail or intern in places of security persons suspected of political disaffection. Many who were jailed languished without a hearing and without even learning of the charges against them.

The most striking departure from standards of due process of law was undoubtedly the Bill of Attainder and Outlawry, drafted by Jefferson in 1778, against the tory officer Josiah Philips and unnamed members of his gang of reputed traitors and murderers. An attainder is a legislative declaration of guilt and punishment, devoid of judicial and procedural safeguards. Outlawry, which had been in bad odor since Magna Carta, was controlled in England by an elaborate common-law process; Jefferson's bill declared an open hunting season on Philips and the unnamed men whose guilt was legislatively assumed. Anyone might be killed with impunity on the mere supposition that he was an associate of Philips. Although Edmund Randolph and others connected with the attainder-and-outlawry subsequently regretted it and expressed their horror at what had been done, Jefferson continued long after to defend his attainder and to insist that an outlaw had no right to the privileges of citizenship or to ordinary legal process. He also sought to exclude from an historical account of the case opinions to the contrary. In 1815, when musing on the bill of 1778, he wrote: "I was then thoroughly persuaded of the correctness of the proceeding, and am more and more convinced by reflection. If I am in error, it is an error of principle." The libertarian standard was the one proposed by Jefferson himself in 1783 when he prepared a new draft constitution for Virginia, explicitly denying to the legislature any power "to pass any bill of attainder (or other law declaring any person guilty) of treason or felony."

The Capitol as it looked when Thomas Jefferson was
President: the House of Representatives at the right
and the Senate at the left. There was a connecting
passage where the Rotunda now stands.

Jefferson's reputation as a libertarian derived in part from his habitual repetition of in-spired reveries about freedom, expressed in memorable aphorisms. On countless occasions, for example, he testified to his belief in liberty of the press; his maxims on the subject earned him a place with Milton and Mill. However, there were significant inconsistencies between his deeds and his words. In the long run his pen was mightier than his practice, for his rhetoric helped to create an American creed and to shape the standards by which even he must be measured. There was, for example, that imperishable remark in his first Inaugural Address in which he said, "If there be any among us who would wish to dissolve this Union or to change its republican form, let them stand undisturbed as monuments of the safety with which error of opinion may be tolerated where reason is left free to combat it." Yet his views on the scope of permissable freedom of political expression were very narrow and did not change even after Madison, Gallatin, and others in his camp had developed a very broad theory of free speech and press.

In 1776 Jefferson proposed a constitution for Virginia without a clause on either speech or press. He also, incidentally, omitted guarantees against exclusive privileges, excessive bail, general search warrants, compulsory self-incrimination, and most of the positive rights of the criminally accused which the Virginia Declaration of Rights included. The restrictive-ness of his thinking on political expression is suggested by a trial clause on religious liberty: "This [the liberty of religious opinions] shall not be held to justify any seditious preaching or conversation against the authority of the civil government." He was groping for a formula to ensure the unfettered right to propagate religious opinions without relinquishing the power of the state to curb dangerous political opinions. He finally settled on the "overt acts" test for religious opinions, but, significantly, he never applied that test to political opinions and never questioned the conventional doctrine that the government can be criminally assaulted by seditious words. In a draft constitution for Virginia in 1783 and again in a letter to Madison in 1788, he proposed that the presses be subject to prosecution for falsity, especially for false facts affecting the peace of the country. This was a particularly dangerous standard or test, because in political matters, one man's falsity is another's truth. Had Jefferson's test prevailed and been taken seriously, its suppressive possibilities can well be imagined in the midst of a foreign policy controversy like the ones provoked by Jay's treaty, or the Louisiana Purchase, or the Embargo. Noteworthy too is the fact that Jefferson did not propose that in trials for seditious libel the jury, rather than the judge, should be empowered to return a verdict on the alleged criminality of the defendant's words.

Jefferson's celebrated opposition to the Sedition Act of 1798, which he did not publicly attack, was primarily based on a states' rights doctrine. His concept of federalism, rather than a theory of free speech, dominated his thinking. Far from assaulting the concept of seditious libel, he contended that the Sedition Act was unconstitutional because the First Amendment intended that the states alone might wield the power of abridging the freedom of the press. On half a dozen instances when he was President, in both his correspondence and public statements, he continued to endorse the exclusive power of the states to prosecute criminal libels against the government. On one occasion he urged a specific state prosecution and hoped that it would be emulated in other states. On another occasion, which his Federalist enemies exaggerated as Jefferson's "reign of terror," he permitted common-law prosecutions

of his critics in a federal court during his Presidency.

Jefferson was a thin-skinned, fierce political partisan. He once remarked that whether his neighbor said that there were twenty gods or none "neither picks my pocket nor breaks my leg." But political opinions could pick his pocket or break his leg. His threshold of tolerance for hateful political ideas was less than generous. Eloquently and felicitously he declared himself in favor of freedom of speech and press, but invariably either in favor of the liberty of his own political allies or merely in abstract propositions. Under concrete circumstances he found it easy to make exceptions when the freedom of his opponents was at stake. To Madison the test of free speech or press was whether a man could with impunity express himself openly even in times of stress and on matters that counted deeply. Freedom for the other fellow was the test, not freedom for the friendly opponent, but for the one with the detested, scurrilous, and outrageous views who challenged on fundamentals and whose criticism cut to the bone. Jefferson simply did not concern himself about such freedom. He cared deeply for the intellectual liberty of religious, scientific, or philosophical heretics – unless political heresies of his own adherence were involved.

During the Burr case he betrayed an insensibility to standards of criminal justice and behaved as if he were prosecutor, judge, and jury. He wanted convictions on the treason charge and was not particularly scrupulous as to how he got them. After Burr had been freed by a federal grand jury in the West, the President mobilized public opinion against him by declaring him to be guilty beyond question, although there were at the time nothing but rumors and suspicions on which to base a judgement – and in any case it was the business of a jury, not of the President, to declare Burr guilty. To secure a conviction, Jefferson accepted the word of a real traitor, General Wilkinson, and praised him as a loyal and honorable patriot. Jefferson found it necessary also to betray a witness by violating a pledge not to reveal or use against him his self-incriminatory statements. The President was also prepared to sign a bill that would have suspended the writ of habeas corpus in order to keep in military custody Wilkinson's illegally held prisoners. Jefferson assaulted the integrity and loyalty of the federal courts which ensured due process in Burr's case, and he accused them of protecting traitors. He supported a constitutional amendment that would have made the judges removable from office by vote of Congress. He favored committing a prisoner to trial on probable suspicion rather than on prima facie evidence of guilt. He yearned for a packed jury in Burr's case. He flirted with doctrines of constructive treason when citing as proof of Burr's guilt the "universal belief" of his guilt, the "rumors" of his guilt, newspaper stories, and Burr's flight from arrest. Yet Jefferson admitted that he did not know what overt acts of treason would be proved by the government three months after he had publicly declared Burr guilty and three weeks after the indictment. He suspected critics of the government's case as being associates in Burr's treason.

Jefferson also condoned Wilkinson's despotic acts in New Orleans. The General defied both the civil authorities and judicial writs of habeas corpus; he arrested men without warrants – including a judge and an editor; he transported his prisoners in chains out of the territory, denying them trial by jury of the vicinage. He rifled the mails in an illegal search for evidence, generally terrified the city, and subordinated the civil to the military, acting as if he were ruling by martial law – and to all this Jefferson applauded and merely cautioned

Wilkinson against arresting on suspicion only for fear that he might lose public support. The President judged his general not by legal or moral standards, but by the extent to which his actions might be supported by public opinion. An officer must risk going beyond the law when the public preservation requires, wrote Jefferson. He informed Governor Claiborne that the political opposition "will try to make something of the infringement of liberty by the military arrest and deportation of citizens, but if it does not go beyond such offenders as Swartwout, Bollman, Burr, Blennerhassett, etc., they will be supported by public approbation." As in the Philips attainder case, Jefferson's position was that bad men do not deserve the benefit of the usual forms of the law. His position was reprehensible on both constitutional and libertarian grounds. His final view on Wilkinson's actions – that there were only two opinions: one held by "the guilty" and the other "by all honest men" – betrayed an impulse to stamp all opposition and criticism as illegitimate.

That same impulse, so dangerous to democratic procedure, was revealed abundantly during the Embargo era, when a national policy of passive resistance was enforced at home by bayonets. Jefferson can not be faulted for the Embargo itself as an experiment in the avoidance of war, but for the manner of its adoption, its execution, and its abridgements of public and private liberty, as well as its failure, he bears the greatest responsibility. The failure was the failure of responsible democratic leadership. The task of the President was to enlist bipartisan support by educating the nation on the need for complying with laws that required a free people to suffer loss of some liberty and acute economic privation for the sake of a national goal. But Jefferson never explained, never gave the facts, and never sought understanding, and he treated Congress as he did the nation, expecting blind, dutiful obedience. His sphinx-like silence during fifteen months of agonizing national trial contributed to the subversion of principles of self-government.

The first four Embargo acts – the last of which was a severe force act – were rammed through Congress almost without debate. Jefferson showed no concern whatever about constitutional questions, not even in regard to the force act which carried the administration to the precipice of unlimited and arbitrary powers as measured by any known American standards. There was an unprecedented concentration of powers in the executive: he could detain vessels on his authority, employ the navy for enforcement purposes, and search and seize on mere suspicion without warrant in disregard of the Fourth Amendment. The President was unable, however, to get from Congress the power that he wanted: to search and seize without court process any goods, any time, any place, and this would have been a power far more despotic than the writs of assistance which the patriot party condemned in the years before the Revolution.

As civil disobedience spread Jefferson was increasingly tempted to more severe measures to force compliance. The Embargo, begun as a means of coercing European powers into respect for American rights, became an instrument of coercion against American citizens, abridging their rights. Gallatin, in the summer of 1808, apprised Jefferson that the Embargo was failing and probably could not be enforced under any circumstances, but that if the attempt were made, "arbitrary powers" that were "equally dangerous and odious" would have to be employed, including enforcement by the regular army. Jefferson, who two months later expressed the opinion that in extreme cases "the universal resource is a dictator, or

by J.R.Smith.   Engraved by J.R.Smith.

WASHINGTON.   A 47255

y Washington, with rows of Jefferson poplars on
nsylvania Avenue. Jefferson copied the Parisian
tice of using rows of trees to separate roads
sidewalks.

martial law," replied decisively: "Congress," he instructed, "must legalize all means which may be necessary to obtain its end." The standing peacetime army, formerly the *bête noire* of republicanism, had already been tripled; now it was used (on a prolonged and systematic basis) to enforce the Embargo at home, without lawful authority in numerous instances. In accord with the dangerous theory that the ends justify the means, Jefferson also permitted his Attorney-General to experiment with a treason prosecution as another means of enforcement, and he deliberately and lawlessly ordered his collectors of the customs to ignore a federal court ruling that he had exercised his detention power illegally. However, he resisted his temptation to adopt the guilt-by-association principle by attaining and blockading entire towns because some of their citizens showed "a general spirit of resistance." Still, he recommended a new and terrible enforcement measure, the Fifth Embargo Act.

In the detention case, it was Justice William Johnson, a Republican of Jefferson's own choosing, who declared that even the President was subject to legal restraints and should not attempt an unsanctioned encroachment upon individual liberty. Jefferson, defying Johnson's ruling, issued orders that it be ignored – a subversion of the concept of the independent judiciary which Jefferson had once valued as a bulwark of liberty against zealous rulers. In the treason case, growing out of a violation of the Embargo, Justice Brockholst Livingston, another Republican appointee of the President, thwarted him by delivering a scorching attack on the theory of the prosecution. Pointing out that the crime at hand was merely a riot and trespass, Livingston declared that the court would not permit the establishment of so dangerous a precedent that would destroy the Constitutional protection against constructive treason.

The Fifth Embargo Act, which like its predecessors was framed by Jefferson and Gallatin, disclosed an ugly spirit. It contained unbelievable violations of many provisions of the Bill of Rights, including the right to be free from compulsory self-incrimination, from unreasonable searches and seizures, and from unfair trial. The statute also authorized the regular army, at the President's discretion and without procedural safeguards, to enforce the Embargo laws. The Federalists were not so wrong in denouncing the act as a step toward military despotism.

In retirement, during his declining years, the fires of Jefferson's faith in his fellow men flickered as if dampened by the ashes of disillusion. Although he still claimed that men would choose wisely if given the facts, his doubts revealed themselves even in the area of intellectual liberty and academic freedom. Afflicted with that occupational vanity of intellectuals, the notion that reading can profoundly influence a man's ideas, he began to worry about dangerous books. Although he wanted citizens to think freely, he wanted them to think Republican thoughts. Blackstone and Hume, he believed, stood in the way, particularly Hume, whose widely read *History of England* was filled with pernicious political heresies. Reading Hume, Jefferson thought, made Americans Tories. For years, therefore, he tried to secure publication of a "republicanised" version of Hume edited by an English radical, John Baxter. What attracted Jefferson to Baxter's edition was its intellectual deception. Baxter had hit upon the "only remedy" for reading Hume: he "gives you the text of Hume, purely and verbally, till he comes to some mispresentation or omission ... then he alters the text silently, makes it what truth and candor say it should be, and resumes the original text again,

as soon as it becomes innocent, without having warned you of your rescue from mis-guidance." For years Jefferson tried to switch American readers from Hume to Baxter, apparently in the belief that truth could not best error in a fair encounter. Eager to influence young minds, future political leaders, Jefferson did not want them exposed to wrong opinions.

His career as a censor continued as founder and rector of the University of Virginia. By that time Jefferson had become a narrow localist, a strict constructionist, a southern advocate. "In the selection of our law professor," he wrote, "we must be rigorously attentive to his political principles." Denouncing northern principles of "consolidation," he pro-claimed it a duty to "guard against such principles being disseminated among our youth, and the diffusion of that poison, by a previous prescription of texts to be followed in their discourses." The law school, which taught the principles of government, became a training ground for the propagation of the Virginia creed of 1798.

That creed made room for human slavery. It was originally a states' rights creed whose purpose was to defend freedom; it remained a states' rights creed but its purpose changed to a defense of slavery. Yet Jefferson abhorred slavery with the same passion that he reserved for any form of tyranny. Anyone

> nursed, educated, and daily exercised in tyranny [he said of the slave system] cannot but be stamped by it with odious peculiarities.... And with what execration should the statesman be loaded, who permitting one half the citizens thus to trample on the rights of the other, transforms those into despots, and these into enemies, destroys the morals of the one part, and the amor patriae of the other.

Jefferson himself was nursed, educated, and daily exercised in tyranny. The system made him a despot – a benevolent one, to be sure, but a despot nevertheless, and it corrupted his political morals. He loathed slavery. It filled him with a sense of shame, guilt, and sin: "this evil thing," he called it. Above all it filled him with a sense of despair; he felt helpless to bring about its end. Yet he did little to try, however much he believed in emancipation.

To describe him as one of the foremost racists of his time, as several historians have in recent years, or to say, as Winthrop Jordan has, that his derogation of the Negro "consti-tuted, for all its qualifications, the most intense, extensive, and extreme formulation of anti-Negro 'thought' offered by any American in the thirty years after the Revolution," is unbelievably present-minded, ununderstanding, misleading, and inaccurate. If Jefferson was a racist, as was every other white man in the South, and perhaps in the North too, he could be no other. He was born white in eighteenth-century Virginia. He was a plantation aristocrat, the master of 10,000 acres, and when he wrote that all men are created equal, he owned 180 slaves (the number had increased to over 260 by the time of his death). He depended upon his slaves for his livelihood and his elegant style of life. The slave system conditioned him. He knew that blacks were human beings and were entitled to the same God-given inalienable rights as whites, yet he could write that he used potatoes and clover "to feed every animal on the farm except my negroes...." But he could also write to the black scientist, Benjamin Banneker, "Nobody wishes more than I to see such proofs as you exhibit, that nature has given to our black brethren, talents equal to those of the other colors

of men, and that the appearance of a want of them is owing merely to the degraded condition of their existence, both in Africa and America." If Jefferson was a racist in his own time, a South Carolina Senator would not have condemned him for "fraternizing with negroes, writing them complimentary epistles, stiling them his black brethren, congratulating them on the evidences of their genius, and assuring them of his good wishes for the speedy emancipation."

The description of Jefferson as a racist depends mainly upon his discussion of slavery and blacks in his *Notes on the State of Virginia* (1787). His views never changed throughout his life. Significantly he began his discussion with a reference to his bill to emancipate all slaves born after its adoption. It did not pass, like similar measures that he recommended. His plan was to free the slaves and to colonize them out of the country, for he did not believe that the two races could live together in peace and equality. "Deep rooted prejudices entertained by the whites," the bitter memories of the blacks, and racial differences would, he believed, result in race wars. He also suspected that blacks were not the equals of whites, especially not intellectually. The remarkable fact is that he only suspected it to be so; he did not hold it as a fixed conviction. It was a "conjecture," an opinion "hazarded with great diffidence," "a suspicion only." His plan to remove the emancipated slaves "beyond the reach of mixture" reflected the white supremacist views of his time. By contrast Jefferson believed that an "amalgamation" between Indians and whites would be beneficial to both races.

Although his opinion on blacks was on balance uncomplimentary, he was in the forefront of Virginia's anti-slavery sentiment. It remained little more than sentiment. After 1784 Jefferson no longer spoke out publicly against slavery. Thereafter he reserved for his private correspondence his denunciation of slavery and his various plans of emancipation and expatriation. Still, no other prominent Virginian did more than he to abolish slavery, and, paradoxically, no other did more than he to confine it and to extend it. He sought to exclude slavery from the West by his abortive Ordinance of 1784, yet when he was President, he did nothing to exclude it from the vast reaches of the Louisiana Purchase and he agreed to its protection there where it already existed. By the time of the Missouri Compromise he had become a bitter and frantic southern apologist. After Congress outlawed slavery in the northern half of the Louisiana territories, Jefferson wrote despairingly that he was about to die in the belief that the sacrifices made by "the generation of 1776" were to be wasted.

His record on the greatest of all civil libertarian issues, the abolition of slavery and equality for blacks, was thus mixed. It too had its darker side. But on one related issue of almost equal importance he did as much or more than any man of his time to make this a free nation. He condemned the importation of slaves from Africa even before the American Revolution, and he consistently urged the end of the foreign slave trade. Virginia, in 1778, enacted his bill to close that trade. The Constitution of the United States permitted a continuance of it until 1808, authorizing Congress thereafter to abolish it, but not making it mandatory to do so. Jefferson was President when that critical year approached. He asked Congress "to withdraw the citizens of the United States from all further participation in those violations of human rights which have been so long continued on the unoffending inhabitants of Africa, and which morality, the reputation, and the best interests of our country, have long been eager to proscribe." Congress responded as the President wished. As a result, tens of

Private

Dear Sir   Washington Feb. 27. 08.

 I inclose you a copy of Armstrong's letter covering the papers sent to Congress. the date was blank as in the copy. the letter was so immaterial that I had really forgotten it altogether when I spoke with you last night. I feel myself much indebted to you for having given me this private opportunity of shewing that I have kept back nothing material. that the Federalists & a few others should by their vote make such a charge on me is never unexpected: but how can any join in it who call themselves friends? The President sends papers to the house which he thinks the public interest requires they should see. they immediately pass a vote implying irresistably their belief that he is capable of having kept back other papers which the same interest requires they should see. they pretend to no direct proof of this. it must then be founded in presumption; and on what act of my life, or of my administration is such a presumption founded? what interest can I have in leading the legislature to act on false grounds? my wish is certainly to take that course with the public affairs which the body of the legislature would prefer. it is said indeed that such a vote is to satisfy the federalists & their partisans. but were I to send 20. letters, they would say 'you have kept back the 21.st send us that'. if I sent 100. they would say 'there were 101.' and how could I prove the negative? their malice can be cured by no conduct: it ought therefore to be disregarded, instead of countenancing their imputations by the sanction of a vote. indeed I should consider such a vote as a charge in the face of the nation calling for a serious & public defence of myself. I send you a copy that you may retain it and make such use of it among our friends as your prudence and friendship will deem best. I salute you with great affection & respect.

The Speaker of the H. of R.   Th:Jefferson

---

thousands, perhaps hundreds of thousands of blacks were saved from slavery. Moreover, by keeping so many from bondage, a scarcity in numbers increased the value of those enslaved in America, thereby preventing their masters from working them to death as if they were cheap, expendable beasts of burden. The practical results of ending the slave trade more than compensated for any belief on Jefferson's part in the inferiority of blacks.

Still, the evidence taken as a whole discloses an anti-libertarian pattern in Jefferson's thought and action extending throughout his long career. How are we to understand it?

A few years after Jefferson's death, John Quincy Adams, upon reading Jefferson's *Autobiography*, yielded to his censorious and cantankerous nature. Jefferson, confided Adams to his diary, told nothing that was not creditable to him, as if he had always been right. Yet he had a "pliability of principle," a "treacherous" memory, a "double dealing character," and was so filled with "deep duplicity" and "insincerity" that in deceiving others, "he seems to have begun by deceiving himself." The curious thing about this massive indictment, which was founded on just enough shreds of truth not to be utterly ridiculous, was that Adams spiced it with a dash of credit and a pinch of praise. Even from his jaundiced view, Jefferson was a great patriot with an "ardent passion for liberty and the rights of man." Thus the image of Jefferson as the apostle of freedom had formed even in his own time.

Unlike the Liberty Bell, that image never tarnished or cracked in any serious way. After all, nations live by symbols and have a need for vital illusions. Thomas Jefferson was by no means ill-suited for the symbolic role in which he has been cast by American history. It was a role that he had cast for himself when he left instructions for the epitaph bearing testimony to the three achievements by which he wished "most to be remembered:"

Here was buried
Thomas Jefferson
Author of the Declaration of American Independence
of the Statute of Virginia for Religious Freedom
& Father of the University of Virginia

The words chosen for inscription on the Jefferson Memorial: "I have sworn upon the altar of God, eternal hostility against every form of tyranny over the mind of man," reflect his enduring spirit and will speak to mankind as long as liberty is cherished on earth. At the dedication of the shrine built by a grateful nation, President Franklin Roosevelt in 1943 quite naturally discoursed on "Thomas Jefferson, Apostle of Freedom." "We judge him," declared Roosevelt, "by the application of his philosophy to the circumstances of his life. But in such applying we come to understand that his life was given for those deeper values that persist throughout all time." The sentiment was a noble one, poetically true. But it was not the whole historical truth.

When judged by his application of "his philosophy to the circumstances of his life," a fair enough test, the saintly vapors that veil the real Jefferson clear away. He himself hated hagiolatry. Posterity, about which he cared so much, had a greater need for a realistic understanding of their heritage than for historical fictions paraded as "images." Jefferson was not larger than life; he was human and held great power. His mistaken judgements were many, his failings plentiful. Much of Jefferson that passed for wisdom has passed out of date. He

was, to be sure, a libertarian, and American civil liberties were deeply in his debt. But he was scarcely the constantly faithful libertarian and rarely, if ever, the courageous one.

The finest moments of American liberty occurred when men defied popular prejudices and defended right and justice at the risk of destroying their own careers. Thus John Adams, at a peak of passionate opposition to the British, defended the hated redcoats against a charge of murder growing out of the Boston Massacre. By contrast Thomas Jefferson never once risked career or reputation to champion free speech, fair trial, or any other libertarian value. On many occasions he was on the wrong side. On others he trimmed his sails and remained silent.

As Secretary of State Jefferson signed the proclamation against the Whiskey Rebels; as Vice President and presiding officer of the Senate, he signed the warrant of arrest for the journalist William Duane for a seditious contempt of that august body. Jefferson chose the easy path of lawful performance of his duties instead of conscientious opposition on the ground that liberty and justice were being victimized. In neither case did he speak out *publicly*. He signed in silence and characteristically complained in his private correspondence about the government's abridgements of freedom. His opposition to the Alien and Sedition Acts is famous: what is not so well known is that he never publicly declared his opposition during the period of hysteria. He kept his participation in the Kentucky Resolutions of 1798–9 a secret. In the winter of liberty's danger there was the greatest need for the heated and undisguised voice of dissent to be heard in the land.

Any depiction of Jefferson as the nearly faultless civil libertarian, the oracle of freedom's encyclicals and model of its virtues, should provoke a critical reader who is reasonably aware of human frailties – from which political figures are not notably exempt – to react with skepticism. Jefferson was no demigod. That he was a party to many abridgements of personal and public liberty should neither shock nor surprise. It would have been surprising had he not on occasion during his long career taken his hatchet in hand and cut down a few libertarian cherry trees. He said himself that he had been bent like a long bow by irresistible circumstances, his public life being a war against his natural feelings and desires. The compulsions of politics, the exigencies of office, and the responsibilities of leadership sometimes conspired to anesthetize his sensitivity to libertarian values. Nor did his own drives have an opposite effect. He yearned for the contemplative intellectual life but he could not resist the temptations of power. He had as great a need for the means of carrying out policies in the national interest, as he understood it, as he did for the quiet life of scholarship.

He was capable of ruthlessness in the exercise of power. As President he behaved as if compensating for his notorious weakness as wartime Governor of Virginia, when constitutional scruples and an inclination to shrink from the harsher aspects of politics had made him incapable of bold leadership. Thereafter he acted as if he had disciplined himself to serve in office with energy and decisiveness, at whatever cost. A hard resolution to lead and triumph certainly characterized his Presidency.

Often the master politician, he was not averse to the most devious and harsh tactics to achieve his ends. Usually gentle and amiable in his personal relationships, he possessed a streak of wilfulness that sometimes expressed itself in flaring temper, violence, and toughness. His grandson portrayed him as a "bold and fearless" horseman who loved to ride

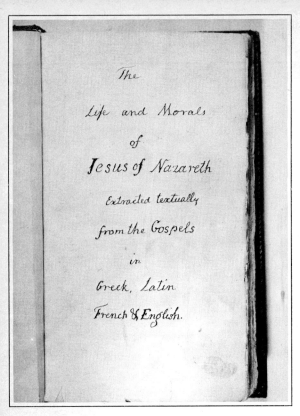

The title page of the so-called Jefferson Bible.

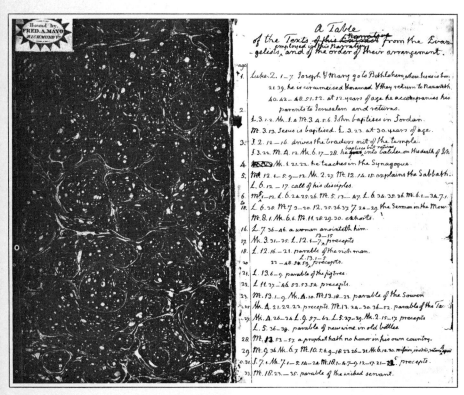

A page of Jefferson's Bible. He took from the four gospels only what he believed were the true words of Jesus and then translated them into Greek, Latin, and French.

booted, with whip in hand. "The only impatience of temper he ever exhibited," recalled Thomas Jefferson Randolph, "was with his horse, which he subdued to his will by a fearless application of the whip, on the slightest manifestation of restiveness." He rode the nation in the same way, booted and spurred during the Embargo days, notwithstanding the fact that one of his most memorable utterances announced his belief that mankind had not been born with saddles on their backs to be ridden booted and spurred by those in power over them.

It is revealing that Jefferson arrogated to himself the power to decide personally how much bread, and with what degree of whiteness, the American people could eat during the Embargo. He regulated the nation down to its table fare, despite an aversion to centralized government and a dedication to the belief that domestic concerns were a matter of personal or local government. The eye of President Jefferson was so prying, his enemies bitterly joked, that a baby couldn't be born without clearance from a government customs house.

Practices once reprehended by Jefferson as shocking betrayals of natural and constitutional rights suddenly seemed innocent, even necessary and salutary, when the government was in his hands. His accession to power seemed to stimulate a fresh understanding of the existence of public dangers requiring forceful measures that often did not result in a union of principle and practice. When, for example, the party faithful were victims of the Sedition Act, unchecked tyranny was abroad in the land with frightening consequences for the future of liberty. When he was in power the uncontrolled licentiousness and malice of the opposition press took on the hideous features of sedition, deserving of a few exemplary prosecutions to protect the public. Jefferson's Presidency, particularly the second term which witnessed the federal sedition prosecutions in Connecticut, the Wilkinson–Burr imbroglio and trials, and the five Embargo acts, was an obligato on the arts of political manipulation and severity.

Some of his anti-libertarianism can be explained by the ironic fact that he was, in the words of a clear-eyed admirer, a "terrifying idealist, tinged with fanaticism." What other sort of man would impersonally applaud a little bloodletting now and then to fertilize the tree of liberty? Jefferson held his convictions with a fierceness that admitted little room for compromise – if he was in a position of power to deny it – and no room for self-doubt. Unduly sensitive to criticism by others, he wore a hair shirt – often a dangerous attire for a politician – which covered a spirit rarely capable of objective disinterestedness.

Jefferson had the mentality and passion of a true believer, certain that he was absolutely right, a marked contrast to the skepticism of modern libertarians such as Justice Oliver Wendell Holmes or Judge Learned Hand. Holmes believed that the first mark of a civilized man was the capacity to doubt his own first principles, while Hand remarked that the spirit of liberty was the spirit which was not too sure that it was right. Jefferson was a product of the eighteenth century which regarded truths as immutable and self-evident. Yet philosophic truths concerning the nature of man or the first principles of government were not on a footing with practical legislation or executive policies. Jefferson had read Locke and the British empiricists as well as the Deists, scientists, and French *philosophes*. He might reasonably have been somewhat more skeptical of the rightness of his own favorite theories that he translated into national policy; he might have been less cocksure, less ready to

subscribe to the proposition that certitude was the test of certainty.

In politics, particularly, where the art of the possible is often the highest value, making compromise a necessity, the capacity to doubt one's own convictions is indispensable. The poorest compromise is almost invariably better than the best dictation which leaves little if any scope of freedom to the losing side and corrupts the spirit of those in power. In his old age Jefferson observed wisely:

> A government held together by the bands of reason only, requires much compromise of opinion; that things even salutary should not be crammed down the throats of dissenting brethren, especially when they may be put into a form to be willingly swallowed, and that a good deal of indulgence is necessary to strengthen habits of harmony and fraternity.

The observation was not an abstract one. Jefferson was arguing at the time in behalf of a constitutional amendment that would authorize the national government (which by then he was denominating the "foreign" department in contrast to the states that composed the "domestic" department) to build roads and canals. He had an utterly exquisite constitutional conscience when he was not in power.

Jefferson's only constitutional qualms during his Presidency concerned what he believed to be his questionable authority to purchase Louisiana. He never doubted for a moment the rightness of his behavior during the Burr and Embargo episodes. The intensity of his convictions and his incapacity for self-criticism propelled him onward, more resolute than ever in the face of outside criticism. The certainty that he was right, combined with his terrifying idealism, led him to risk the fate of the nation on the chance that an experiment in commercial sanctions might prove a substitute for war. Opposition only goaded him to redouble his efforts to prove himself right. He behaved as if a prisoner of his ideas, or, to put the thought less charitably, as a doctrinaire "tinged with fanaticism."

The self-skeptic, the practical politician, and the democrat conduct themselves otherwise. Any one of them in a position of power tends to operate with an understanding of the necessity of compromise and the obnoxiousness, not to mention the immorality or political stupidity, of cramming legislation "down the throats of dissenting brethren." Legislation, as William James once observed about democracy generally, is a business in which something is done, followed by a pause to see who hollers; then the hollering is relieved as best it can be until someone else hollers. Jefferson, however, was faintly doctrinaire. Exhilarated by the experience of putting an idea in motion and backing it by force, he could not back down or admit that he had been wrong. What counted most was the attainment of his objective, the validation of his conviction, not its impact on those who, failing to appreciate his idealism or personal stake, hollered long and loud. He reacted not by relieving their hollering but by a stretch of the rack that increased their protests and his own power to override them.

Jefferson tended to stretch his political powers as he stretched his mind in intellectual matters, leaving his conscience behind – and sometimes his good sense. His voluminous correspondence showed no hint that he suffered from uncertainty or was tormented by his conscience when he so readily used the army to enforce the Embargo and recklessly disregarded the injunctions of the Fourth Amendment. Lincoln, in the greatest of all crises in American history, had a supreme moral objective as well as a political one to sustain him;

but he was constantly racked by self-doubt. The exercise of power, not always constitutionally justifiable, exacted of him a price that included melancholy and an agonized soul. In moments of despair he could doubt that Providence was with him and even that his position was indeed the morally superior one.

The contrast with Jefferson was towering. Thwarted by the courts in Burr's case, Jefferson doubted not himself but the loyalty of the judges. Evasions of the Embargo filled him with astonishment not that his policy could have such a result but that the people could be so rankly fraudulent and corrupt. Rumors of resistance were matched by his impulse to crush it by force. There was no inner struggle in Jefferson; the tragedy of his antilibertarianism lacked poignancy. He was oblivious of the tragedy itself, symbolized by that moment of enormity when he approved of the use of any means, even if odious and arbitrary, to achieve his end.

Vanity, the enemy of self-doubt, also played its role in fashioning his darker side. His *amour-propre* prevented him from checking an illiberal act once begun or from admitting his error after the event. Witness his conduct of the Burr prosecutions and the way in which he was driven to defend Wilkinson. His persistent defense of his role in the case of Josiah Philips bears testimony to the same trait. When caught in a flagrancy, as when it was revealed that he had hired the journalistic prostitute Callendar to poison the reputations of political opponents, or when he was accused of permitting sedition prosecutions in a federal court, he denied the truth. In deceiving others, as John Quincy Adams said, he deceived himself. In deceiving himself he denied himself insight into his abridgements of liberty, though he was acutely perceptive of abridgements by others.

Perhaps the chief explanation of his darker side was his conviction that the great American experiment in self-government and liberty was in nearly constant danger. He completely identified with that experiment, to the point that an attack on him or on the wisdom of his policies quickly became transmuted in his mind as a threat to the security of the tender democratic plant.

During the Revolution, coercive loyalty oaths and proscription of tory opinions seemed a cheap price to pay when independence was the goal and the outcome was in doubt. The Alien and Sedition Acts, following the enactment of Hamilton's economic policies, forever convinced Jefferson that his political opponents were unalterably committed to the destruction of public liberty in America. In the flush of victory, at that splendid moment of the First Inaugural, he admitted the Federalists into the camp of loyal Americans, but not for long. If the scurrilousness of the Federalist press did not convince him that his magnanimous judgement had been mistaken, opposition to the purchase of Louisiana, coupled to threats of secession, proved his belief that popular government in America was imperiled. Burr's conspiracy brought the ugly menace to a head, justifying drastic countermeasures.

Open defiance of the Embargo once again threw the Union's future into grave doubt. That defiance seemed to sabotage majority rule and the only hope of avoiding a war that might end the democratic experiment. In time of such acute crisis, when insurrection existed on a widespread basis and treason itself again loomed, the methods of Dracon were tempting. The behavior of the Essex Junto during the War of 1812 reconfirmed Jefferson's worst fears. In the postwar period, from his hilltop at Monticello, he imagined that a monarchistic,

THE AMERICAN CAPITAL.

"The American Capital." In Jefferson's design,
classical motifs were replaced by tobacco flowers
and leaves.

clerical cabal had re-formed under a new party guise, employing doctrines of nationalistic consolidation to destroy public liberty.

Over the years he constantly sensed a conspiracy against republicanism. He had a feeling of being besieged by the enemies of freedom who would use it to subvert it. The face of the enemy changed: now that of a Tory; later that of a monarchist, a political priest, an Essex Juntoman, a Quid, or a Burrite; still later that of a judicial sapper-and-miner, an American-system consolidationist, or a Richmond lawyer. The face of the enemy or his name might change, but not his tory principles nor his subversive goal.

To the experiment of democracy in America, as Jefferson called it, he was committed heart, mind, and soul. Believing that experiment to be in grave jeopardy throughout most of his public life, he was capable of ruthlessness in defeating its enemies. His own goal was free men in a free society, but he did not always use freedom's instruments to attain it. He sometimes confused the goal with self-vindication or the triumph of his party. On other occasions instability and a lack of faith were revealed by his doubts of the opposition's loyalty. They were prone, he believed, to betray the principles of the Revolution as expressed in the Declaration of Independence. On still other occasions his eagerness to make America safe for democracy made him forgetful of Franklin's wise aphorism that they who seek safety at the expense of liberty deserve neither liberty nor safety.

The terrible complexities of any major issue, such as Burr's conspiracy or the Embargo, particularly as seen from the White House, also help to explain Jefferson's conduct. The strain and responsibilities of the highest office did not stimulate the taking of bold risks on the side of liberty when it seemed to be pitted against national security. Moreover, problems had a way of presenting themselves in a form that mixed conflicting political considerations and obscured clearcut decisions on libertarian merits. To a mind that was keenly alerted against the conspiracies of Federalist bogeymen and sensed a union between self, party, and nation, the virtue of an independent judiciary became the vice of judicial interference with majority rule; fair trial and a strict interpretation of treason became obstacles to the preservation of the Union; academic freedom became a guise for the dissemination of pernicious doctrines.

Jefferson's darker side derived in part, too, from the fact that he had no systematic and consistent philosophy of freedom. He was neither a seminal nor a profound thinker. Part of his genius consisted of his ability to give imperishable expression to old principles and to the deepest yearnings of his fellow citizens. Style, as much as substance, accounted for his staying power. He once defended himself against the accusation that there was not a single fresh idea in the Declaration of Independence by replying that the objective was not to find new principles or arguments never before thought of. It was, rather,

> to place before mankind the common sense of the subject, in terms so plain and firm as to command their assent.... Neither aiming at originality of principle or sentiment, nor yet copied from any particular and previous writing, it was intended to be an expression of the American mind, and to give to that expression the proper tone and spirit called for by the occasion. All its authority rests then on the harmonizing sentiments of the day.

As a distinguished admirer has written, "Jefferson's seminal achievement was to institutionalize familiar eighteenth-century ideas. He made abstract notions about freedom a

The Maison Carrée at Nîmes which Jefferson used as a model for the Virginia capitol at Richmond.

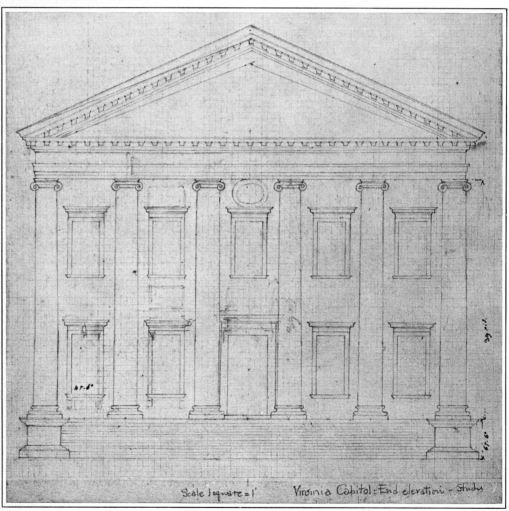

Scale ¼ square = 1'   Virginia Capitol: End elevation – Study

Jefferson called the Maison Carrée "the most perfect model existing of what may be called Cubic architecture . . .".

dominating faith and thereby the dynamic element in the strivings of men." Moreover he had the superlative talent of organizing a party that might realize his ideals by infusing the new nation with a sense of its special democratic destiny. But his failure to develop a theory of liberty existed and more than likely influenced his anti-libertarian thought and action.

In the thousands of pages of his published works there is a notable scarcity of extended treatments on a single subject. Insatiably curious, he knew a little about nearly everything under the sun and a great deal more about law and politics than any man of his time. But in all his writings, over a period of fifty years of high productivity, there is not a single sustained analysis of liberty. He was pithy, felicitous, repetitive, and ever absorbed by the subject, but never wrote a book or even a tract on the meaning of liberty, its dimensions, limitations, and history.

That he made no contribution of this kind is not *per se* a criticism, for the brief preambles to the Declaration of Independence and the Virginia Statute of Religious Freedom are worth all the books that have been written on liberty. He had not, however, thought through the tough and perplexing problems posed by liberty: the conditions for its survival and promotion; the types of liberty and conflicts between them; the validity of various legal tests for measuring the scope of liberty or its permissible area of operation; and the competing claims of other values.

Jefferson contented himself with a dedication to the general principle, apparently without realizing that general principles do not satisfactorily decide hard, concrete cases. Only in the area of religious liberty did he have a well-developed philosophy, replete with a usable and rationalized test for application to specific cases. There his contribution was pre-eminent, even if derived from English sources. It is significant, however, that he did not apply the "overt acts" test outside of the realm of the free exercise of religion. It is even more significant that his literary remains show no evidence that he ever tried to work out a usable test for cases of verbal political crimes.

A philosopher of freedom without a philosophy of freedom, Jefferson was ill-equipped, by his ritualistic affirmations of nebulous and transcendental truths, to confront the problem posed by General Wilkinson's conduct in New Orleans, or the circulation of Hume's *History of England* in the colleges, or the savage distortions of the opposition press. He reacted expediently on an *ad hoc* basis and too often hastily. Then his *amour-propre* prevented his candid acknowledgement of a mistaken judgement that demeaned the libertarian values he symbolized to the nation.

Regret and remorse are conspicuously absent from Jefferson's writings, as is reflective reconsideration of a problem. Something in his make-up, more than likely a stupendous ego, inhibited second thoughts. Whether he would deny the plain facts or stubbornly reiterate his original position, he failed to work out fresh guide lines for future conduct. Restatement, not re-evaluation, marked his thinking, and beneath an eloquently turned phrase there lurked a weary, problem-begging cliché. That it was commonplace rarely deprived it of its profundity as a libertarian principle. The "self-evident truths" of the Declaration of Independence will continue to survive all scorn of being "glittering generalities." They tend, however, to overarch real cases.

Jefferson, for example, might declare in his first Inaugural Address that enemies of the

Republic should be free to express themselves, but the principle was so broad that it failed to have pertinence for him when he learned that a few "political Priests" and "Federal printers," who had been confident that no federal court would take cognizance of their seditious calumnies, were being criminally prosecuted for their libels against him and his administration. His awareness of the general distinction between preparation and attempt, or between conspiracy to commit treason and overt acts of treason, escaped application in the case of the Burrites, though not in the case of the Whiskey Rebels. A commitment to the large principle of intellectual liberty had no carry-over when the possibility arose that a "Richmond lawyer" might be appointed professor of law at the University of Virginia.

Maxims of liberty – "glittering generalities" – were frail props for a sound, realistic libertarianism. A mind filled with maxims will falter when put to the test of experience. A mind filled with maxims contents itself with the resonant quality of a noble utterance. Such a mind, although libertarian, cannot produce a libertarian analysis such as Madison's *Report* of 1799–1800 on the Alien and Sedition Acts, or Wortman's *Treatise Concerning Political Enquiry*. Jefferson's only tracts and books were *A Summary View of the Rights of British America* which was a protest against British encroachments on colonial freedom at the eve of the Revolution; *Notes on the State of Virginia*, a guidebook and utilitarian history; the *Manual of Parliamentary Practice*; his *Autobiography* and *The Anas*, which comprise his memoirs; *The Life and Morals of Jesus of Nazareth*; and the philological work, *Essay on Anglo-Saxon*. Despite his interest in freedom, its meaning did not interest him as a subject for even an essay.

A plausible but not wholly convincing explanation of Jefferson's darker side may be founded on the argument that he lived at a time when the understanding of civil liberties was quite different from that of our own. Libertarian standards were also quite new and inchoate, making modern yardsticks of judgement anachronistic as well as unfair and ununderstanding. The first bills of rights did not come into existence until 1776; the national Bill of Rights not until 1791. The meanings of their provisions were not always clear; their restraints in that formative era constituted an experiment in government. Deviations, inconsistencies, and even gross abridgements were to be expected when experience provided few guides. It was a time of testing, of groping and growth, of trial and error, out of which issued the improved wisdom of subsequent generations. In any case, counsels of perfection and hindsight come rather cheap when aimed by those not on the firing line or of a later time.

This explanation is certainly a plausible one. Yet it is like the theory that was spoiled by the facts. During the revolutionary war, only tory voices – and they were not necessarily wrong – could be found in opposition to loyalty tests, bills of attainder, and suppression of "traitorous" speech. Thereafter there were always respectable, instructive voices, even if heard only in dissent, to sound the alarm against abridgements of liberty. Jefferson needed only to hear or read in order to know that a particular measure could be seriously construed as a threat to the Bill of Rights or the undermining of a libertarian value. For every example of his darker side that has been mentioned in this essay, a congressional speech, a popular tract, a letter, a newspaper editorial, a judicial opinion, or, more likely than not, a pronouncement by Jefferson himself can be adduced to show a judgement of his own time placing his action in an anti-libertarian light. By 1800 or thereabouts the standards of his own

Jefferson's seal with which he closed his letters.

time did not noticeably differ from those of ours on the kind of civil-liberty questions that he confronted.

Though contributing little to any breakthrough in libertarian thought, except in the important realm of freedom of religion, Jefferson more than any other man was responsible for the public sensitivity to libertarian considerations. If the quality of the new nation was measured by the ideals and aspirations that animated it, Jefferson had erred only slightly in confusing his own reputation with that of the democratic experiment. Notwithstanding the reciprocal scurrilities and suspicions of the opposed parties, or more importantly their conflicting interests, Americans were indeed all Federalists, all Republicans. They were equally attached to the "experiment in freedom" and the "empire of liberty." Anyone who depreciates the national commitment to libertarian values, which were based on an extraordinary legal and political sophistication, deprives himself of an understanding of the times – and of the impact of Thomas Jefferson upon it.

That Jefferson's libertarianism was considerably less than perfect or that his practice flagged behind his faith, does not one whit diminish the achievements by which he is and should be best remembered. That he did not always adhere to his libertarian principles does not erode their enduring rightness. It proves only that Jefferson often set the highest standard of freedom for himself and posterity to be measured against. His legacy was the idea that as an indispensable condition for the development of free men in a free society, the state must be bitted and bridled by a bill of rights which should be construed in the most generous terms, its protections not to be the playthings of momentary majorities or of those in power.

JEFFERSON: ARCHITECT
AND EMANCIPATOR

Thomas Jefferson: engraving after Gilbert Stuart's
portrait of 1805.

Poplar Forest: the octagonal home that Jefferson
designed and retreated to when crowds began to
overwhelm Monticello. A garden elevation (*above*)
and section (*below*) are shown.

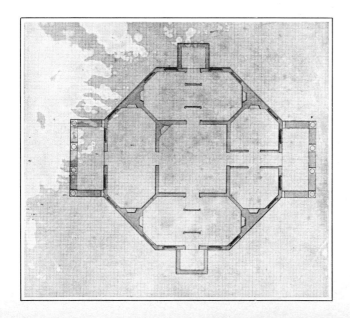

Monticello as depicted in the mid-nineteenth century.

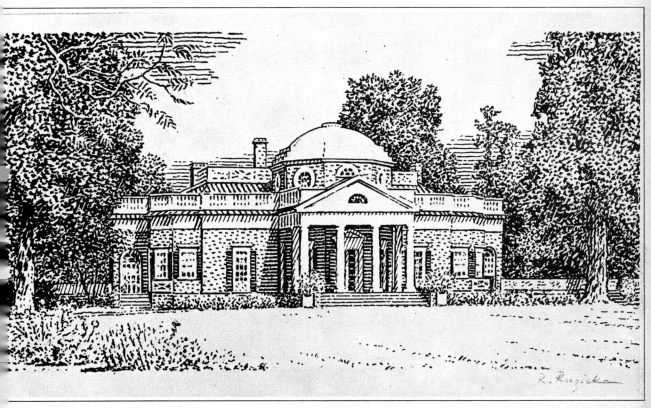

Ruzicka's drawing of Monticello, 1957.

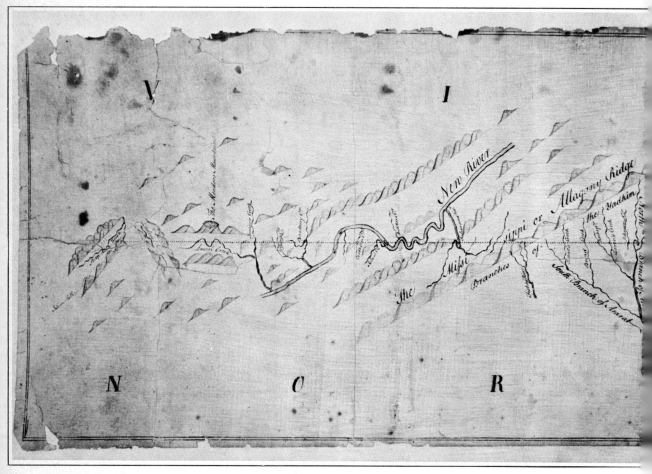

Above and overleaf A map of the border of Virginia and
North Carolina done by Peter Jefferson and Joshua Fry
in 1749. "My father's education had been quite
neglected," wrote Jefferson, "but being of a strong
mind, sound judgment, and eager after information, he
read much and improved himself, insomuch that he
was chosen . . . to continue the boundary line between
Virginia and North Carolina, which had been begun
by Colonel BYRD. . . ."

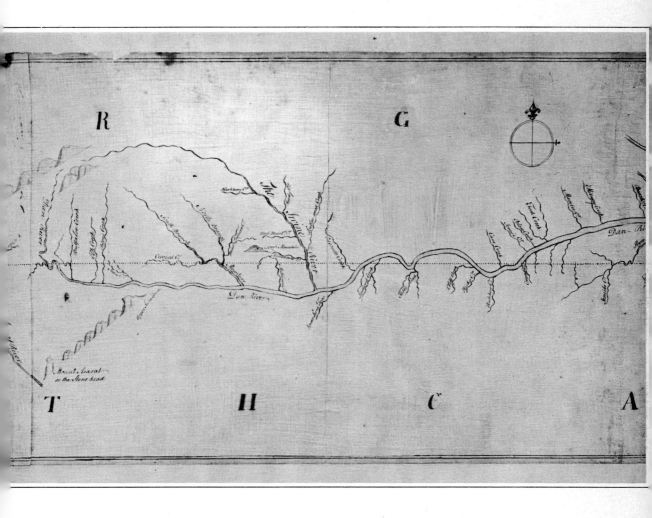

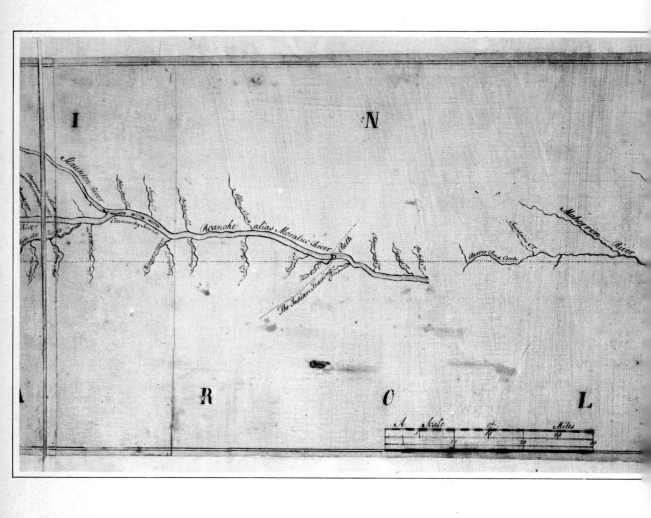

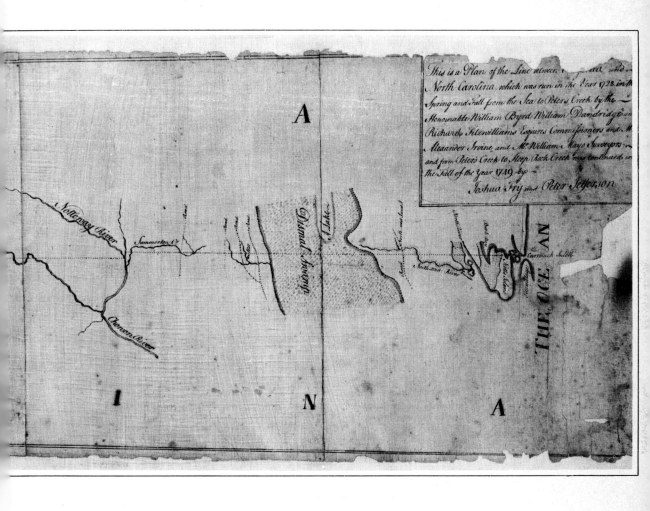

This is a Plan of the Line between [Virginia] and
North Carolina, which was run in the Year 1728, in the
Spring and Fall from the Sea to Peter's Creek, by the
Honourable William Byrd William Dandridge and
Richard Fitzwilliams Esquires Commissioners and Mr
Alexander Irvine, and Mr William Mayo Surveyors,
and from Peter's Creek to Steep Rock Creek was continued, in
the Fall of the Year 1749, by
Joshua Fry and Peter Jefferson

Battle of Lexington.

The Battle of Lexington: 1775.

Georgetown and Washington, D.C. in 1800, the year
Jefferson was elected President.

AN EXACT VIEW of THE LATE BATTLE AT CHARLESTOWN June 17th 1775.
In which an advanced party of about 700 Provincials stood an Attack made by 11 Regiments & a Train of Artillery & after an Engagement of two hours retreated to their Main body at Cambr.
Leaving eleven Hundred of the enemy killed and Wounded upon the field.

A view of the battle at Charlestown, 17 June 1775.
A small provincial army at Charlestown withstood
an attack by two British regiments.

The action off Mud Fort on the Delaware River in 1777. The British attacked American forts and ships in an attempt to get supplies to Philadelphia which they had captured.

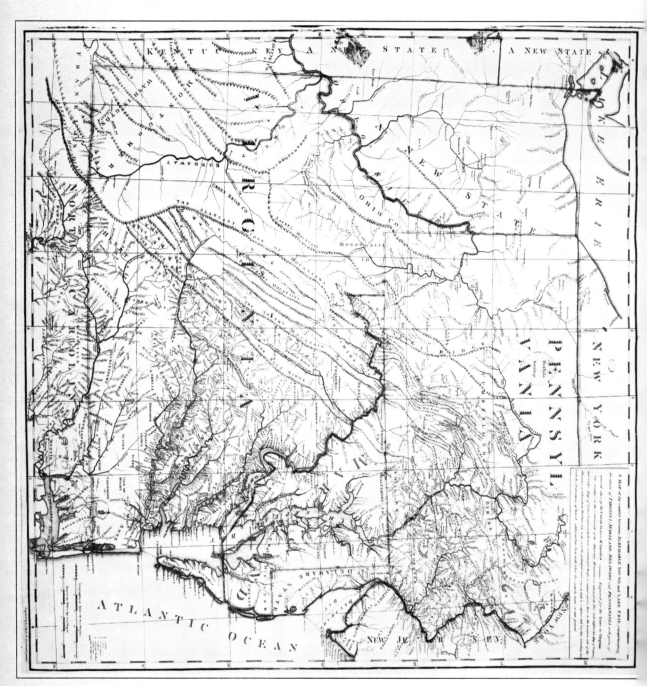

A map of Virginia and surrounding states compiled
by Jefferson and engraved for *Notes on the State
of Virginia.*

THE JEFFERSONIAN LEGACY

Christopher Lasch

Probably none of the other founding fathers has been so often invoked as Jefferson, in such diverse and even conflicting causes. The extraordinary range and suggestiveness of his practical activity, together with the flexibility of his opinions, has made it possible to see Jefferson in any number of ways: as the noblest exponent of religious and intellectual freedom; as a staunch defender of minority rights; as a conscience-stricken slaveholder who foresaw the inevitability of emancipation at a time when most of his countrymen still took slavery for granted; as the patron saint of that embattled and beleaguered faith, southern liberalism; as examplar of American individualism and the creed of self-reliance; as founder of a persisting tradition of popular republicanism. States-rights conservatives, liberals, and even socialists have all claimed descent from Jefferson. Faced with so many conflicting claims, interpreters of early American history have searched inconclusively for the real, the essential Jefferson. He remains, however, an elusive and many-sided figure, and his reputation in any case is too firmly entrenched in the popular imagination to be radically altered or undone by the work of historians.

Even during his lifetime, three distinct varieties of "Jeffersonian democracy" emerged, all of them recognizably Jeffersonian in origin – a pure agrarian version, which later became identified with the defense of states' rights; a mercantile version, somewhat more kindly disposed to the positive uses of central power; and a popular version associated with the rights and interests of the common man.

Among Jefferson's early adherents, certain purists – notably the Virginians John Randolph, William B. Giles, Joseph H. Nicholson, and John Taylor – expected his rise in national politics to vindicate their own exclusively agrarian interpretation of the republican creed. These men, many of whom saw the Constitution itself as a betrayal of the "spirit of '76," seized on Jefferson's agrarianism, his opposition to Hamilton, and above all his authorship of the Kentucky resolutions as evidences of a pristine republicanism uncorrupted by compromise with the mercantile leaders who had engineered the coup d'état of 1787 and then rallied to Washington and Hamilton. If Jefferson in the 1790s became the leader of a coalition of discordant elements united chiefly by hatred of Federalism, by far the most devoted and fanatical of his followers were men who were scandalized by the corruption and intrigue that seemed to them to have characterized the Washington administrations – by Hamilton's funding scheme, which would have enriched unscrupulous

speculators at the expense of revolutionary veterans; by the rapprochement with England, culminating in Jay's treaty; by the encouragement given to manufactures; and by the establishment of a national bank and the emergence of a "paper aristocracy" based on credit – based, that is (in their eyes), on organized deception and fraud.

Those who saw Jefferson as first and foremost the representative of the "Virginia school" in national politics acclaimed his election in 1800 as a restoration of republican virtue, a return to economy, simplicity, strict construction, and zealous devotion to local rights and traditions. They were soon disappointed. Jefferson's purchase of Louisiana, as he himself admitted, stretched presidential authority beyond even the loosest construction of the Constitution (although Randolph, for one, said nothing against it). Acquisition of Louisiana plunged the country once again into the thick of diplomatic entanglements. It whetted Jefferson's appetite for West Florida, which some authorities regarded as properly part of Louisiana in the first place, and impelled him to ask Congress to make a secret appropriation of two million dollars in the hope that Napoleon, for a suitable price, would extort West Florida from Spain. Deeply offended by this revival of secret diplomacy, Randolph and Taylor denounced the administration. They were further antagonized by its attempt to arrange a compromise with the Yazoo claimants, who had bought land under a fraudulent sale enacted by the legislature of Georgia and later rescinded. The Yazoo frauds, perpetrated in 1795 at the height of the Federalist period, epitomized everything the old republicans despised in Federalism, and Jefferson's temporizing confirmed their worst suspicions about his course in office.

Underlying the rift between Jefferson and the "Tertium Quid" within his own party was an issue more profound than these conflicts between principle and expediency. Jefferson's policies as President drifted away from pure agrarianism toward a compromise with mercantile interests, who were themselves unhappy with a rigidified Federalism aligning itself more and more with the defense of a purely regional outlook and in these years sliding toward outright secession. Jefferson astutely perceived that "the mercantile interests" could be "detached" from Federalism. Writing to his Secretary of Treasury Albert Gallatin in 1803, he declared himself "decidedly in favor of making all the banks republican by sharing deposits among them in proportion to the [political] dispositions they show." The incorporation of new elements into the Republican party, made possible by the party's flexibility, encouraged the emergence of a sort of republican mercantilism, still opposed to standing armies and national debts but taking over from the Federalists a solicitude for the orderly development of the country's resources and commercial possibilities. Jefferson and his followers never relinquished their suspicions of "a consolidated government," which, they believed, unreconstructed Federalists continued to favor as "the next best point" to "monarchism." In office, however, the Jeffersonian Republicans moderately but firmly exercised federal control of the economy through regulation of banking and credit, regulation of land settlement, encouragement of science and technology, and unintentionally through the Embargo.

In the eyes of Randolph and Taylor, Jefferson was a traitor not only to republican principles but to Virginia – which was saying the same thing. Their republicanism sprang from a hatred of foreign influences and a fierce localism that defined foreign influences so

LANDING OF GEN. LA FAYETTE
At Castle Garden, New York,
16th August 1824.

Entered According to Act of Congress the 27th Day of October 1824 by Samuel Maverick of the State of New York

The landing of General Lafayette in New York,
16 August 1824. Lafayette made a triumphant tour of
the United States and went to Monticello to see his
friend Jefferson. "Teach your children to be as you
are," Jefferson wrote Lafayette, "a cement between
our two nations."

broadly as to embrace anything originating outside the Old Dominion. Like Jefferson, they were individualists on principle (in their case, to the point of eccentricity); but their individualism was that of the planter accustomed to lord it over his slaves. Booted and spurred, leading a brace of hunting dogs, Randolph would stride imperiously into the House of Representatives to harangue his colleagues on the dangers of aristocracy. The most eloquent attack on the aristocracy of "paper and patronage" (and the most impressive theoretical statement of early republican doctrine) was written by another Virginia nabob, John Taylor of Caroline.

Somewhat excessively praised by Charles A. Beard as an "economic interpretation" of politics and social classes, Taylor's *Inquiry into the Principles and Policy of the Government of the United States* (1814) argues not that classes arise from control over production but that they are created by special privilege and official favoritism. The *Inquiry* was directed in part against John Adams, who had argued in his *Discourses on Davila* that classes originate in the unequal distribution of intelligence and talent. Taylor's exposition of republican doctrine helps to clarify the distinction between conservatism and classical liberalism, with its insistence that politics is based on rational self-interest rather than irrational instinct and "emulation," as Adams would have said. Jefferson's celebrated proposition that "that government governs best which governs least" – a principle consistently violated, according to Taylor, by Jeffersonian practice – rests on the premise that men are capable of self-government in the most literal sense, subordinating their passions to the intelligent pursuit of their own self-interest. Traditional conservatism, strongly rooted in a theological view of the world, assumed on the other hand that men need government and plenty of it, since they are unable to govern their irrational, self-destructive propensities.

Jeffersonian liberalism no doubt introduced into political theory an element of economic realism that had been lacking before – though at the expense of the psychological realism present in the older view of human nature – but it stopped well short of a fully developed theory of class, attributing the growth of inequality to misguided governmental policy. "Monopoly" is the great enemy against which Taylor inveighs; and a belief that monopoly is artificially created by "special privilege," rather than arising out of the very conditions of capitalist competition, continued to be the hallmark of economic liberalism down to the time of William Jennings Bryan – a faithful adherent of these doctrines – and even beyond.

Taylor's book stated principles that were shared by republicans of every variety. By laying particular stress on the rights of minorities, however, it stated them in a form particularly well suited to the needs of the South, already at the end of the War of 1812 a minority interest increasingly defensive about its "peculiar" institutions. The careers of Taylor and Randolph pointed the way toward the adoption of "Jeffersonian democracy" as a militantly pro-slavery ideology – a development consummated in the next generation when Jeffersonian doctrines were invoked on behalf of nullification and finally of secession. Detached from any larger commitment to freedom of speech, Jefferson's defense of minority rights could be twisted into the defense of the South as a sectional minority, at the same time that the southern ruling class was actively suppressing discussion of slavery and the rights of petition and assembly, to say nothing of the rights of the slaves themselves. A wholesale intellectual regression accompanied the rise of southern sectionalism in politics, with its

appeal to "Jeffersonian" principles. From eighteenth-century rationalism to southern romanticism and neo-chivalric pretensions, from religious tolerance to the revival of evangelical emotionalism, from the detachment and precision of Jefferson's *Notes on the State of Virginia* to Calhoun's logic-chopping, was a long declension – in many ways a declension that afflicted the entire country, not only the South.

It would be short-sighted, however, to see southern sectionalism simply as a perversion of Jeffersonianism, an opportunistic appropriation of Jefferson's ideas wrenched out of context and applied to political objectives he would presumably have abhorred. That the defense of minority rights happened to coincide with the selfish interests of the planting class does not mean that the defense of minority rights was therefore wholly specious or that other people besides slaveholders did not have good reason to fear the growth of centralized power. For all their involuted argumentation, a succession of southern statesmen foresaw very clearly the dangers of centralization, particularly Alexander H. Stephens in his *Constitutional View of the Late War Between the States* – a work that defends slavery and secession but still bears a recognizable relation to the Jeffersonian tradition.

That tradition continued to have a real influence, not merely a rhetorical influence, on southern politics and thought. Its persistence helps to explain the anomaly that the South justified secession in 1861 by appealing to the traditions of the American Revolution – government rests on consent and can be dissolved when it becomes arbitrary – rather than to George Fitzhugh's intensely conservative political economy. As a competitor of the minority-rights tradition for the allegiance of the slaveholding elite, Fitzhugh's argument had the advantage that it combined a defense of slavery with a scathing indictment of northern capitalism. Moreover, it carried the pro-slavery argument to its logical conclusion and defended slavery not as a means of racial control but on the general principle that a paternalistic and hierarchical society was more humane than a society resting on brutal, unrestricted economic competition. In this way Fitzhugh raised the "peculiar" interests of the South to the level of universal truths. He provided a consistently conservative rationale for a landed elite threatened with extinction by the accumulating energies of economic and political modernization.

In the best conservative fashion, Fitzhugh argued that the social order is an organism and that

> the great error of modern philosophy is the ignorance or forgetfulness of this fact. The first departure from it was ... the doctrine of the right of private judgment.... Human equality, the social contract, the let-alone and selfish doctrines of political economy, universal liberty, freedom of speech, of the press, and of religion, spring directly from this doctrine, or are only new modes of expressing it. Agrarianism, Free Love, and No Government, are its logical consequences: for the right to judge for ourself implies the right to act upon our judgments ...

If on the whole the South rejected Fitzhugh in favor of Jeffersonian liberalism (however debased), this choice presumably reflected not merely the continuing prestige of the foremost Virginian but the persistence, in southern society, of a rich and popular tradition of individualism, more easily attracted to liberalism than to the vision of hierarchical peace and

quiet. This individualism, indeed, contributed in the end to the South's own undoing, causing southerners themselves to complain during the Civil War that although southern soldiers "have courage, woodcraft, consummate horsemanship, and endurance of pain equal to the Indians ... [they] will not submit to discipline."

The mercantile version of Jeffersonian democracy emerged, as we have seen, as a result of compromises made by the Jeffersonians in power. The practical requirements of governing forced the Jeffersonians to temper the more visionary aspects of their faith. As Henry Adams observed, "The republican party, when in opposition, set up an impossible standard of political virtue, and now that they were in power found that government could not be carried on as they had pledged themselves to conduct it."

Jefferson's early writings are strewn with effusions on the moral sublimity of agricultural life accompanied by strictures on cities and urban "mobs." In a letter of 1785 to John Jay, he denounces "the class of artificers as the panders of vice, and the instruments by which the liberties of a country are generally overturned." Again and again he urges his countrymen to develop only those crafts and industries that are directly necessary to agriculture. "Carpenters, masons, smiths are wanting in husbandry; but, for the general operation of manufacture, let our workshops remain in Europe." Himself one of the engineers of the Revolution, Jefferson did not seem to grasp its economic implications. He wished to preserve precisely the international division of labor (in which British North America would remain strictly agricultural) that was envisioned by the British colonial policy the colonists had just overthrown. Before the Revolution, Americans still had the choice of remaining agricultural, at the price of remaining part of the British Empire; but after independence a purely agrarian America belonged to the realm of fantasy.

The Jeffersonians, like most other Americans, imagined that independence would enable them to escape what they took to be the fate of Europe – class conflict, poverty, and war. Albert Gallatin wrote in 1798, when the United States seemed to be on the verge of war with France:

> I had conceived, when contemplating the situation of America, that our distance from the European world might have prevented our being involved in the mischievous politics of Europe, and that we might have lived in peace without armies and navies and without being deeply involved in debt. It is true in this dream I had conceived it would have been our object to have become a happy and not a powerful nation, or at least no way powerful except for self-defence.

An attractive vision, but one that rested on a fundamental misreading of the country's "situation." Notwithstanding America's distance from Europe, independence unavoidably embroiled the country in the "politics of Europe," for America was a new and unknown but by no means negligible quantity in the global power struggle between France and England. Only as a colonial backwater could Americans have hoped to remain "a happy and not a powerful nation." The winning of independence, seemingly the triumph of republican principles, had already sealed the doom of the republican "dream," at least in its purest form.

The slightly chastened and modified republicanism that emerged after 1800, of which

Thomas Jefferson's clothes.

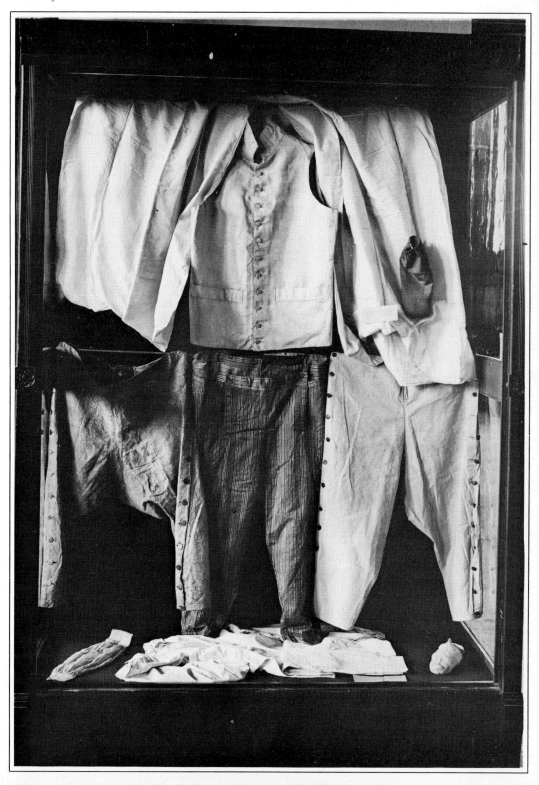

Gallatin himself was perhaps the most consistent exponent, implicitly acknowledged that in some ways Federalists had understood more clearly than Jeffersonians the implications of American independence. The question now was not whether the United States would develop her resources, expand her commerce, perfect manufactures, and become a powerful nation, but whether the country's growth would be measured and orderly or unplanned and chaotic. Only the diehard agrarians sought any longer to resist the pressures for growth and development; the main-line Jeffersonians, as they may be called, sought merely to regulate them – to control the expansion of credit, national indebtedness, and the settlement of the West while judiciously encouraging public "improvements" of every kind. The Lewis and Clark expedition, the coastal survey, and Gallatin's report on roads and canals attempted to explore the natural resources of the country and the most intelligent means of using them. In his annual message of 1806, Jefferson recommended that the Treasury surplus be spent on a national system of roads and canals. Ten years later the Republicans went so far as to enact a moderate protective tariff – over the objections of New England Federalists. In the same year they rechartered the Bank of the United States, which they had opposed in 1791 but which men like Gallatin now perceived had acted as a check on speculation.

The new model republicanism was by no means incompatible with the spirit of improvement and enterprise. At the same time it retained a flavor of the eighteenth century, the eighteenth century not so much of Rousseau and the physiocrats as of Addison and Steele – a certain worldliness, even a sense of the "romance of trade," mixed with a classical reluctance to allow trade to become an engrossing passion. Nicholas Biddle, the President of the Second Bank of the United States, exemplified very well this aspect of Jeffersonian democracy. Born into a solid revolutionary family, elected to the Pennsylvania legislature in 1810 as a Republican, Biddle presided over an institution designed to promote a cautious and sensible expansion of industry and commerce. It was appropriately housed in a building designed after the Parthenon. Biddle's country house near Philadelphia and the structures he was instrumental in building for Girard College were widely admired as models of Greek revival architecture. Jefferson – who had, he said, "an excellent opinion" of Biddle – believed that his travels (to Paris as secretary to the American Ambassador, to Italy, to Greece, to London as secretary to James Monroe) "must have given him advantages." A year after his appointment as head of the bank in 1823 we find Biddle writing satirical verses to a female acquaintance, favorably contrasting the allurements of commerce to the literary life he had abandoned:

> And Cecilia herself, though her lyre was divine,
> Never gave to the world notes equal to mine.

Urbane, witty, traveled, slightly dandified in a style reminiscent of the Hartford Wits, a man of affairs who was determined to be a man of letters as well, Biddle embodied a side of the republican tradition that adapted itself to the new requirements of the nineteenth-century economy without losing touch with its Enlightenment origins.

In the same speech in which he recommended a program of internal improvements, Jefferson urged Congress to create a national university. None of his projects – unless it was his act disestablishing the Anglican church in Virginia – was more characteristic of the

cosmopolitan and worldly (as opposed to the agrarian and parochial) side of the Jeffersonian tradition. Repeatedly spurned by Congress, something of the original ideal survived in Jefferson's plans for the University of Virginia, instituted in the 1820s. The distinguishing features of Jefferson's conception of higher education were the organization of the university into "faculties" of law, medicine, modern languages, moral philosophy, commerce, etc., each offering instruction at the highest level; the absence of custody, discipline, ranking of students by class, and other paraphernalia of the early nineteenth-century denominational college; the absence of administration ("avoid too much government"); refusal to grant degrees; and unlimited latitude for the student to study what he chose, a freedom based on the premise that specialization had to be related to the whole of knowledge. In recruiting a faculty for the University of Virginia, Jefferson tried to find men who combined practical experience with intellectual breadth (men like Nicholas Biddle, in other words). These policies show that Jefferson was attempting to bring into being a national intelligentsia competent to direct the practical life of the nation but also capable of reflection – a professional class liberally educated. Utterly foreign to this conception was the split between practical life and "culture," shortly to become so pervasive in America. Although in some rather superficial ways the initial organization of the University of Virginia anticipated later experiments at Johns Hopkins and elsewhere (themselves soon abandoned in practice), essentially Jefferson's university was an eighteenth-century conception, already old-fashioned by the 1820s. By that time most Americans were no longer able to understand a form of higher education at once rigorously professional – oriented toward practice – and opposed to specialization. The practical and the interpretive or "meaningful" components of culture, as they have been called, were now so badly split that it would take more than Jefferson's beautiful design to bring them together again.

By the 1830s the University of Virginia was granting degrees, teaching the standard classical curriculum, and conducting itself like any other American college. In the same decade, the Jacksonians overthrew that other eighteenth-century survival, the Bank of the United States. Jackson's veto of the bill rechartering the bank declared that "banking, like farming, manufacturing, or any other occupation or profession, is a *business*, the right to follow which is not originally derived from the laws." Together with other Jacksonian reforms, the destruction of the bank swept away the last of the mercantilist system erected by the Federalists and preserved in modified form by the Jeffersonians. It removed the last effective restraint on speculation and competitive enterprise, inaugurating a period of untrammeled commercial and industrial expansion accompanied by the brutal subjugation of nature and of the growing class of industrial laborers. Huge fortunes began to accumulate in private hands as business became enormously profitable and at the same time enormously risky. Enterprises of unprecedented size and power rose on the ruins of smaller ones. In the Panic of 1837 – first fruit of the Jacksonian monetary policies – Gallatin's own bank suspended payments, a failure in the highest degree humiliating to a man who regarded indebtedness with puritanical horror.

The old-line Jeffersonians, overwhelmed by the triumph of laissez-faire capitalism in the 1830s, either retired from political struggles or drifted into the Whig party, an amorphous anti-Jacksonian coalition itself to be soon torn apart over the slavery question. Henry Clay's

American system, a program of aid to internal improvements, protective tariffs, and liberal but by no means unlimited encouragement to the settlement of western lands, owed something to Jeffersonian mercantilism, but it owed much more to the sectional diplomacy – the need to balance the interests of West, South, and East – through which Clay hoped to capture the Presidency. Clay himself, though he began his career as a Jeffersonian of sorts and always regarded himself as such, had no fixed principles and could hardly be taken seriously, even by himself, as a worthy successor to the Virginia school. Still, he represents a tenuous link between Jefferson and Abraham Lincoln.

Lincoln idealized Clay ("the Nestor of the old Whig party," he picturesquely called him in 1856), and filled his early writings and speeches with references to Jefferson, "the most distinguished politician in our history." What the Jeffersonian legacy had come to mean to politicians of Lincoln's whiggish opinions – the men who later founded the Republican party and named it after Jefferson's party – emerges quite clearly from an examination of these references. In a speech of 1839 Lincoln compared the economies of the first four Presidents with the spendthrift policies of Jackson and Van Buren. In a campaign circular defending the protective tariff (1843) he quoted from a well-known letter written by Jefferson in 1816, in which the former agrarian declared that "manufactures are now as necessary to our independence as to our comfort." Defending internal improvements, Lincoln pointed out that Jefferson never questioned the expediency of federal aid, although in his annual message of 1806 he did question their constitutionality, recommending that the Constitution be amended accordingly. (President Polk, quoting the same passage in his veto of a rivers-and-harbors bill, had tried to make it appear that Jefferson opposed federal aid to internal improvements as a matter of policy.) The young Whig made a similar point regarding Jefferson's views on the acquisition of Louisiana. In general he sought to portray Jefferson as a man of large and flexible views whose constitutional scruples did not prevent him from recognizing the need for bold federal action on a whole variety of issues. Thus it was Jefferson, Lincoln insisted, who in his Northwest Ordinance of 1787 originated "the policy of policing slavery in new territory" – the doctrine around which the anti-slavery movement rallied in the late forties, and in the fifties the central tenet of the new Republican party.

As the slavery controversy intensified and Lincoln was forced by Douglas and by events into a more radical position, a different aspect of Jefferson's thought – of which I have so far said almost nothing – began to figure more prominently in Lincoln's rhetoric. Condemning the Dred Scott decision on the grounds that the courts have no business deciding political issues, Lincoln repeatedly invoked "Jefferson's fears of a political despotism." In the face of Douglas's assertion that the Declaration of Independence was not meant to apply to Negroes, Lincoln insisted that it was unthinkable that Jefferson could have held so restricted a view of the rights of man. He quoted passages from Jefferson's writings showing a deep concern with the moral dimension of slavery. Finally, in a public letter commemorating Jefferson's birthday, written in April 1859, Lincoln declared with great feeling that the essence of Jeffersonian democracy was the principle that personal rights take precedence over property rights. Forgotten by the Democratic party, this principle, according to

Th: Jefferson

presents his compliments to

and requests the favour of his company
to dinner on   next
at half after three oclock

The favour of an answer is requested

An invitation to the main meal of the day at Monticello
which was held at three-thirty in the afternoon.

Lincoln, was now honored only by the Republicans, who stood "for both the *man* and the *dollar*; but in cases of conflict, the man *before* the dollar." The events of the fifties, Lincoln maintained, had placed this doctrine in grave jeopardy. "It is now no child's play to save the principles of Jefferson from total overthrow in this nation."

In this period of his career Lincoln and the Republicans in general identified themselves more and more with the interests of the "common man," in particular the interests of artisans, laborers, and mechanics. Drawing on one of the most cherished traditions of the working-class movement, they maintained that acquiring land was the workingman's great hope of self-improvement. Accordingly the extension of slavery, by closing the West to free settlement, directly threatened the northern working class: such was the view of a growing number of Republican spokesmen. Pro-slavery apologists, increasingly intemperate in their efforts to open the entire West to slavery, played into the hands of men who opposed slavery extension on these grounds. George Fitzhugh's ideas probably had more influence in the North than in the South, by confirming Republican suspicions that the "slave-power conspiracy" aimed at nothing less than the enslavement of white workers. In 1856 the Republicans put out a campaign pamphlet entitled: *The New Democratic Doctrine: Slavery Not to Be Confined to the Negro Race, But to Be Made the Universal Condition of the Laboring Classes of Society*. About this time Lincoln pasted in his scrapbook an editorial from a southern paper condemning "free society" as "a conglomeration of greasy mechanics, filthy operatives, small-fisted farmers, and moon-struck theorists." When Lincoln debated Douglas at Galesburg, Republican supporters carried a banner inscribed "Small Fisted Farmers, Mud-sills of Society, Greasy Mechanics for A. Lincoln." In his address to the Wisconsin State Agricultural Society in 1859, Lincoln upheld the rights of "free labor" against the "mud-sill theory," according to which society always rests on a class of uneducated, degraded, and semi-servile workers – the logical conclusion, he contended, of the pro-slavery argument.

Forced by the fierce partisan conflicts of the 1850s to give the "free soil position" a strongly popular emphasis, and even to identify it with the interests of the working class, the Republican party in the sixties would find it difficult to retreat to the position that the Civil War was purely and simply a war to preserve the Union. In its own right, therefore, the growing radicalism of Republican leaders in the fifties had more than temporary significance, precluding the complete triumph of a conservative interpretation of the northern cause and laying the groundwork for radical Reconstruction. What is particularly interesting here, however, is that the name of Jefferson could so easily be linked to this Republican radicalism. A third strand of Jeffersonian influence, distinct from the agrarian republicanism of Randolph and Taylor and from the neo-mercantilism of Gallatin and Biddle, had descended from the radical democrats of the revolutionary period through the Jacksonians to the radical Republicans, persisting into the later nineteenth and even into the twentieth centuries in the form of populism.

Jefferson's low opinion of artisans and mechanics – "panders of vice" – had not prevented his movement from attracting support from these very elements. During the Revolution the urban "mob" played a considerable part. Stirred by the ideas of Sam Adams, Tom Paine, and Jefferson himself, it tried to direct the Revolution against inequalities at home as well as against the British. The Constitutional Convention attempted among other things to thwart

JEFFERSON'S BEDROOM, IN WHICH HE DIED.

Jefferson's bedroom, published in *Harper's New Monthly* in 1853.

this movement, but the struggle continued in the 1790s, fueled by the French Revolution. In the international conflict growing out of the upheaval in France the Federalists tended to side with the counter-revolution led by the British, while Jefferson and his allies were perceived as standing with the French. Whether or not this perception was wholly accurate, many artisans and mechanics gravitated to the Jeffersonian movement because they saw Jefferson as a champion of the rights of man, a freethinker, a leveler, in short as a radical democrat courageously resisting the arrogance and power of the propertied classes.

Jefferson's writings, if not always his actions, gave plenty of support to this view of his leadership. He subscribed to one of the cardinal tenets of the eighteenth-century revolution, that "the earth," in his words, "belongs to the living generation." He defended the right of revolution as a general principle – not merely as a tactic to which it was convenient for the colonists to resort in their quarrel with England – and urged frequent use of it, on the grounds that "between society and society, or generation and generation, there is no municipal obligation, no umpire but the laws of nature." Jefferson believed that "a little rebellion, now and then, is a good thing, and as necessary in the political world as storms in the physical." He once said that no country ought to go for much longer than a century without one. Like all eighteenth-century liberals, he believed in the rights of property, but his defense of property rights, when combined with his belief in the sovereignty of the present generation, was susceptible of a radical democratic interpretation that condemned inherited wealth and insisted that all men have the right to enjoy the fruits of their own labor – that is, to acquire property.

Many of Jefferson's ideas were thus absorbed into a current of working-class radicalism that was itself deeply committed to the ideals of the bourgeois revolution. In the 1830s it was easy for popular spokesmen like William Leggett, Orestes Brownson, Thomas Skidmore, and Robert Rantoul, Jr, to see Jacksonian democracy – to which they were attracted because, in Rantoul's words, it stood out "against monopolies, against exclusive privileges, against unequal taxes, against all other usurpations and oppressions" – as a continuation of Jeffersonian democracy, even though, as we have seen, many former Jeffersonians opposed Jackson.

"Jacksonism," said Rantoul, "is but a revival of Jeffersonism." Following a practice common to all radicals of his time, Rantoul divided society "into two classes – those who do something for their living and those who do not." This definition of the "producing class" was broad enough to include practically everybody, not only the workingman but the industrious capitalist as well, who "superintends the employment of capital acquired by diligence and prudence," in Rantoul's words, and "sends its fertilizing streams through the community...." The definition excludes only the idler, the speculator, the gentleman of hereditary leisure, and the "vagabond demagogue," as Rantoul calls him. There was no contradiction, therefore, between a working-class movement that defined the workingman as a small producer, and the yeoman ideal derived from Jeffersonian democracy. Both stressed "the rights of man to property," as Thomas Skidmore put it in 1829 in a book bearing that title. Both insisted, in the words of Horace Greeley, that "man has a *natural* right to produce and acquire property." They condemned only "artificial" interferences with that right, such as monopoly and "special privilege" – symbolized for "Jeffersonians" of this

type in the Second Bank of the United States.

Partly because many workingmen were themselves dispossessed farmers and partly because the existence of "free land" in the West served as a magnetic influence on American workers, the idea of the workingman as a small property holder fused with the myth of the sturdy yeoman, giving a strongly agrarian flavor to the early working-class movement. The popularity of the safety-valve theory contributed to this merging of agrarianism and working-class radicalism. As George Henry Evans explained it, land in the West, if it were made freely available to eastern workingmen, would drain off surplus labor and thus "prevent such a surplus of workmen in factories as would place the whole body (as now) at the mercy of the factory owners." Evans's career illustrates very clearly the influence of natural rights doctrines on nineteenth-century petty bourgeois and working-class radicalism. Born into a lower middle-class family in Herefordshire, this "agrarian" leader migrated to the United States in 1820, apprenticing himself to a printer in Ithaca, New York. He became an atheist after reading Tom Paine. One of the founders of the Workingmen's Party of New York, from 1829 to 1845 he edited *The Working Man's Advocate*. No more than his associates in what has been termed the labor-reform community did Evans perceive any contradiction between his championship of the workingman and his advocacy of homestead legislation. He reasoned that man's right to life, source of all his other rights, implies the right to use the materials of nature and that the right to land, accordingly, is inalienable.

Such ideas had enduring appeal for American radicals. Men like George W. Julian and Thaddeus Stevens saw the Civil War and Reconstruction as a struggle to make land freely available to the common man, black as well as white. After the collapse of Reconstruction and the middle-class radicalism that had helped to sustain it, radical agrarianism survived in populism and in the working-class movement itself. The Knights of Labor advocated the right to own land as a natural and inalienable right. Henry George's enormously influential *Progress and Poverty* argued that monopoly of land ownership underlay all other forms of monopoly. It is easy to see why the nineteenth century often used "agrarianism" and "socialism" as synonymous terms. As late as 1899 we find Eugene V. Debs – an admirer of Jefferson, by the way – advocating what might be called socialism in one state, a program that owed much more to the westward movement and the dream of free land than to Karl Marx.

> Give me 10,000 men, aye 10,000 in a western state with access to the sources of production, and we will change the economic conditions, and we will convince the people of that state, win their hearts and their intelligence. We will lay hold upon the reins of government and plant the flag of socialism upon the State House.

By the end of the nineteenth century, working-class radicals had become in many ways the most consistent upholders of the bourgeois values of equality before the law, equal opportunity, the right of revolution, and the rights of man in general – the values, in short, of the bourgeois revolution, exemplified in America by Thomas Jefferson. The bourgeoisie itself, having consolidated its power, spurned its own revolutionary past. For the new mercantile and manufacturing elite, the Civil War represented the victory of the principle of legitimacy over disloyalty and revolution. "The glory of our system," wrote a northern conservative

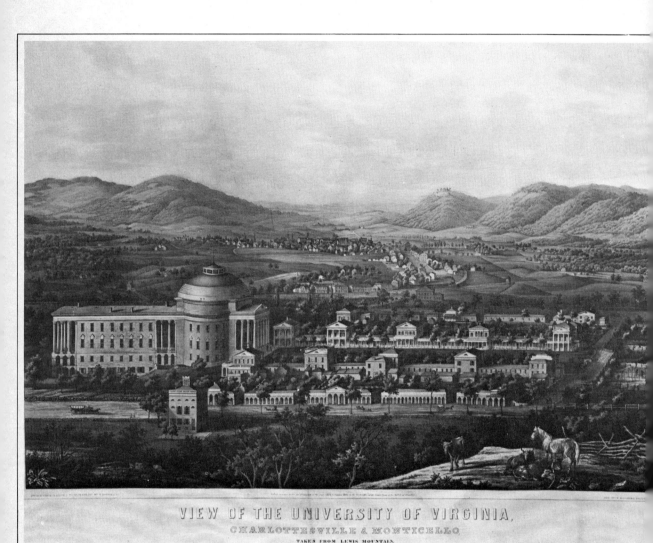

A view of the University of Virginia. "This institution
of my native state, the hobby of my old age, will be
based on the illimitable freedom of the human mind."

in 1863, "is, that there is nothing revolutionary about it, and that when properly understood, it contains within itself every necessary means, founded on a purely historical and legal basis, of perpetuating our national life." Historians rewrote the early history of the Republic in order to minimize its revolutionary origins, stressing the moderation of the founding fathers, the far-sighted statesmanship of the Federalists. Henry Adams portrayed Jefferson as a visionary, an amiable enthusiast. Theodore Roosevelt and Henry Cabot Lodge saw him as a doctrinaire pacifist indifferent to the needs of a great power. Denigration of Jefferson was an important element in the revised version of liberalism that emerged at the turn of the century under the name of progressivism. Albert Beveridge's *Life of John Marshall* extolled Marshall's realism over Jefferson, the fuzzy-headed idealist. Herbert Croly called for a synthesis of the Hamiltonian and Jeffersonian traditions but admitted that his own sympathies lay overwhelmingly on the side of Hamilton.

Those who called themselves liberals now sought to stabilize the economy through state intervention and to build the United States into an imperial nation. Accordingly they had little need of the Jeffersonian legacy. Democratic Presidents would continue to invoke Jefferson's name on ritual occasions, but it would be absurd to take these professions seriously or to regard the modern Democratic party as in any way the heir of Jefferson's party. Beginning with Woodrow Wilson, Democratic Presidents expanded the powers of the executive and of the federal government as a whole, created a vast war machine, and set themselves up as the guardians of world order – actions that bear not the faintest resemblance to the Jeffersonian ideals of limited central power, avoidance of war, and avoidance of standing armies. When Wilson dismissed Bryan as Secretary of State in order to prepare for war with Germany, he showed – what later experience has only confirmed – that the Democratic party could no longer accommodate men who took Jefferson's principles seriously. As for the Republicans, their fondness for the rhetoric of classical liberalism does not conceal an underlying commitment to the welfare-warfare state.

Under these conditions Jeffersonian traditions have survived only as a minor current of opposition, among those who retain an old-fashioned commitment to equality, who find Jefferson's suspicions of centralized power as pertinent as ever, or who believe, perhaps perversely, that the rights of free speech and free inquiry have not been altogether superseded by the exigencies of world power. J. William Fulbright, one of the last of a long line of senatorial mavericks, has recently reminded us that the founders of this country believed democracy to be suitable only for small countries. "War and conditions of war," he adds, "are incompatible and inconsistent with our system of democracy." Such bluntness is unfashionable. Those who preside over a global empire find it embarrassing to be reminded of these quaint notions, this rustic wisdom of the fathers – voices from a dead but not quite forgotten past.

ACKNOWLEDGEMENTS

The editor and the publishers would like to thank the trustees and the owners of the museums and collections listed below for granting permission for the photographs to be reproduced.

THOMAS JEFFERSON: A BRIEF LIFE

12	Thomas Jefferson Memorial Foundation
15	The Assay Office, Birmingham, Alabama
opp p. 16,	Henry Wolf
17	The Metropolitan Museum of Art, The William H. Huntingdon Collection
18	The R. W. Norton Art Gallery, Shreveport, Louisiana
20	University of Virginia Library
25	New York Public Library, Stokes Collection
30	Thomas Jefferson Memorial Foundation
opp p. 32,	Henry Wolf
33	Massachusetts Historical Society
36	University of Virginia Library

JEFFERSON AND THE ENLIGHTENMENT

38	The Metropolitan Museum of Art, The Michael Friedson Collection, 1931
42	The Library of Congress
48	Massachusetts Historical Society
53	University of Virginia Library
58	Thomas Jefferson Memorial Foundation
63	Virginia State Library (top), University of Virginia Library (bottom)
66, 67	University of Virginia Library

PROLEGOMENA TO A READING OF THE DECLARATION

68	University of Virginia Library
73	Thomas Jefferson Memorial Foundation
77	The Library of Congress
78	The Smithsonian Institution

INDEX

— to top of impost, ranging with top of architraves of doors
— to top of arch, ... within ½ I. ... with soffites of windows, that half inch being lost to accomodate it to ... panes of glass ... architrave.

... pa. 20. the impost in height = breadth of ... = ½ ... = 13½
... only the Abacus (4½ I.) go across the ... to ... the glass
then the doors must be 7 f. 2½ I. high.

... measured on ... side of the ...

... heights measured on the doors
Abacus 4½ I. not included.

6 - 2. upper rail
... - 0 upper pane
1 - 6 .25 fillet
... pane
.25 fillet
1 - 6. ... pane
.25 fillet
1 - 6. bottom pane
1 - 5.75 bottom rail
7 - 2.5 height of door.

breadths measured on door
4. outer style
4 0.75 4. panes
... 3. fillets
2.25 middle or mountstyle
4. 7.

... in the N.E. side must ... the same measures in height ... arch in the N.W. ...

... 3 I. architrave above we must show the pannel .025 I. ... the cornetto. the bottom architrave must range with the cap ... of the basement.
Abacus (to be made in a single rail from side to side of room) break 1½ I. at the edge ... and to show a fair projecting impost and let the Abacus over the jamb be solid pieces tenanted in the ... of the outer & inner face to bind all together ... of the Abacus ... thickness of the rail ... its length will be 10 f. ... I.

Count Rumford fire places in the square rooms
... with its ... is 5 f. ... wide which must come ... back to the ...
7 + 6.5 + ... + 6.5 + 7 = 66

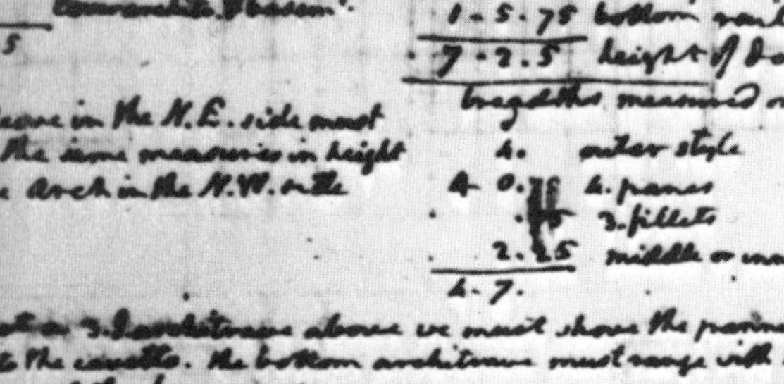

... wide ... high

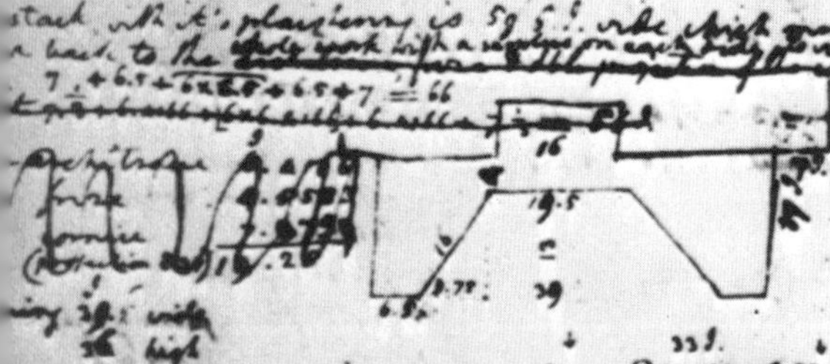

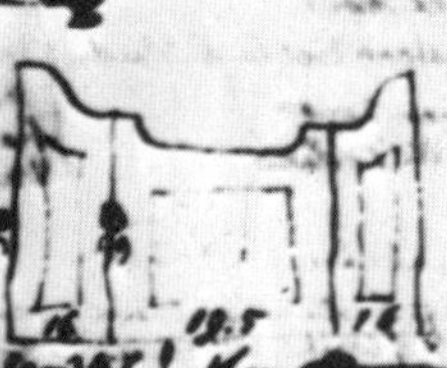

... back must go up perpendicular 3 ... I. then ... fall back horizontally to the back of the flue

... backs & sides wanting. for new rooms ...

... back for the parlour 2 f. wide & 30 I. high & at the ... another of the same size for the Dining room with sides 18 I. broad

... Pleasant's paper of Nov. 27. 98.
the dimensions of the Parlour & Dining room hearths as follow
the opening of the parlour fire place is 3 f. 7 I. high

rules for railings on the terrasses.

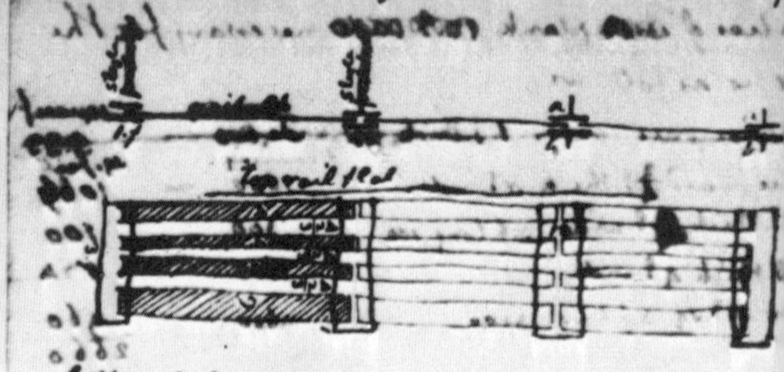

laths 1. I. thick 4. I. wide. 8 f. long
uprights or styles 12 I. wide 3 f. long 1. I. thick
the laths to be nailed ... alternate pannels, the one pann... next on each side to the style b
the pannels being separately prepared, are nailed fa... so that the rails of all are in a line. Nails 3½ I. both styles and the intervening rail clinch ...
c are brackets at the foot of each stile to steady it to the ...
a hand rail on the top laid on flat 4. I. broad and a little rounded on the top thus

* a neat and secure better for ... to place

another plan. June. 23. 24.
do the work in pannels.

a. are styles 1. I. thick, ... I. wide, with triangular bra... to fasten them to the floor and brace them from moving
b is a mopboard 8 I. wide & ½ I. thick nailed on ... to the stiles, to steady them more, with triangular br... wise to steady them the other way. c are laths ... I. nailed in like manner to the styles, one on each ... there is a vacancy then of 1. I. between the 2 lath... between the 2. mopboards. between these drops in d.d. &c. 1. I. square, and 2 I. apart. ... the ... pannel is put edge to edge to the next and sec... collar at top or by a square staple driven ... each. long slender nails should go through ... the upright bar, and through both mopboards. the styles may be fastened together by bits of bo... nailed to both. or by having the laths and mopboar... 2. pannels, and ... joints alternately in nailing ... brackets should be ... I. on their square sides.

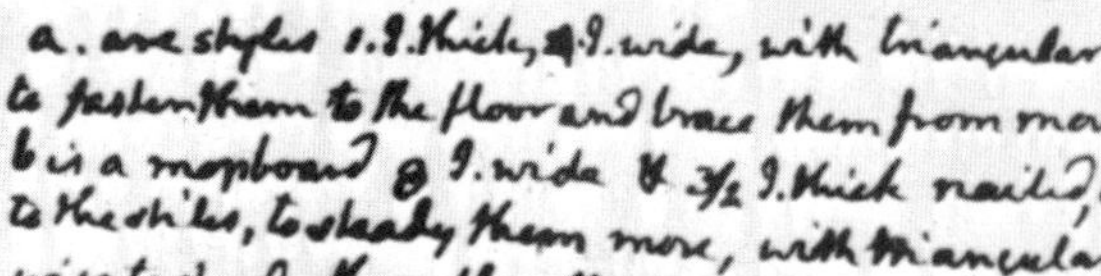

these actual measures rendered it necessary to make each arch a semicircle of 15 I. radius in the clear, with a brick arch of 3. I. thick
order 100. key bricks 3½ I. on the inner or ... edge
900. arch bricks 3. I. on the inner & 3.6 on the outer
3. I. wide & 9. I. long
May. 23. 06.